Aftershock

Aftershock

PROTECT YOURSELF AND PROFIT IN THE NEXT GLOBAL FINANCIAL MELTDOWN

David Wiedemer, PhD
Robert A. Wiedemer
Cindy Spitzer

WILEY

John Wiley & Sons, Inc.

Published by John Wiley & Sons, Inc., Hoboken, New Jersey.
Published simultaneously in Canada.

For general information on our other products and services or for technical support, please contact our Customer Care Department within the United States at (800) 762-2974, outside the United States at (317) 572-3993 or fax (317) 572-4002.

Wiley also publishes its books in a variety of electronic formats. Some content that appears in print may not be available in electronic books. For more information about Wiley products, visit our web site at www.wiley.com.

Library of Congress Cataloging-in-Publication Data

Wiedemer, David.
 Aftershock : protect yourself and profit in the next global financial meltdown / David Wiedemer, Robert Wiedemer, Cindy Spitzer.
   p. cm.
 Includes bibliographical references and index.
 ISBN 978-0-470-48156-1 (hardback)
  1. Finance, Personal. 2. Investments. 3. Financial crises. I. Wiedemer, Robert A. II. Spitzer, Cindy S. III. Title.
 HG179.W5264 2009
 332.024—dc22

                                                                    2009029124

Printed in the United States of America
10 9 8 7 6 5 4 3

Contents

Executive Summary

What Is a Bubble?

An asset value that temporarily booms and eventually busts, based on changing investor psychology, rather than underlying, fundamental economic drivers that are sustainable over time.

What Is a Bubble Economy?

An economy that grows in a virtuous upward spiral of multiple rising bubbles (real estate, stocks, private debt, dollar, and government debt) that interact to drive each other up, and that will inevitably fall in a vicious downward spiral as each falling bubble puts downward pressure on the rest, eventually pulling the economy down.

What Is the Bubblequake?

Phase I of the popping of the bubble economy, including the fall of the real estate bubble, private debt bubble, stock market bubble, and discretionary spending bubble.

What Is the Aftershock?

Phase II of the popping of the bubble economy. Just when many people think the worst is over, next comes the Aftershock, when the dollar bubble and the government debt bubble will burst.

Acknowledgments

The authors thank John Silbersack of Trident Media Group and John Wiley & Sons editors David Pugh and Laura Walsh for supporting this book. They also want to thank John Douglas for his very special role in making this book a reality.

David Wiedemer

I thank my co-authors Bob and Cindy for being indispensable in the writing of this book. Without them, this book would not have been published, and if written, would have been inaccessible for most audiences. I also thank Dr. Rod Stevenson for his long-term support of the foundational work that is the basis for this book, which hopefully will be the second of many. I also thank Ruth Pritchard for her review of the manuscript. And I am especially grateful to my wife Betsy and son Benson for their on-going support in what has been an often arduous and trying process.

Robert Wiedemer

I, along with my brother, want to dedicate this book to our father, the original author in the family, who died earlier this year. We also want to thank our brother Jim for his lifelong support of the ideas behind this book and our mother for inspiring us both with the joy in discovering the world and writing about it. I thank Ron Everett, my business associate, for his enthusiastic support of this project. I also want to thank Stan Goldstein, Bradley Rosenberg, Phil Gross, and Michael Lebowitz for their support and help in reviewing this book. I am also grateful to Weldon Rackley, who helped my father to become an author and who did the same for me.

Of course, my gratitude goes to Dave Wiedemer and Cindy Spitzer, for being quite clearly the best collaborators you could ever have. It was truly a great team effort. Most of all, I thank my wife

Serap, and children, Seline and John, without whose love and support, this book, and a really great life, would not be possible.

Cindy Spitzer

Thank you, David and Bob Wiedemer, for the true privilege of collaborating with you on two brilliantly insightful books. I can't wait until the world fully discovers just how right you have been.

My love and deep appreciation go to my wonderful husband Philip Terbush, my precious children, Chelsea, Anya, and Zachary, and my dear friend Cindi Callanan.

I am also filled with indescribable gratitude for two fantastic teachers, the kind that make you cry years later when you realize just how much they changed your life: Christine Gronkowski, who at SUNY Purchase in 1985 forced me to discover something in myself that I couldn't see on my own; and to my phenomenally gifted UMCP journalism mentor, two-time Pulitzer Prize winner Jon Franklin, whom I haven't seen in more than two decades but still learn from daily.

Introduction

BY ROBERT A. WIEDEMER

We are going through a series of popping financial bubbles, led by a housing price bubble collapse, not a down financial cycle. Unlike a down cycle which is naturally followed by an up cycle, a bubble pop isn't followed by an up cycle—it simply pops and any profit is gone forever.

This is how I begin many of my presentations to financial and non-financial audiences. As this book is being finalized for printing, we are being bombarded by the news that there are signs that the recession is coming to an end. Headlines from leading financial figures saying "Bet on America" or "The Recession is Almost Over" are the norm.

Also, the numbers are showing that the decline in GDP is slowing and there are other indicators of a slowdown in the contraction. Of course, the assumption is that this slowdown in decline presages an up cycle.

But, even if the decline slows down or stops, and even if there is a small increase, the recession is not over for the long term. Saying the recession is over is more like saying "Mission Accomplished" before the real Iraq War even began. It's hiding from the underlying problems that have been created by thinking we can cheerlead our way through it.

The economy won't bounce back. It is a bubble economy. With the popping of the housing bubble will go the consumer spending bubble and private credit bubble and the stock market bubble and then the dollar bubble and finally the public debt bubble. It won't all pop at once, it will pop over time, but it won't bounce back, not very much at least, before the popping resumes. Once the bubbles start popping, as they have with housing, it's not over until the fat lady sings, and the fat lady is the dollar and its evil twin, the government debt bubble.

More than any time since I was born, the United States is in denial of the truth. We are assuming that by cheerleading, we can solve our problems. Even during the Vietnam War era, when cheerleading in the face of reality was very popular, we still had major national figures, like Walter Cronkite, who were willing to step in and give us a reality check.

I don't see it this time. Not from any national figure on the left or the right.

We are extraordinarily confident in the power of cheerleading to solve our ills and, hence, so many of our national figures are simply cheerleading.

Yet, at the same time we seem to be so confident, we also seem to be scared to death that something terrible is going to happen. We say this more by our actions than our words.

For example, why is the Fed so worried that it would do something so reckless as to buy over $1 trillion of our Treasury bonds, Fannie Mae bonds, and Freddie Mac bonds with printed money? That's a big number to print in six months and they have said they will buy even more if necessary to keep mortgage rates low. That means they are willing to *double* our entire money supply (the size of the money supply (M_1) is about $1 trillion) just to keep mortgage rates down a couple of points. What are they so concerned about? We certainly didn't worry about it that much in the last big recession in the early 1980s. In fact, interest rates were allowed to go over 15 percent! By the way the Fed is acting, you would think the world would come toan end if rates went to 15 percent. Why are they so worried now and they weren't then?

Maybe because, unlike what their cheerleading words are saying, they are concerned about a bigger problem. They are concerned that there aren't nearly enough buyers for all that debt, either in the United States or overseas, and that means the possibility of a failed Treasury auction. And they know that in this environment that could be a big problem. Or maybe they realize that interest rates might pop up much more than a couple percentage points to as high as 10 percent. That would be devastating.

High interest rates weren't devastating in the early 1980s because we didn't have a housing bubble. Now we have a housing bubble and high interest rates would absolutely puncture much of what's left of that bubble and put enormous pressure on the other bubbles in the economy—private credit, discretionary spending, stock market, dollar, and public debt. Maybe, subconsciously, they and others outside the Fed realize that it is a bubble economy and that is why the Fed and others are trying so hard to cheerlead. And, that is why they are so willing to do things like printing massive amounts of money to buy our own government's bonds—something they would never have considered only a year ago. Because, in a bubble economy, cheerleading does help—for a while. Because the economic fundamentals are bad, the only thing holding up the bubbles is confidence that they won't pop. When that confidence fails, the reality of the bad fundamentals comes blazing through.

And, again, few people talk about the very real problems of taking such irresponsible actions as buying our own bonds with printed money—nah, it's just a smart strategy of "quantitative easing." Many say "the Fed knows exactly what they're doing and can handle any inflationary problems down the road." Both the right and the left seem to have great confidence in the Fed's abilities to handle such problems.

However, I don't think they have confidence so much as they know in the back of their minds that the Fed is in a desperate situation that requires desperate solutions. They simply hope that they won't cause problems too big to solve. But, of course, they will. Same for the huge deficits we are running for stimulus programs. The cheerleaders say, "No problem there—sure, long term we'll have to deal with the problem, but it's nothing we need to worry about now. It's not nearly as important as the need to throw money at the economic problems we have now."

Both Republicans and Democrats seem to strongly agree on these points. Both conservatives and liberals seem to think that government has tremendous power to solve economic problems. Yet, that has not been proven in the past. The reality is that the government has two main economic powers—the ability to print money and a credit card with a much, much higher limit then you or me.

But, printing a lot of money really will cause inflation and their credit card is not limitless. In fact, as we make the case in this book, for a variety of reasons, we may reach that credit limit in just a few short years. The reality is that the government's power to solve economic problems right now is really quite limited. And, ultimately, when the government acts too recklessly, it actually becomes the source of the biggest economic problem of all, when the government debt bubble pops.

Despite all the cheerleading, people seem to know we are in a very dangerous situation. They don't want to talk about it but they know the danger is there. As one of my friends who works at a major hedge fund in New York said when I was talking about the dollar bubble, "It's the hydrogen bomb in the middle of the room."

It's an eerie time and I get an eerie feeling reading the papers—yes I am one of the few who still read papers! It's almost as if people know that America really does have a bubble economy and that an Aftershock could happen even though, unfortunately, most Americans haven't read this book or *America's Bubble Economy*.

All the cheerleading, all the lack of concern over the Fed buying treasury bonds, no more talk about the "moral hazard" of bailing out large financial institutions, and no concern over giving $100 billion to the auto industry when in the last big recession we argued for months over a puny $1 billion loan.

It all seems to point to one thing—that many people sort of know what we've been talking about is true. They think that by not talking about it, somehow it will go away, like Bernie Madoff thinking he won't get caught. He fooled investors and the SEC so many times before, he expected he could fool them again.

We've gotten away with all these bubbles so far and it's never caused us much problem until recently. In fact, just the opposite, it's given us one of the best economies we've ever had. So, we expect nothing bad will happen. Of course, that plan of action has never worked before and it won't work now.

It's time for investors to talk about it—a lot! It's the best and only way to protect yourself and make some money. With this book, we hope to throw a little gasoline onto the fire of that conversation and make it really burn. We expect it to be an exciting and fruitful conversation.

Long term, we expect to carry on this conversation in future books and contribute to solving the problem by building a much wealthier and stronger economy the way the United States has done so masterfully and successfully in the past. Not by blowing bubbles, but by improving productivity. But unlike bubble money, productivity money is real money and creates real growth that lasts.

The world will be a much better place as a result, but we are in for a hell of ride getting there. Don't let the ride surprise you. Read this book. As an Eagle Scout, I can say to investors with no greater conviction that you should follow the Scout's motto, "Be Prepared."

PART

I

FIRST THE BUBBLEQUAKE,
NEXT THE AFTERSHOCK

CHAPTER 1

America's Bubble Economy

UNDERSTANDING HOW WE PREDICTED THE CURRENT BUBBLEQUAKE FOUR YEARS AGO IS KEY TO UNDERSTANDING WHY OUR LATEST PREDICTIONS ARE CORRECT

When our first book, *American's Bubble Economy,* came out in 2006 (the book proposal was actually submitted 18 months earlier), we were right and almost everyone else was wrong. We don't say this to brag. We say it because it's important for understanding why you should bother to pay attention to us now.

America's Bubble Economy (John Wiley & Sons), accurately predicted the popping of the housing bubble, the collapse of the private debt bubble, the fall of the stock market bubble, the decline of consumer spending, and the widespread pain all this was about to inflict on the rest of our vulnerable, multi-bubble economy. We also predicted the eventual bursting of the dollar bubble and the government debt bubble, which are still ahead. In 2006, these and our many other predictions were largely ignored. Two years later, it started coming true.

How did we see it coming? Certainly not by looking only at current conditions, which, at the time we wrote the first book, still looked pretty darn good. In fact, real estate prices were close to their record highs in 2006. With home values high and credit flowing, American consumers were still happily tapping into their home equity and credit cards to buy all manner of consumer products, from diapers to flat screen TVs, importing goods from around the world, boosting the economies of many nations. Businesses and banks appeared to be in good shape (very few banks were even close to failing), unemployment was relatively low, and Wall Street was still on an upward climb toward its record closing high (Dow 14,164) a year later on October 9, 2007.

With so much seemingly going so well back in 2006, how could we have been so sure that the housing bubble would pop, private credit would start drying up, the stock market would begin to fall, and the broader multi-bubble economy, here and around the globe, would begin a dramatic decline in 2008 and beyond? Our accurate predictions were not a matter of blind luck, nor were they merely a case of perpetual bearish thinking finally having its gloomy day. In 2006, we were able to correctly call the fall of the U.S. housing bubble and its many consequences because we were able to see a *fundamental underlying pattern* that others were—and still are—missing.

In this pattern, we saw bubbles. Lots of them. We saw six big economic bubbles linked together and holding one another up, all supporting a seemingly prosperous U.S. economy. And we also saw that each conjoined bubble was leaning heavily on the others, each poised to potentially pull the others down if any one of these economic bubbles were to someday pop.

In this pattern, we also saw the opposite of big airborne bubbles; we saw the evolving economic facts on the ground. As is always the case with bubbles, the facts on the ground did not justify the volume of the bubbles; therefore sooner or later, we knew they would have to burst. In a little while, we will tell you more about our six big economic bubbles (the first four have already begun to burst and the other two will shortly) and how we knew they were bubbles. For now the point is that economic bubbles, by nature, do not stay afloat forever. Sooner or later, economic reality, like gravity, eventually kicks in, and bubbles do fall. After they burst, they never are able to re-inflate and lift off again. In time, new bubbles may grow, but old popped bubbles generally do not take off again. When the party is over, it's over.

Most people, even most "experts," find it much easier to recognize a bubble (like the Internet bubble of the 1990s) *after* it pops. It is a lot harder to see a bubble *before* it bursts, and much harder still to see an *entire multiple-bubble economy* before it bursts. A single, not-yet-popped bubble can look a lot like real asset growth, and a collection of several not-yet-popped bubbles can look a whole lot like real economic prosperity.

We wrote *America's Bubble Economy* because, based on our unique analysis of the evolving economy, the facts on the ground did not match the bubbles in the sky. By that we mean high-flying asset growth that is not firmly pinned to some underlying real economic driver is not sustainable. For example, real estate prices are typically driven higher by a growing population (increasing demand) and the growing incomes of homebuyers (increasing ability to buy). When populations increase and incomes increase, home prices also increase. On the other hand, if you see home prices increasing, let's say, twice as fast as incomes, then that could mean something unusual is happening to the value of real estate. Why? Because home prices that high are not sustainable without a similar rise in the ability of buyers to keep paying those prices.

Asset bubbles are not always bad. On the way up, they can lift part or all of an economy and spur future economic growth. This certainly was the case with the housing bubble. On the way down, however, they can cause real problems. In fact, the bigger the bubble, the harder the fall.

Our first book identified several economic bubbles that were once part of a seemingly *virtuous upward spiral* that first lifted and supported the U.S. economy over many decades, and are now part of a *vicious downward spiral* that will inevitably harm the U.S. and world economies as these sagging, co-linked bubbles weigh heavily on each other and ultimately burst. These bubbles included: the real estate bubble, stock market bubble, discretionary spending bubble, dollar bubble, and government debt bubble. Despite how well the economy appeared to be doing in 2006, we predicted it would only be two or three years before America's multiple bubbles would begin to decline and eventually even burst.

And that is just what happened. By the third quarter of 2008, home prices and sales had fallen significantly, mortgage defaults and home foreclosures were skyrocketing, commercial and investment banks were going under, unemployment was rising, and the stock market bubble had fallen from its peak of 14,164 in

October 2007 to under 7,000 (DJIA) not much more than a year later. We now offer you this second book in late 2009, as the rest of our conjoined economic bubbles are under tremendous downward pressure and about to fall.

Unlike at any other moment in our history, there is something *fundamentally different* going on this time. Even people who pay no attention to the stock market or the latest economic news say they can just feel it in their gut. Something is different. This is *not* merely a down market cycle, nor is it a typical recession. The difference is the *multi-bubble economy*. With so many linked bubbles now on the descent, the impact of their combined collapse will be far more dangerous than any downturn or recession we've experienced in the past. Unlike in a healthy economy, in this falling *multi-bubble* economy, the usual strategies for returning to our previous prosperity no longer apply. We have, in fact, entered new territory.

We call it a Bubblequake. As in an earthquake, our multi-bubble economy is starting to rumble and crack. Clearly, the real estate, credit, and stock market bubbles have already taken a serious fall, and the financial consequences for the broader U.S. and world economy have been terrible.

Next comes the *Aftershock*. Just when most people think the worst is behind us, we are about to experience the cascading fall of several, co-linked, bursting bubbles that will rock our nation's economy to its core and send deep and destructive financial shock waves around the globe. The Bubblequake fall of the housing, credit, consumer spending, and stock bubbles significantly weakened the world economy. But the coming Aftershock will be far more dangerous. A multi-bubble economy cannot be easily re-inflated. Rather than home prices stabilizing and the U.S. economy recovering in the next year or two, as many "experts" want you to believe, we see serious, groundbreaking new troubles ahead. In fact, the worst is yet to come.

That's the bad news. The good news is the worst is yet to come (with emphasis on the word *yet*). There is still time for individuals and businesses to cover their assets and even find ways to profit in the Bubblequake and Aftershock. But first you have to see it coming.

Prescient Quotes from Our First Book, *America's Bubble Economy*

Stock Market

Bottom line: Most stocks are overvalued and on their way down. Will there be some ups and downs? Of course. Is it worth taking a chance on it? We think not. As with real estate, although there may be some potential growth left in the stock market, the timing is very tricky and it's not worth taking the risk. In the short run, you are about as likely to lose as gain. And in the long run, all you will do is lose significantly when stock values begin to seriously plummet. Again, we will show you much better places to put your money. (p. 139)

The Dow was at 12,100 when published in October 2006.

Real Estate

In the near term, the slow collapse of the Real Estate Bubble (in some markets it won't be so slow) will weigh heavily on the stock market. The loss of housing construction jobs, plus the factory and service jobs that support housing construction, will further slow the economy, putting more downward pressure on the stock market. (p. 73)

Housing prices were at 205 according to Case-Shiller Top 20 Cities Index when published, and are now at 150; we're now losing construction jobs at a rate of 50,000 to 100,000 per month.

Private Credit

All adjustable rate loans, credit cards and adjustable or variable mortgages will become an absolute disaster when the bubbles burst. Interest rates will rise dramatically and so will your mortgage and other payments if you don't get out of these soon. Now is a great time to lock in your low long-term interest rates. Don't take a chance; get rid of your evil variable rate mortgage and other big debts now! (p. 141)

Adjustable rate mortgages helped kick off the housing price collapse and are still one of the leading causes of mortgage default and foreclosure.

Stock Market

It is important to point out that all asset bubbles (such as the Stock Market Bubble and Dollar Bubble) will burst in two stages. The first stage will be the bursting of the recent over-valued price bubble. The second stage will be the additional fall in value due to the significant coming downturn in the economy. (p. 10)

The Dow was at 12,100 when this was published in October 2006.

Collectibles

All collectibles crash in value. In fact, if possible, postpone any collectible purchase until after the bubble crash when everything is at bargain basement prices. Not only will they be far cheaper, but your selection becomes huge because so many people need to sell their collectibles to raise money. (p. 173)

Sotheby's auction revenues fell over 70 percent from the first quarter of 2008 to the first quarter of 2009.

Stock Market

Of course, the idea that the stock market at any time is risk free is completely false. Every market has downside risk. Back in the 1950s, 1960s, and 1970s that was understood. It's been a very long time since the experts have tried to tell us there is no risk in the stock market. Guess when it happened before? The last time market cheerleaders tried to get Americans to think of the stock market as risk-free was just before the big 1929 stock market crash that led to the Great Depression. Coincidence?

A bloated overvalued market (Dow up tenfold in 20 years), now "stable" from mid 2000 to 2005 (also known as stagnant), plus cheerleaders telling us that there is no downside risk, all add up to one thing: a Stock Market Bubble on the edge. (p. 110)

The Dow was at 12,100 when this was published in October 2006.

Because We Were Right, Now You Can Be Right, Too

Most people think the economy will get better soon. It won't. We can tell you what you want to hear, or we can help you enormously by showing you how to prepare and protect yourself while you still can, and find opportunities to profit during the dramatically changing times ahead. We may not give you news you like, but it will definitely be news you can do something about.

Now is not the time to look for someone to cheer you up. Now is the time to get it right because you won't care in three years if someone cheered you up today. What you will care about is that you made the right financial decisions. It matters more now than ever before that you get it right today. Please remember this important point as you go through the rest of the book: *It's only bad news for your personal economy if you don't do anything about it.*

Before we go on, we should take a moment to assure you that we are neither bulls nor bears. We are not gold bugs, stock boosters or detractors, currency pushers, or doom-and-gloom crusaders. We have no particular political ideology to endorse, and no dogmatic future to promote. We are simply intensely interested in patterns, big evolving changes over broad sweeps of time. And because we look for patterns, we are willing to see them—often where others do not.

At the time we wrote *America's Bubble Economy*, we saw, and continue to see, some patterns in the U.S. and world economies that others are missing. We see these patterns, in part because we are very good at analyzing the larger picture. In fact, co-author David Wiedemer has developed a fascinating new "Theory of Economic Evolution" (introduced briefly in Chapter 8) that helps explain and even predict large economic patterns that most people simply don't see.

But there's more to it than that. We can see things happening in the economy right now that many others do not because at this particular moment in history, it's very hard for most people—even most experts—to face what is actually going on. The U.S. economy has been such a strong and prosperous powerhouse for so long, it's difficult to imagine anything else. Our goal is not to convince you of anything you wouldn't conclude for yourself, if you had the right facts, based on objective science and logical analysis. Most people don't get the right facts because most financial analysis today is based on preconceived ideas about a hoped-for positive outcome. People want analysis that says the economy will improve in the future, not get worse. So they look for ways to create that analysis, drawing on outdated ideas like repeating "market cycles," to support their case. Such is human nature. We all naturally prefer a future that is better than the past, and luckily for many Americans, that is what we have enjoyed.

Not so this time.

Again, just to be clear, we are not intrinsically pessimistic, either by personality or by policy. We're just calling it as we see it. Wouldn't you really rather hear the truth?

At an April 2008 presentation about *America's Bubble Economy* to Hogan & Hartson, one of the nation's largest law firms, co-author Robert Wiedemer said he wished people would treat economists and financial analysts as doctors rather than people trying to cheer you up. What if you had pneumonia and all your doctor did was just slap you on the back and say, "Don't worry about it. Take two aspirin and you'll be fine in a couple days." Wouldn't you prefer the most honest diagnosis and best treatment possible? But when it comes to the health of the economy, most people only want good news. Even in the face of some very damning economic facts, people still want convincing analysis of why the economy is about to turn around and get better soon. The vast majority of financial analysts and economists are simply responding to the market. That's what people want and that's what they get.

Despite this universal desire for good news, and despite the fact that the housing and stock markets were both near their peaks in 2006, our first book did remarkably well. In fact, *America's Bubble Economy* has been discussed in articles in Barron's, Reuters, Bottom Line, and the Associated Press. The book was also selected as one of the 30 best business books of 2006 by Kiplinger's. Co-author Robert Wiedemer has been invited to speak before the New York Hedge Fund Roundtable, The World Bank, and on CNBC's popular morning show *Squawk Box*. So clearly there are people who are interested in unbiased financial analysis, even when that analysis says there are fundamental problems in the economy that won't be resolved easily or soon.

Yet even within this supportive audience, and among our most devoted fans, there is still a wish for optimism, a deep-down feeling that the future couldn't possibly be as bad as we say. We understand that. All we can offer is realism, based on facts and logical analysis. In the end, that is what's best for all of us.

Our original analysis showed us that the real estate bubble would be the first to burst, putting downward pressure on the stock market and discretionary spending bubbles, kicking off a major global recession. Now, in this book, we want to tell you more details about the next round of bubbles to fall while there's still time to protect your assets and position yourself to survive and thrive in this dangerous, yet potentially highly profitable new environment. Just like in the first book, our analysis is based on a reliable theory of economic evolution, backed up by cold, hard facts, and not random guesses.

Although much of what we predicted has come true, there is still much that we predicted in our first book that hasn't happened yet because most of the impact of the multi-bubble collapse is still to come. This is good news because it means you still have time to get prepared.

Didn't Other Bearish Analysts Get It Right, Too?

Not really. Back in 2006, there was a small group of more bearish financial analysts and economists who correctly predicted some slices of the problems we are seeing now. We say hats off to them for having the courage and insight to make what they felt were honest, if not popular, appraisals of the economy. It takes guts to yell "fire" when so few people believe you because they can't even smell the smoke.

However, there are times when smart people make the right predictions for the wrong reasons, or for incomplete reasons, and that makes them less likely to be right again in the future. In this case, there are some important differences between our way of thinking and the typical "bear" analysis, which we think you ought to know about. For one thing, a lot of bear analysis tends to be apocalyptic in tone and predictions, sometimes going so far as to call for drastic survivalist measures, such as growing your own food. Unlike these true Doom-and-Gloomers, we see nothing of the kind occurring.

Another important difference is that so much bear analysis seems to carry moralistic overtones, implying that, individually and collectively, we have somehow sinned by borrowing too much money and we will eventually have to pay a hefty price for our immoral ways. We certainly disagree that borrowing money is morally wrong. In fact, depending on the circumstances, borrowing money can be the best course of action for an individual, a business, or a government. Without the leveraging power of credit, it's very difficult to start business, go to medical school, build a bridge, or lift an economy. Borrowing is not intrinsically "wrong." Clearly, some debts are a lot smarter than others. For example, borrowing money to go to college for four years en route to a lucrative career is smart. Borrowing the same amount to spend four years at Disney World is not. (More on "smart" versus "dumb" debt in the next chapter.) For now, the point is that borrowing money, in and of itself, is not the biggest problem—*stupidity* is. Other bearish analysts who complain about too much borrowing tend to miss this vital distinction entirely.

The biggest difference between our predictions and the rest is that the other bearish analyses tend to ignore the bigger picture of our *multi-bubble economy*. Even the most realistic bearish thinkers fail to see all the bubbles in today's economy, and they certainly miss the critically important *interactions* between them. Instead, if they mention any bubbles at all, they often focus on one singular bubble—like the credit crunch, or the housing bubble, or the growing federal debt. They are right to point out that all is not well, but they generally don't connect the dots from their single complaint to the larger multi-bubble economy. More importantly, they don't see the crucial interactions between all these bubbles that are currently pulling our economy down.

Honestly, if all we had was a credit crunch or a fallen housing bubble, our economy could get past it fairly unscathed. Unfortunately, our multi-bubble problem is much bigger than any one of its parts. As we discuss in more detail in the next chapter, these bubbles worked together in a seemingly *virtuous upward spiral* to lift the economy up in the longest economic expansion in U.S. history, and together these linked bubbles will work in concert in a *vicious downward spiral* to bring the economy down.

Partly because of their single-bubble focus and partly because of the general market need to be more optimistic about the future, most bears predict an upturn in the economy coming shortly, perhaps as early as 2010. Grumpier bears say it could take as long as four or five years, but most see a turnaround ahead fairly soon.

Unfortunately, that's not the way it works in a multi-bubble economy. Even healthy economies don't naturally grow bigger and bigger without end. Multi-bubble economies certainly cannot stay afloat forever. There are real forces that push economies up and real forces that push economies down. These forces are not static, like repeating market cycles, but evolve over time. Based on our science-backed analysis of the evolving economy, which is neither bullish nor bearish, but simply realistic, the U.S. economy is in the middle of a long-term fundamental change. It is evolving, not merely cycling back and forth between expansion and contraction. Therefore, the multi-bubble economy will not automatically turn around and go back up again in the next few years. The idea that the economy is evolving, not merely expanding and contracting and expanding again, is a key difference between us and other bearish analysts, and it is certainly a huge difference between us and the bullish "experts."

We Said, They Said: Our Score Card

In Oct 2006, we said	Experts said	What actually happened from October 2006 to December 2008
Stocks will fall	Stocks will rise	Dow 12,100 went to 8600 NASDAQ 2350 went to 1575
Housing will fall	Housing will rebound	Case-Shiller Top 20 Cities Composite Index 205 went to 150
Commercial real estate will fall	Commercial real estate will rise rapidly	Dow Jones U.S. Real Estate Index 82 went to 37
Dollar will fall (euro and yen will rise)	Dollar stable	Euro $1.29 went to $1.40; Yen $0.85 went to $1.10
Gold will rise	Gold at peak	Spot Gold $600/ounce went to $880
Bear funds will rise	Bear funds will not rise	ProFunds Ultra Bear Fund (UPPIX) rose 9.13 percent annually for last 3 years (as of 12/31/08)
International bond funds safe	International bond funds not safe	T. Rowe Price International bond fund (RPIBX) had an average annual return of 4.28 percent for last three years, as of March 31, 2009
Foreign stocks will go down	Foreign stocks will rise	FTSE 100 (London) down 30 percent
Commodities will fall	Commodities will rise	Copper down almost 50 percent

What Did the "Experts" Say?

We enjoyed an article in the January 12, 2009 issue of *BusinessWeek* magazine so much that we thought we'd include some of it for you here. What follows are observations and predictions about the economy in 2008 by well-known and highly trained financial professionals, writers, investors and economists. It is interesting to note that, in the course of our research for this book, we keep a file of predictions and observations that well-known analysts, investors and economists make. In reviewing the file for this section of the book, we noticed that it is very hard to find *anyone* who will predict economic movements beyond a year. Hence, it limits just how wrong they can be. It also makes it very hard to compare our long-term predictions that were made in October 2006 with anyone else since so few people in 2006 made predictions for 2008 or 2009. That we can show the accuracy of our predictions against much easier short-term predictions that other people make shows the power of our financial and economic analyses in understanding our economy. For most investors, long-term predictions are really the most important because most investors are investing for the long term, whether it be for capital appreciation, capital preservation, or for retirement. Financial analysis has to be accurate long-term to really be valuable.

Stock Market

"A very powerful and durable rally is in the works. But it may need another couple of days to lift off. Hold the fort and keep the faith!" A quote from Richard Band, editor, *Profitable Investing Letter*, Mar. 27, 2008.

What Actually Happened: At the time of Band's comment, the Dow Jones industrial average was at 12,300. By December, 2008 it was at 8,500.

AIG

AIG "could have huge gains in the second quarter." A quote from Bijan Moazami, distinguished analyst, Friedman, Billings, Ramsey, May 9, 2008.

What Actually Happened: AIG lost $5 billion in the second quarter 2008 and $25 billion in the next. It was taken over in September by the U.S. government, which will spend or lend $150 billion to keep it going.

Mortgages

"I think this is a case where Freddie Mac and Fannie Mae are fundamentally sound. They're not in danger of going under. . . . I think they are in good shape going forward." From Barney Frank (D-Mass.), House Financial Services Committee chairman, July 14, 2008.

What Actually Happened: Within two months of Rep. Frank's comments, the government forced the mortgage giants into conservatorships and pledged to invest up to $100 billion in each.

GDP Growth

"I'm not an economist but I do believe that we're growing." President George W. Bush, in a July 15, 2008 press conference.

What Actually Happened: Gross domestic product shrank at a 0.5 percent annual rate in the July-September quarter. On December 1, the National Bureau of Economic Research declared that a recession had begun in December 2007.

Banks

"I think Bob Steel's the one guy I trust to turn this bank around, which is why I've told you on weakness to buy Wachovia." Jim Cramer, CNBC commentator, March 11, 2008.

What Actually Happened: Within two weeks of Cramer's comment, Wachovia came within hours of failure as depositors fled. Steel eventually agreed to a takeover by Wells Fargo. Wachovia shares lost half their value from September 15 to December 29.

Homes

"Existing-Home Sales to Trend Up in 2008" from the headline of a National Association of Realtors press release, December 9, 2007.

What Actually Happened: NAR said November 2008 sales were running at an annual rate of 4.5 million—down 11 percent from a year earlier—in the worst housing slump since the Depression.

Oil

"I think you'll see [oil prices at] $150 a barrel by the end of the year" a quote from T. Boone Pickens, one of the wealthiest and most respected oilmen today, on June 20, 2008.

What Actually Happened: Oil was then around $135 a barrel. By late December it was below $40.

Banks

"I expect there will be some failures. . . . I don't anticipate any serious problems of that sort among the large internationally active banks that make up a very substantial part of our banking system." Ben Bernanke, Federal Reserve chairman, Feb. 28, 2008.

What Actually Happened: In September 2008, Washington Mutual became the largest financial institution in U.S. history to fail. Citigroup needed an even bigger rescue in November.

Madoff

"In today's regulatory environment, it's virtually impossible to violate rules." Famous last words from Bernard Madoff, money manager, Oct. 20, 2007.

What Actually Happened: About a year later, Madoff—who once headed the NASDAQ Stock Market—told investigators he had cost his investors $50 billion in an alleged Ponzi scheme.

More Wrong Predictions

Following is another collection of predictions made about 2008 that was published in *New York* magazine. Again, these are all professional financial analysts that represent the opinions of many, many others, even if they are not quoted directly.

Stock Market

"Question: What do you call it when an $8 billion asset write-down translates into a $30 billion loss in market cap? Answer: an overreaction . . . . Smart investors should buy [Merrill Lynch] stock before everyone else comes to their senses." From Jon Birger in *Fortune's Investors Guide 2008*.

What Actually Happened: Merrill's shares plummeted 77 percent and it had to be rescued by Bank of America through a deal brokered by the U.S. Treasury.

Housing

"There are [financial firms] that have been tainted by this huge credit problem . . . . Fannie Mae and Freddie Mac have been pummeled. Our stress-test analysis indicates those stocks are at bargain basement prices." Sarah Ketterer, a leading expert on housing, and CEO of Causeway Capital Management, quoted in *Fortune's Investors Guide 2008*.

What Actually Happened: Shares of Fannie and Freddie have lost 90 percent of their value and the federal government placed these two lenders under "conservatorship" in September 2009.

Stock Market

"Garzarelli is advising investors to buy some of the most beaten-down stocks, including those of giant financial institutions such as Lehman Brothers, Bear Stearns, and Merrill Lynch. What would cause her to turn bearish? Not much. 'Our indicators are extremely bullish.'" Quote from Elaine Garzarelli, president of Garzarelli Capital and one of the most outstanding analysts on Wall Street, in *Business Week's Investment Outlook 2008*.

What Actually Happened: None of these firms still exist. Lehman went bankrupt. J P Morgan and Chase bought Bear Stearns in a fire sale. Merrill was sold to Bank of America.

General Electric

"CEO Jeffrey Immelt has been leading a successful makeover at General Electric, though you wouldn't know it from GE's flaccid stock price. Our bet is that in a stormy market investors will gravitate toward the ultimate blue chip." Jon Birger, senior writer, in *Fortune's Investors Guide 2008.*

What Actually Happened: GE's stock price fell 55 percent and it lost its triple-A credit rating.

Banks

"A lot of people think Bank of America will cut its dividend, but I don't think there's a chance in the world. I think they'll raise it this year; they have raised it a little in each of the past 20 to 25 years. My target price for the stock is $55." A quote from Archie MacAllaster, chairman of MacAllaster Pitfield MacKay in *Barron's 2008 Roundtable.*

What Actually Happened: Bank of America saw its stock drop below $10 and cut its dividend by 50 percent.

Goldman Sachs

"Goldman Sachs makes more money than every other broker-age firm in New York combined and finishes the year at $300 a share. Not a prediction—an inevitability." A quote from James J. Cramer in his "Future of Business" column in *New York* Magazine.

What Actually Happened: Goldman Sachs' share price fell to $78 in December 2008. The firm also announced a $2.2 billion quarterly loss, its first since going public.

Despite the hit to its stock (which has almost doubled by July 2009) Goldman has by far the best management and skills on the Street and will have a consistently better performance than any other major firm.

Predictions from Ben Bernanke and Henry Paulson— We Trust These Officials With Our Economy

Federal Reserve Chairman Ben Bernanke and former Treasury Secretary Henry Paulson unfortunately make an incredible team for wrong forecasts. With the performance below, you have to wonder why they are given so much credibility.

March 28th, 2007—Ben Bernanke: "At this juncture . . . the impact on the broader economy and financial markets of the problems in the subprime markets seems likely to be contained."

March 30, 2007—Dow Jones @ 12,354.

April 20th, 2007—Paulson: "I don't see (subprime mortgage market troubles) imposing a serious problem. I think it's going to be largely contained." "All the signs I look at" show "the housing market is at or near the bottom."

July 12th, 2007—Paulson: "This is far and away the strongest global economy I've seen in my business lifetime."

August 1st, 2007—Paulson: "I see the underlying economy as being very healthy."

October 15th, 2007—Bernanke: "It is not the responsibility of the Federal Reserve—nor would it be appropriate—to protect lenders and investors from the consequences of their financial decisions."

February 28th, 2008—Paulson: "I'm seeing a series of ideas suggested involving major government intervention in the housing market, and these things are usually presented or sold as a way of helping homeowners stay in their homes. Then when you look at them more carefully what they really amount to is a bailout for financial institutions or Wall Street."

May 7, 2008—Paulson: "The worst is likely to be behind us."

June 9th, 2008—Bernanke: "Despite a recent spike in the nation's unemployment rate, the danger that the economy has fallen into a 'substantial downturn' appears to have waned."

July 16th, 2008—Bernanke: "[Freddie and Fannie] . . . will make it through the storm." "[are] . . . in no danger of failing.", ". . . adequately capitalized."

July 31, 2008—Dow Jones @ 11,378

August 10th, 2008—Paulson: "We have no plans to insert money into either of those two institutions" (Fannie Mae and Freddie Mac).

September 8th, 2008—Fannie and Freddie nationalized. The taxpayer is on the hook for an estimated $1–1.5. Over $5 trillion is added to the nation's balance sheet.

Where We Have Been Wrong

There is one area in which we have been wrong before and we will likely be wrong again. Timing exactly when each bubble will pop in the Bubblequake and Aftershock is nearly impossible to accurately predict. Timing is always tricky when making any forecast but if you know what to look for, the *overall trends* of each phase are predictable, even if the exact moments when specific triggers that will activate them are not. That's why, throughout this book, we give general time ranges for our ideas about future events, and we attempt to link these to other signs and events, rather than trying to predict specific dates.

Recognizing the overall trend is absolutely essential. If you know winter is coming, you can prepare yourself without knowing exactly when the first snowflake will fall. On the other hand, if you are expecting summer, that first winter storm is really going to snow you.

An old stock market saying is "the trend is your friend." We say "the trend is your best way to defend" against the dangers of trying to time the Bubblequake and Aftershock. If you know the general trend, your asset protection and investment timing will, on average, be fine (see Chapters 5–7). Even if the trend seems to go against you for a while, if you follow a fundamental trend that you know may take years to play out, you will do fine. This type of fundamental, long-term trend thinking is key for success during each stage of the Bubblequake.

Within an overall trend, there will be moments, or trigger points, when dramatic shifts occur. For example, in the fall of 2008, the stock market dropped more than 20 percent of its value within a few weeks of Lehman Brothers going bankrupt. Predicting the occurrence or the timing of that kind of specific event is essentially impossible. What we did predict with complete accuracy was the overall trend of an over-valued stock market bubble poised for a fall.

Specific trigger points are so hard to predict because their activation usually involves a high psychological component, and try as we might, the timing of human psychology is not especially predictable. For example, if you objectively analyzed the Internet stock bubble prior to its fall, you'd know that it was bound to pop at some point, but you'd be hard pressed to know when and what would kick it off. Even today, well *after* the fact, it is still hard to figure out exactly what triggered the pop of the dot-com bubble in March 2000. Was it the collapse of Microstrategy's stock price due to the restatement of earnings forced on it by Price Waterhouse Coopers in March? That's a good guess, but not necessarily correct. Other people have their own guesses, but in talking to many investment bankers and venture capitalists, we have found no unified agreement on what the actual trigger point was, even though they are experts in this area and this was a major economic event that affected each of them quite personally. All we know with certainty is that we had a bubble in Internet-related stock prices, and in March 2000 investor psychology dramatically changed.

When thinking about how bubbles in general tend to burst, it's interesting to note that during the fall of the Internet bubble, NASDAQ didn't just collapse and go straight down. Over the course of nine months, it fell and recovered, at one point rising not too far from its peak, before its eventual final fall. Even right in the middle of the dot-com crash, most people didn't see it. In fact, the mantra among investors at the time was that we were simply moving away from a business-to-consumer model toward a business-to-business model, and then to an infrastructure play. The infrastructure play begat the rise of the fiber–optic companies in the summer of 2000, most notably JDS Uniphase, before it, too, collapsed. Ultimately, NASDAQ would rise and fall again many times until it had fallen 75 percent from its all-time high of nearly 4700 in early 2000 until finally hitting its low point of 1170 in September 2002.

The moral of the story is that it's hard to predict specific triggers before they happen. Even *after* the fact, it can be hard to understand the timing of specific events. Why did investors change their psychology in March 2000 instead of in August 1999? After March 2000, why did people think that infrastructure was the next big thing? Did they just want to keep the old Internet boom alive or were they really sold on infrastructure? Most investor decision-making turned out to be based on psychology, not real analysis of the underlying trends. Eventually, all the stocks in the infrastructure play collapsed. Even wishful thinking can't grow a bubble forever.

So when people challenge us to tell them exactly when each phase of the Aftershock will begin, we don't take the bait. All we can say with certainty is that the transitions from each phase to the next will involve triggering events, the timing of which will be as hard to predict as the popping of the Internet bubble.

We do know that trends can take years to assert themselves fully, and along the way, long-term trends can be temporarily delayed, even briefly reversed, by a short-term trend. For example, the long-term trend of a falling stock market bubble was temporarily delayed by the short-term trend of the rise of the private equity company buyout bubble. With easy credit at very low interest rates, private equity and hedge funds raised enormous amounts of money and went on a company buying spree the likes of which we've never seen. Total merger and acquisition transaction values went from $441 billion in 2002 to $1.4 trillion in 2006 and $1.3 trillion in 2007, according to Mergerstat. This, plus generally good investor psychology, drove stock prices higher, helping to boom the Dow above 14,000 in 2007. Of course, it also made the stock market bubble much bigger, and therefore, much more vulnerable to the credit crunch, caused by the fall of the housing bubble and the private debt bubble (see Chapter 2).

In another example, the potential full negative impact of the collapse in home prices on the economy and stock market in 2008 was blunted by the short-term trend of lenders making much riskier loans in 2006. Historically, July 2005 was when home prices stopped going up in many places or slowed their growth dramatically. They weren't falling, but they weren't rising rapidly anymore, thus setting the stage for the sub-prime and adjustable-rate mortgage collapse. Lenders' willingness to participate in riskier home loans in 2006 and early 2007 to some extent, slowed the fall of the housing bubble and delayed its impact on the economy and the stock market for a while. In our first book, we couldn't give the exact timing of the housing bubble fall because it was hard for us to predict just how crazy lenders would get. We did know they could not keep it up forever, and in fact, they didn't. Lenders pulled back on their risky loans very dramatically in 2007, triggering an even bigger collapse in real estate prices.

Thus, our 2006 prediction of the long-term trend of falling housing and stock market prices began to emerge with a vengeance by the end of 2007 and early 2008, firmly establishing the start of the Bubblequake. And, if it were not for emergency measures by the Federal Reserve to lower interest rates in the spring of

2008, which were almost unprecedented, the stock market would have fallen much further. *But the dramatic government intervention only served to temporarily blunt (not stop) the effects of the underlying fundamental trend, which is why the falling housing, private debt, and stock market bubbles are still on their way down.* In time, these trends will also include a major Aftershock that few others are anticipating: the bursting of the dollar and government debt bubbles. When will that happen? All we can say with any reasonable degree of confidence is that the full force of the Aftershock will likely begin in the next one to three years.

Love us or hate us—the fact is we got it right before, while others got it wrong. And unfortunately, we will be right again, for the very same reasons. As Paul Farrell, senior columnist for Dow Jones *MarketWatch*, said about our first book in February 2008, "*America's Bubble Economy*'s prediction, though ignored, was accurate."

Leave 'em Laughing

After reading some of the quotes from senior financial analysts and financial leaders you may be laughing or crying. But, to be sure you start the book with a little humor in an otherwise difficult situation, we thought we would close out the first chapter of the book with the following bit of humor. We were e-mailed this by one of our supporters. It's not ours, but we honestly don't know who to give credit to. So, if someone knows who wrote this, e-mail or call us and we'll post it on our web site.

You Know It's a Bad Economy When . . .

1. Your bank returns your check marked as "insufficient funds" and you have to call them and ask if they meant you or them.
2. The most highly-paid job is now jury service.
3. People in Beverly Hills fire their nannies and are learning their children's names.
4. McDonalds is selling the quarter- ouncer.
5. Obama met with small businesses—GE, Chrysler, Citigroup, and GM—to discuss the stimulus package.
6. Hot Wheels and Matchbox cars are now trading at higher prices than GM's stock.
7. You got a predeclined credit card in the mail.
8. Your "reality check" bounced.

9. The stock market indexes have been renamed: the Dow is now the "Down-Jones" and the S&P is the "Substandard & Very Poor".

10. Webster's is keeping its dictionary length constant by adding words that are commonly used, such as Twitter, tweet, and Facebook, and dropping those no longer needed, such as retirement, pensions, and Social Security. The continuing evolution of the experts' predictions is covered at our web site, www.aftershockeconomy.com/chapter1

He Said What?!

In an appearance on CNBC's "Squawk Box" in February 2008, co-author Bob Wiedemer offered what must have seemed like a whacky investment idea: *Start shorting housing stocks.* The analysts on the program cringed at what they considered yesterday's news—perhaps good advice the year before, but clearly no longer valid. Bob stood his ground. Based not on a lucky guess or some morbid wish for a crash, but based on the science-backed analysis of our first book, Bob knew the full collapse of the housing bubble (and therefore the construction industry) still lay ahead.

By now, we all know he was very right. Homebuilders' stocks fell by almost 50 percent over the next year, according to the Dow Jones U.S. Home Construction Index, which fell from 20 in February 2008 to 10 in December 2008. It would have been a tidy profit for any investor, especially if you were wise enough to use LEAPs (Long-Term Equity Anticipation Securities, which are publicly traded options contracts with expiration dates longer than one year)—one of our many investment suggestions. If you have an underlying theory that predicts overall trends, based on cold, hard facts, you don't have to run with the pack. Without trying to precisely "time the market," if you know the overall trend, you can stay out in front of the curve.

In fact, while the cameras were still rolling and the experts were still telling him he was dead wrong, Bob knew that eventually *all* the major publicly traded homebuilders would not just decline, they would eventually go bankrupt. Naturally, he didn't dare say such a thing. (You don't get invited back on these shows if you are too pessimistic about stocks.) But, on that particular prediction, we know Bob will be quite right again. Without an underlying theory of economic evolution to base one's investment ideas on, even the "experts" don't realize just how fundamental the coming changes will be.

CHAPTER 2

Phase I: The Bubblequake

POP GO THE HOUSING, STOCK, PRIVATE DEBT, AND SPENDING BUBBLES

What in the world happened? There we were, with the Dow over 14,000, U.S. home prices close to their all-time highs, and consumer and commercial credit flowing like honey on a hot summer day. Then, seemingly overnight, things weren't so sweet. It may feel like the proverbial rug was randomly pulled out from under us, but in fact, we've been setting ourselves up for this multi-bubble fall over many years. Beginning with our decision in the early 1980s to run large government deficits, six co-linked bubbles have been growing bigger and bigger, each working to lift the others, all booming and supporting the U.S. economy:

- The real estate bubble
- The stock market bubble
- The private debt bubble
- The discretionary spending bubble
- The dollar bubble
- The government debt bubble

The first four of these bubbles began to burst in the Bubblequake that rocked the U.S. and world economies in late 2008 and 2009. Next, while most people think the worst is over, the coming Aftershock will bring down all six bubbles in the next two to four years. We know this is hard to believe, and we wish it weren't true, but as you will see in this and the next chapter, all the evidence is right there, plain as day. You just need to know what to look for.

Bubbles "R" Us: A Quick Review of America's Bubble Economy

What is a bubble? This should be an easy question to answer but there is no academically accepted definition of a financial or economic bubble. For our purposes, we define a bubble as an asset value that temporarily booms and eventually bursts, based on changing investor psychology rather than underlying, fundamental economic drivers that are sustainable over time.

For the last several years, America's multi-bubble economy has been growing because of six co-linked bubbles, some of which you may find easier to believe than others. These six bubbles are outlined below.

The Real Estate Bubble

Now that it's popped, the housing bubble is easy to see. As shown in Figure 2.1, from 2000 to 2006, home prices grew almost 100 percent

Income Up 2%   Housing Prices Up 80%

Figure 2.1   Income Growth versus Housing Price Growth 2001–2006
Contrary to what some experts say, the earlier rapid growth of housing prices was not driven by rising wage and salary income. In fact, from 2001 to 2006, housing price growth far exceeded income growth.
Source: Bureau of Labor Statistics and the S&P/Case-Shiller Home Price Index.

according to the Case-Shiller Home Price Index, while the inflation-adjusted wages and salaries of the people buying the homes went up only 2 percent for the same period, according to the Bureau of Labor Statistics. The rise in home prices so profoundly outpaced the rise of incomes that even our most conservative analysis back in 2005 led us to correctly predict that the vulnerable housing bubble would be the first to fall. We have a lot more to say about what's ahead for the housing market later in this chapter. (Hint: It's not what they tell you to think.)

If nothing else, just looking at Figure 2.2 on inflation-adjusted housing prices since 1890, created by Yale economist Robert Shiller, should make anyone suspicious that there was a VERY big housing bubble in the making. Note that home prices barely rose on an inflation-adjusted basis until the 1980s and then just exploded in 2001.

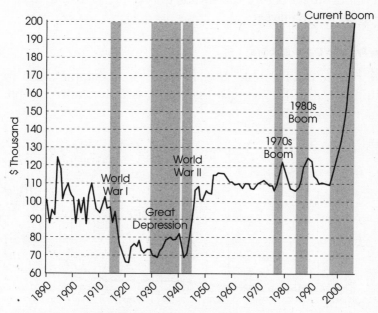

Figure 2.2   Price of Homes Adjusted for Inflation Since 1890
Contrary to popular belief, housing prices do not ordinarily rise rapidly. In fact, until recently, inflation-adjusted home prices haven't increased that significantly, but then they just exploded after 2001 (1890 index equals 100).
Source: Irrational Exuberance, second edition, 2006 by Robert J. Shiller.

The Stock Market Bubble

This one was almost as easy for us to spot as the housing bubble, yet many times harder to get other people to see. Stocks can be analyzed in so many different ways. We find the state of the stock market is easier to understand by looking at Figure 2.3. After decades of growth, the Dow had risen 300 percent from 1928 to 1982 (54 years). Yet in the next 20 years the Dow increased an astonishing 1200 percent, growing four times as fast as before, but without four times the growth in company earnings or our GDP. We call that a stock market bubble.

Shown in a different way in Figure 2.4, the value of financial assets as a percentage of GDP held relatively steady at around 450 percent since 1960. But starting in 1981 it rose to over 1000 percent in 2007, according to the Federal Reserve. We call that prima facie evidence of a stock and real estate bubble.

Readers of our October 2006 book who followed our advice and got out of stocks before the Bubblequake hit, were able to sell near the peak of the market.

The Private Debt Bubble

The private debt bubble, like all bubbles, is complex. But we will simplify it a bit by saying it essentially is a derivative bubble that

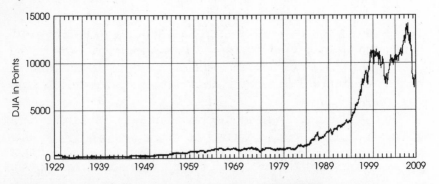

Figure 2.3   Dow Jones Industrial Average 1928–2007
Despite massive growth in the U.S. economy between 1928 and 1981, the Dow only rose about 300 percent. But after 1981 it rose an astonishing 1400 percent.
Source: Dow Jones.

Figure 2.4   Financial Assets As a Percentage of GDP
The exploding value of financial assets as a percentage of GDP is strong
evidence of a financial bubble.
Sources: Thomson Datastream and the Federal Reserve.

was driven by two other bubbles: the rapidly rising home price
bubble and the rapidly rising stock market bubble, which combined to make for a strong and growing economy. In both cases,
lenders of all forms (not just banks) began to feel very comfortable with the false idea that the risk of a falling economy had been
essentially eliminated and the risk of any lending in that environment was minimal. This fantasy was supported for a time by the
fact that very few loans went into default. Certainly, at the time we
wrote our first book, commercial and consumer loan default rates
were at historic lows.

The problem was not so much the amount of private debt
that made it a bubble, but having too much debt under the false
assumption that nothing would go wrong with the economy. That
also meant that lenders assumed asset prices would not fall. Lenders
felt very comfortable increasing the amount they lent for consumer
credit card loans, home mortgages, home equity loans, commercial
real estate loans, corporate loans, buyout loans, and just about every
kind of loan, due to increasing asset values and a healthy economy
that no one thought would change.

For us, it was easy to see in 2006 that if the value of housing or stocks were to fall dramatically (as bubbles always eventually do), a tremendous number of loan defaults would occur. The private debt bubble was a derivative bubble par excellence that was bound to pop when the housing and stock market bubbles popped.

The Discretionary Spending Bubble

Consumer spending accounts for about 70 percent of the U.S. economy (depending on exactly how you define consumer spending). A large portion of consumer spending is "discretionary spending," meaning it's optional (How big a portion depends on exactly how you define discretionary). Easy bubble-generated money and easy consumer credit made lots of easy discretionary spending possible at every income level. Now, as the housing, stock market, and private debt bubbles pop and people lose their jobs, or are concerned they may, consumers are reducing their spending, especially unnecessary, discretionary spending.

This is typical in any recession, but this time it is much more profound for two key reasons. First, the private debt bubble allowed consumers to spend like crazy due to huge growth in housing prices and a growing stock market and economy, which gave them more access to credit than ever before, via credit cards and home equity loans. As the bubbles pop, that credit is drying up, and so is the huge consumer spending that was driven by it.

Secondly, much of our spending on necessities has a high discretionary component, which is relatively easy for us to give up. We need food, but we don't need Whole Foods. We need to eat, but we don't need to eat at Bennigans or Steak & Ale (both now bankrupt). We need refrigerators and countertops, but we don't need stainless steel refrigerators and granite countertops. The list of necessities that have a high discretionary component goes on and on. And all that discretionary spending is on top of completely discretionary spending, such as entertainment and vacation travel.

The combined fall of the first four bubbles (housing, stock market, private debt, and discretionary spending) make up what we call the Bubblequake of late 2008 and 2009. Unfortunately, our troubles don't end there. Two more giant bubbles are about to burst in the coming Aftershock.

The Dollar Bubble

Perhaps the hardest reality of all to face, the once mighty greenback has become an unsustainable currency bubble. Due to a rising bubble economy, investors from all over the world were getting huge returns on their dollar-denominated assets. This made the dollar more valuable——but also more vulnerable. Why? Because we didn't really have a true booming economy, we had a multi-bubble economy. The value of a currency in a multi-bubble economy is linked, not to real, underlying, fundamental drivers of sustainable economic growth (like true productivity gains), but to the rising and falling bubbles. For many years our dollars rose in value because of rising demand for dollars to make investments in our bubbles. Now the falling bubbles will eventually create falling-value dollars, despite all kinds of government efforts to stop it. (Don't believe us? You will by the end of the next chapter.)

The Government Debt Bubble

Weighing in at more than $8.5 trillion when our 2006 book came out, and expected to exceed $12 trillion by the end of 2009 as shown in Figure 2.5, the whopping U.S. government debt bubble is currently the biggest, baddest, scariest bubble of all, relative to the other bubbles in our economy. Much of this debt has been funded by foreign investors, primarily from Asia and Europe. But as our multi-bubble economy continues to fall and the dollar starts to sink, who in the world will be willing, or even able, to lend us more? (Much more on the fall of the impossibly huge government debt bubble in the next chapter.)

From Boom to Bust: The Virtuous Upward Spiral Becomes a Vicious Downward Spiral

On the way up, these six linked economic bubbles helped co-create America's booming bubble economy. In a seemingly virtuous upward spiral, the inflating bubbles helped the United States maintain its status as the biggest economy the world has ever known, even in the last few decades, when declines in real productivity growth could have slowed our expanding economic growth. Instead, these bubbles helped us ignore slowing productivity growth, boost our prosperity, disregard some fundamental problems, and keep the party going.

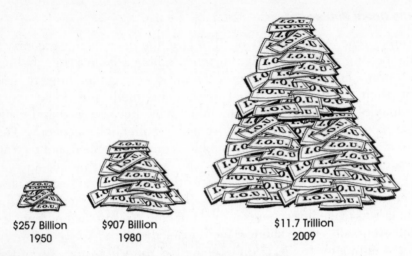

$257 Billion
1950

$907 Billion
1980

$11.7 Trillion
2009

Figure 2.5   Growth of the U.S. Government's Debt
The U.S. Government's debt is massive and growing rapidly. With no plan
to pay it off and not much ability to pay it off either, it is quickly becoming
the world's largest toxic asset.
Source: Federal Reserve.

Not only did the U.S. economy continue to grow and remain
strong, the rest of the world benefited as well. Money we paid for
rapidly increasing imports poured like Miracle-Gro into developing
countries like China and India, quickly expanding their burgeoning economies. The developed nations benefited as well. Because
America's bubble economy was booming along with the developing nations, Japan and Europe were able to sell lots of their cars
and other high-end exports, which helped their home economies
prosper. The growing world economy created a rising demand for
energy, pushing up oil prices, which made some Russian billionaires, among others, very happy. Growing demand for minerals, like
iron, oil, and copper, pumped money into every resource-producing
country. China and India's expanding appetite for steel boosted
iron exports from the Australian economy. And on, and on. All combined, America's rising bubble economy helped boom the world's
rising bubble economy.

Now, as our intermingled global party bubbles are beginning
to deflate and fall, the virtuous upward spiral has become a vicious
downward spiral. Linked together and pushing hard against the others, each time any one bubble sags and pops, it puts tremendous

downward pressure on the rest. First, we had the fall of the U.S. housing bubble and its downward impact on the stock market bubble, the private debt bubble, and the discretionary spending bubble—what we call the Bubblequake. Next, in the Aftershock, the dollar bubble and the U.S. government debt bubbles will begin their unavoidable descents (Chapter 3). And as the final bubbles in America's bubble economy begin to burst, so will the world's bubble economy (Chapter 4).

It is important to understand that the Bubblequake problems we are now facing are due to much more than merely a popped real estate bubble. If all we had were a burst housing bubble, it would not have created so much financial pain here and around the globe. In addition to the housing bubble, the private debt bubble and the stock market bubble also fell. And these problems are not going to be resolved anytime soon. Rather than the housing bubble, private debt bubble, and stock market bubble magically re-inflating, they will instead continue to fall. This will continue to put downward pressure on the already vulnerable dollar bubble and bulging U.S. government debt bubble, eventually forcing both to burst, creating a worldwide mega-depression. Unless you know what to look for, the coming Aftershock will be hard to see until it's too late to protect yourself (Chapters 3–7).

Once all six of our economy-supporting bubbles are fully popped, life in the post-dollar-bubble world (discussed in Chapter 10) will look quite different than the relatively quick recovery most analysts are now predicting. The vicious downward spiral of multiple popping bubbles will move the economy from the current Bubblequake to the coming Aftershock faster than the onset of the troubles we've already seen. And moving from the Aftershock to the post-dollar-bubble world will go quite quickly indeed. So although there is much more economic change ahead, it will increasingly happen in shorter and shorter periods of time.

While it may seem chaotic and unpredictable, all this change will not be entirely random but will happen as part of a much bigger picture of ongoing economic evolution. That evolution will eventually involve some very effective solutions for the economy's problems that would be politically impossible to implement today (discussed in Chapter 8).

If you've read the last few pages, you now know more than nearly everyone else about how we got ourselves into this mess. Now the big question is how bad will this Bubblequake get? How low will U.S. real estate, private credit, and stocks go? The rest of the chapter focuses on these three bursting bubbles.

Pop Goes the Housing Bubble

The most important thing to understand about the current housing crunch is that it's not a subprime mortgage problem whose contagion spread to other mortgages; it is a *housing price collapse.* If home prices had not declined there would never have been a subprime mortgage problem at all. If home prices had continued rising as they had in the past, the low introductory, adjustable-rate subprime loans would have simply been re-financed into new low introductory, adjustable-rate subprime loans based on the higher equity in the home, and everything would have been just fine.

But, if there is a housing price collapse, the low introductory, adjustable-rate subprime loans are doomed. These subprime mortgages are not the cause of the problem; they are merely the first to get hit. If you have a housing price collapse and not just a subprime mortgage problem, then as housing prices continue to collapse, the Alt-A, no documented income, "liar loans" start to fail. Loans made on investment properties also get hit. Fancy mortgages to people with good credit that allow the payer the option of paying less than the interest owed and no principal at all (so called option ARM mortgages) take a hit, too. Home equity loans get pinched. Eventually, as the housing price collapse continues, perfectly good prime mortgages get hit, as well. It's not a "spreading contagion" from the subprime problem, as they so often try to tell us in the press. It's just the fallout from a continuously declining housing price bubble that is impacting more and more people.

Falling equity value (not subprime mortgages) is the single most important factor leading to mortgage default and foreclosure. Falling equity values make refinancing any adjustable loan very difficult. Home equity has been falling dramatically with the Bubblequake. As of the second quarter of 2007 it passed a milestone, with the percentage of equity Americans have in their homes falling below 50 percent for the first time since 1945 according to the Federal Reserve. It has fallen below 45 percent since then and continues to fall at a rapid rate today.

Because of the housing price collapse and the damage it caused to home equity, the number of mortgages that are *underwater,* meaning they have no equity or negative equity, is increasing extremely rapidly. Today almost a quarter of all mortgages in the United States are underwater, with many more being added daily.

As the housing bubble pops, more homeowners will lose all of the equity in their homes. As of Q2 2009 more than 33 percent had no equity or were underwater, up from 14.3 percent in Q3 2008, according to Zillow.com.

Even more ominous, a report by Deutsche Bank published in August 2009 forecasted that by 2011 almost half of mortgage holders, about 25 million borrowers, will be underwater on their mortgages.

Co-author Bob Wiedemer likes to demonstrate the impact of falling home values on the economy by pushing a pencil into a balloon. The pencil represents declining home value; the more home prices falls, the deeper the pencil pushes in to the balloon. The balloon represents the economy. As the pencil goes further and further into the balloon, more mortgages of the higher grade are taken down at an increasing rate, taking the economy down with them. Ultimately, the balloon pops because house prices can only go down so far before they will trigger a major collapse in the mortgage market and the economy, a process we will describe in more detail later.

No One Thought Home Prices Would Decline

It was always assumed that subprime loans were risky loans, and so they carried a higher interest rate than non-subprime. What was not factored into anyone's calculations was the possibility (to us, the probability) that home prices would eventually fall. The models used by the bond-rating firms and investment banking firms that rated and sold the complex mortgage-backed securities that included subprime loans never anticipated home prices falling, at least not to any significant degree. As their analysts now readily admit, they anticipated various levels of home price increases—some low, some medium—but certainly not much of a home price decrease. Were these people crazy? Not a bit. After all, home prices have almost never declined in recent history. You would have to go back to the post-World War I recession to find any serious inflation-adjusted home price decline, and even then only for a short period of time. From 1916 to 1921 home values fell about 30 percent, according to data from the Case-Shiller Home Price Index. Inflation-adjusted home prices actually rose during most of the Great Depression.

Virtually no one in the investment world, or even outside the investment world, thought home prices in the United States would ever decline significantly, and certainly not for any extended length of time. There was no historical precedent for it to happen.

But, just as we predicted, happen it did. How come? Because home prices were in a *bubble*. As mentioned earlier, home prices were up 100 percent and income was up only 2 percent from 2000 to 2006. If that isn't a textbook example of an asset bubble, we don't know what is. That kind of price growth without comparable income growth to support it is just not sustainable for very long. It had to be a bubble; therefore, it had to pop.

People will give you a thousand reasons to justify the growing real estate bubble: "People love San Francisco," "There is limited land in Boston (or Manhattan, or LA)," "Washington, DC has a very stable job base," or "People enjoy living close to the city."

None of these reasons ever explained why prices were increasing so much in a fairly flat economy. And the economic growth that did occur in 2003 and 2004 was due in large part to rising home equity spending and rising home construction.

"Innovations" in the Mortgage Industry Made the Housing Bubble Possible

An important ingredient for growing such a large real estate bubble so quickly was the highly "innovative" mortgage industry. The industry developed new products and enhanced previous ones, such as the adjustable-rate mortgage, which had been around for a while but now was taken to a whole new level. Innovations included a low introductory interest rate—the same idea credit card companies used to hook consumers. Start with a low rate of 1 percent or 2 percent for the first two or three years and then jump to a normal adjustable-rate mortgage.

Another "innovation" was the willingness to give these mortgages to people who could only afford them at the low introductory rate, not the rate that was coming later. This made more expensive homes much easier for people to buy, often with the idea of selling them later for a big profit when home prices continued to climb.

The mortgage industry also innovated with no-documentation loans, called Alt-A loans or "liar loans." These loans had been around before but they were pushed much harder during the housing boom. Also, low credit scores were increasingly acceptable, and with the housing bubble on the rise more people lied about their incomes in order to get their hands on the keys to a piece of the housing boom.

Option ARMs were another incredible innovation. Every month you get the choice of paying a full payment of interest and principal, or an interest-only payment, or—get this—a smaller payment that didn't even cover the interest! The interest you didn't pay would be added to the principal of the loan until the loan value reached 110 percent or 125 percent of the original amount, at which point you would have to jump to full payment of interest and the payment on the new, much larger principal. No wonder they called them "suicide loans." More than 80 percent of folks who took these deadly loans paid the lowest option possible (who takes these loans if you want to pay more than the least possible?). Not surprisingly, the default rates on these loans will soon reach 90 percent by some estimates.

Mortgage brokers became much more prevalent during the housing boom and they became much more aggressive in selling as many mortgages as possible. Bad loans were not their problem. The quality of the loan was for the underwriter to decide. As long as the broker could place the loan with an underwriter, that's all that was necessary for the broker to get paid. What happened to the loan after that was not their worry.

Amazingly, in many cases, it was not the worry of the underwriter either. Many underwriters just wanted to repackage these loans into mortgage-backed securities and sell them in big multimillion dollar bundles to large investors, often in other countries. The underwriter collected their underwriting fees and never had to worry if the poor suckers who took out the mortgages could ever make payments to the poor suckers who bought the mortgage-backed securities. The foreign and other investors who bought these mortgage-backed securities considered them as secure as government bonds, but with a higher interest rate. *The bond rating agencies, like Moody's and Standard & Poor's, encouraged these sentiments by giving most of the bond packages their highest AAA rating—same as the U.S. government.* The high rating was often required for many investment funds to buy the bonds.

All of this and even more "innovations" by the mortgage industry were key to making the housing bubble possible. Now that these "innovations" are gone, lending has decreased substantially. In 2003, lending for single-family homes was $3.9 trillion. In 2008 it was half that amount, according the Mortgage Bankers Association. That huge decrease in lending has put enormous downward pressure on the housing bubble.

Had Home Prices Kept Going Up Rapidly, the Mortgage Industry Would Still Be Fine

In fairness to the mortgage industry, if home prices had kept going up and up, none of this would have been much of a problem. People could have easily re-financed their way out of all their fancy mortgages into other new fancy mortgages based on the huge rise in home equity. Had home prices continued going up in value there would have been little risk in making these higher risk innovative mortgages. That is, the risk that was not offset by higher fees and slightly higher interest rates.

Had Home Prices Kept Going Up Rapidly, Home Buyers Would Still Be Fine

In all fairness to the home buyer, if home prices had kept going up, it would have made tons of sense to buy the most expensive house you could possibly get away with. As long as you could make the monthly payments for at least a year (low introductory rate payments really helped with that) and as long as your home's price was going up 10 or 20 percent a year, you would be practically minting money.

For example, for a $500,000 house, a 10 to 20 percent rise in home prices annually created an increase of $50,000 to $100,000 in home equity every year. All you had to do was convert that growing equity into cash via a refinancing or a home equity loan, and you would have had plenty of money to make your house payments and buy a lot of toys along the way. When the housing bubble was rising, you were actually getting paid to buy a home—paid a *lot* of money. What could be better? So please do not blame homebuyers; they were making excellent investment decisions—*as long as home prices kept rising rapidly.*

Had Home Prices Kept Going Up Rapidly, Wall Street Would Still Be Fine

No one thought housing prices would stop rising rapidly and actually go down. Even the best minds on Wall Street seemed blind to the bubble that they were helping to create. Remember, bubbles are a lot easier see *after* they pop. And remember, too, that not noticing the housing bubble was making a lot of people very, very rich. So no one complained or criticized. Quite the opposite; they sang the praises of the brilliant new Wall Street mega-millionaires. Bear Stearns' profits were enormous and many Wall Street insiders made out like bandits. And if the housing bubble had just kept rising, Wall Street would have been just fine.

But, as it turned out for Bear Stearns and the rest of Wall Street, making money by making bad investments and then selling those bad investments to others is a very bad long-term strategy. Even if the federal government comes along and partially bails you out, it's very painful when the boom dies.

And die it did, because even the most "innovative" mortgages and creative new investment instruments could not get around one fundamental fact: Home prices cannot rise dramatically faster than incomes rise over any significant amount of time. It flies in the face of basic economic principles and has never happened before and never will again. Real estate bubbles don't last.

That is the kind of excellent and honest analysis that Wall Street could have really used before the housing bubble popped, but would have been laughed at and ignored. Their lack of interest in such analysis has cost them very heavily indeed.

" Honey, We're homeless."

Where Do Home Prices Go from Here?

Even now, smart people continue to make the same mistakes as before. They feel that the fall in home prices has to stop and turn around fairly soon and they want to get a "bargain." That's why so many people are still buying homes. In 2008, Alan Greenspan announced that home prices would stop falling by spring 2009. He was wrong, of course. He was just cheerleading. But even if he were right for a short period of time and real estate values did begin to temporarily stabilize, they would only start declining again. Why? Because it's a bubble! That means home prices are still higher than is justified by underlying, fundamental economic drivers. There are only two ways to get home values to rise again: Either re-inflate the bubble, which at this point is not possible, or have real economic reasons for a rise in home prices, which currently do not exist. So, like it or not, home prices will continue to go down, along with all the other bubbles in our multi-bubble economy.

Bubbles don't rise and fall in a straight line because psychology has so much to do with it. As we mentioned before, it is hard to predict the exact timing of the next leg down, but you can be sure that projections and proclamations by various economic experts that falling home prices are stabilizing and turning around are mostly conjecture. You will notice that there is never much of a reason given for the predicted about face. They don't say why home prices will stop falling and start rising, or offer any analysis based on the fundamental forces driving real estate prices. Perhaps they just feel it "can't get any worse" so it has to get better soon. Home prices, after all, normally go up, and so the current decline has to be just a temporary aberration. This sounds a lot like what Wall Streeters might have said a few years ago. Instead of doing a careful analysis of the economics behind the asset values, they simply relied on the fact that, in the past, stock prices and home prices went up, so in the future, they would have to go up too. Apparently, they don't listen to their own disclaimer: "Past performance is no guarantee of future results."

All these projections by Greenspan and others are optimistic conjecturing at best and pure cheerleading at worst. Either way, they are telling people what they want to hear because that's what gets the biggest audience. (By the way, we like to hear it, too.

We also own houses.) As a useful alternative to simple conjecture and wishful cheerleading, we offer a point by point analysis of what we believe are the key drivers of U.S. home prices and the other bubbles, in "Appendix A: Forces Driving the Collapse of the Bubbles."

Pop Goes the Stock Market Bubble

The fall of the housing bubble caused many mortgages to go into default, particularly the riskier subprime mortgages given to people who often could not afford them. Some of these subprime mortgages probably would have gone into default even if the housing price bubble were still afloat because they were risky loans. But once the housing bubble started to fall and lots of people had mortgages greater than the value of their homes, mortgage defaults began to rise dramatically. This caused unexpectedly large losses in the massive mortgage-backed securities market felt both by the investors who bought mortgage-backed securities and the investment banks that held mortgage-backed securities. Because the mortgage-backed securities market was so big, these losses roiled the entire credit market.

The credit markets began to freeze up partly due to fear of not knowing which financial institutions were holding what losses (the financial institutions themselves didn't even know, so it was hard for anyone else to know). More importantly, credit froze because investors who thought they were buying highly secure AAA bonds lost confidence. If AAA bonds could go bad, what was next?

The collapse in credit market confidence and in the value of the banks began to pop the stock market bubble. Had the stock market not been in a bubble, it would not have fallen so far so quickly. Not only were stock prices in a bubble, but about two-thirds of the increase in the value of the stock market from 2005 to 2007 was due to increases in financial and energy stocks. With these financial institutions losing the value of many of their assets, their stock prices began to plummet. This spread to the rest of the stock market as investors began worrying about a major market correction. Rising financial stocks had been the key driver of the rising stock market, so now that financial stocks were collapsing, their fears were quite valid.

The Collapse of the Mortgage-Backed Securities Market Popped the Private Equity Buyout Bubble, Creating the Credit Crunch

In addition to harming the value of financial stocks and overall investor confidence in the stock market in general, toxic mortgage-backed securities also punched a hole in the private equity buyout bubble, which on its way up had helped boom the stock market in 2006 and 2007. Back then, private equity firms were able to take on massive amounts of debt on incredibly favorable terms to buy increasingly larger companies. New records for the sheer size of these transactions were being made monthly. At its peak in 2006, 11,750 deals valued at $1.48 trillion were completed according to Mergerstat. It seemed as if every few days another large public company would be bought, and always at a big premium to the market price. The name of the game wasn't to pay a low price; instead the private equity masters of the Universe competed to pay the highest price possible for a company.

It was all very exciting and the stock market loved it. The market didn't need many reasons to go up. The economy was good and the market players were in a good mood. The private equity buyout bubble was just the tonic needed to push the Dow from the 11,000 range in 2006 to a peak of 14,164 in late 2007. Even after the private equity buyout bubble began to slow, the momentum it had created in the market continued.

Like all bubbles, it eventually popped, too. Ultimately bondholders, frightened by the credit crunch, were beginning to worry about the incredibly favorable terms being offered by buyout firms. Many of the loans to do the deals required little equity, and were called "covenant lite," meaning the borrowers had few benchmarks that they had to meet in order to maintain their loans in good standing. Even riskier, many loans did not even require that interest be paid in cash. Instead, the interest could be paid in more debt, or payment-in-kind (PIK).

But, as the mortgage-backed securities debacle continued, investors became increasingly afraid. All of a sudden, there was a greater perception and awareness of risk, which amazingly, investors did not have during the peak of the private equity buyout bubble. Lenders started asking for better terms. They quit agreeing to covenant lite loans and most importantly, they wanted more equity. They wanted the buyout firms to share more of what they now saw as a growing perceived risk. This, of course, put the kibosh on the private equity buyout bubble. Many deals in negotiation fell apart. Even some already agreed to deals were called off.

An even bigger problem, many investment and commercial banks were on the hook for transactions that had recently taken place. They had lent out the money to complete the transactions, fully expecting to be able sell that debt to other investors. When the money musical chairs came to a halt, a lot of that debt became un-saleable, except at a loss, and sometimes at a very big loss.

For the stock market, the party had been ruined. The private equity buyout boom had ended and so had the glorious tonic that had driven up the market to record highs. The decline of the mortgage-backed securities market and the popping of the private equity bubble caused the Bear Stearns implosion in spring 2008, and then the fall of Lehman Brothers in fall 2008.

It Isn't a Liquidity Problem, It's a Bad Loan Problem!

The mantra during the credit crunch following the collapse of Bear Stearns, and the even worse global credit crunch after the collapse of Lehman Brothers, was that we had a "liquidity" problem and all the U.S. Federal Reserve and other central banks had to do was inject liquidity into the markets. However, it wasn't a liquidity problem at all—it was a bad loan problem.

A liquidity problem occurs when a bank has sound financial assets, but for some reason people want to pull money out of the bank. This used to be called a "run on the bank" and happened frequently before the Fed was created to help prevent such a problem. By loaning the bank money (aka "injecting liquidity"), the Fed made it possible for the bank to pay off the people who wanted their money back. But, that assumed that the bank's underlying assets were sound. It was only the people who wanted their money back that were unsound in their fears.

In the case of the latest credit crunch, quite the opposite is true. The bank's assets are unsound, while the people who want their money back are very sound, indeed. Therefore, this is not a liquidity crisis, but a *bad loan crisis*. Investment and commercial banks made a lot of bad loans and hence, they had a lot of bad assets. It is not a crisis of confidence; but a crisis of bad investments that is scaring people. Interestingly, bankers are *still* making a lot of bad loans on the false assumption that the economy will turn around and asset values will not fall much more.

The loans the Fed and other central banks, primarily the European Central Bank (ECB), made to these banks were essentially to cover losses. How much of a loss is still unknown, but one thing we do know: These losses will continue to increase as the value of the assets decline further. As the bubbles pop and asset values decline, these loans will also decline in value and the Fed and the ECB will face horrendous mounting losses. The central banks will take a write-off—meaning they will let the money they have created to make these loans to the banks simply remain in the money supply, eventually causing future inflation.

So, when you hear the experts talking about the "credit crunch" in relation to the stock market or the banks, simply insert these words, instead: "Bad loans going south." These bad investments ultimately impacted the stock market most directly and initially on the most vulnerable part of the stock market—the private equity buyout bubble.

The Key Forces Driving the Stock Market Bubble

The private equity buyout bubble was the first part of the stock market bubble to get hit because it was the *most vulnerable* part of the market. However, there are other stock market drivers putting downward pressure on the stock market, such as the dramatic decline in large, high priced merger and acquisition activity by corporations and the massive decline in corporate stock buy-backs.

As with the real estate market, most stock market analysts don't like to look at these fundamental drivers of price but, instead, assume the stock market will rebound because it has gone up before and it "inevitably" will continue to go up again. The implication is that the gains will be significant even if not at the level of the last few years before the recent market collapse.

However, just like housing, all of these projections of a rebounding stock market are mostly conjecture. There is never much of a reason given for the coming positive change. It's not an analysis based on the fundamental forces driving the stock market. Like real estate, it is more of a feeling that stock prices have gone up a lot in the past 30 years and sooner or later they will begin that inevitable rise again. However, as we know, past performance is no guarantee of future performance!

So, as an alternative to simple optimistic conjecturing and cheer-leading, we will do for stocks what we did for real estate, and put a more detailed analysis in Appendix A. In this chapter, we want to keep you focused on the broader picture of what is happening in the Phase I Bubblequake. But, the details behind all this are important.

When Will the Stock Market Turn Around and Go Back Up Again?

Because we had a bubble in stock prices, there are only two ways to go back to high prices again: Either re-inflate the bubble, which is not possible at this point (the previous drivers of the stock bubble are gone), or have real, underlying economic reasons for a rise in stock prices (like significantly rising company earnings), which currently do not exist. So, like it or not, the stock market bubble—just like the housing bubble—will continue to fall along with all the other bubbles in our multi-bubble economy. Why? Because just like real estate, the stock market is a bubble on the way down.

We know the stock market is a bubble in part because the Dow rose 14-fold from 1982 to 2007, while company earnings rose only three-fold for the same period. That means we had a stock bubble. And the rise in company earnings has been a bubble. Over the long term, as Nobel Prize winning economist Milton Friedman and others have shown, earnings rise about as fast as GDP. Certainly the GDP didn't rise 300 percent during that period. So that means stock prices have been too high compared to earnings, and earnings have been too high compared to real economic growth.

For some visual proof, it's worth looking again at the chart in Chapter 1 on the growth of the Dow, which shows relatively normal growth since the 1920s until 1982 when it skyrockets upwards. Also, look at the chart near it that shows financial assets as a percentage of GDP skyrocketing upward at the same time. It is the classic picture of a bubble.

Of course, even after looking at the evidence and the charts you may still be saying, "but, the Dow did go up almost 3000 points in the spring and summer of this year." That's true, but it's not that much above where it started the beginning of the year and it could easily fall back down below where it started the year by the time this book is published. The earnings certainly aren't there to justify such an increase in the market and neither is the earnings outlook.

What this emphasizes is that you have to be able to differentiate short term volatility from long term trends and the long term economic fundamentals that ultimately drive those trends. We will certainly continue to have volatility, including, quite likely another bear market rally, possibly in spring 2010. But, the long term trends for the market based on the economic fundamentals are definitely negative.

Pop Goes the Private Debt Bubble

The full credit crisis hasn't kicked in yet. That will only happen in the Aftershock, when the dollar bubble and the government debt bubbles pop. When consumers can still get 0 percent financing on a new car, as they can right now, you don't have a credit crisis. When you can get a 5-percent, 30-year fixed-rate mortgage, you don't have a credit crisis. In spring 2009, Toll Brothers was even offering a 3.99 percent 30-year fixed-rate mortgage on the homes they built. Of course, these loans are only to qualified buyers. During 2002—2006, mortgage and auto loans often went to unqualified buyers, so that is a bit of a change. We got so used to credit flowing to anyone willing to take it that now we actually think if an *unqualified buyer* cannot get a loan or cannot get the best interest rates possible, then we have a credit crisis.

We also do not have a credit crisis for business loans. Companies like Wal-Mart do not have to pay 20 percent interest on their inventory loans, and they aren't being turned down for loans entirely. It's true that construction loans for buildings that won't make money are being turned down as are loans for buying commercial real estate at prices that are way too high. But we can't exactly call that a credit crisis. It's more of a return to credit rationalism, which apparently is very foreign to many of us.

However, when the dollar bubble pops, we will most definitely have a massive credit crunch. Very few businesses or individuals will be able to get loans at that point. More importantly, not long after the dollar bubble pops, the massive government debt bubble will burst and the U.S. government will no longer be able to get any credit either.

The Private Debt Bubble Will Pop Twice: In Phase I, Bad Loans Go Bad. In Phase II, Good Loans Go Bad

In Phase I (the Bubblequake), the private debt bubble started to pop in 2008 and 2009, with some bad loans going into default. This will become an even bigger problem in 2010 and 2011 when many more bad loans go bad with the help of a continuing downturn in the economy.

However, in Phase II (the Aftershock), the private debt bubble will more fully collapse when the dollar bubble pops and *good* loans go bad. This is because even good loans (the ones that have reasonable leverage ratios that normally could withstand a modest economic downturn) will not be able to survive the kind of high interest rates, inflation and economic collapse that will follow the popping of the dollar bubble (explained in the next chapter). In this chapter, we are focusing only on the first stage of the private debt bubble pop in Phase I.

The Basis for Many Bad Loans Was the Good Times—And Thinking They Would Go on Forever

This was the basis for the colossal bad loan collapse in mortgages. As we mentioned many times before, *everyone, including bankers,* thought home prices would just keep rising no matter how fast they had already risen above people's incomes. This same mentality affected commercial real estate loans as well. Plus, many of those loans were all short-term because it was a "sure bet" they could always be refinanced, thus keeping rates very, very low.

Huge corporate buyout loans with very high leverage ratios were fine, too, because who ever thought the value of these companies would ever go down? Why not loan 90 percent or more of the value of the company—it never goes down, right? And history was on their side. Bob recalls calling a friend at one of the largest banks in the United States in 2006. He was in the workout group which handles bad commercial loans. When Bob spoke with him he joked that he wasn't in the workout business anymore. He said there was no more need for workouts. If they had the rare bad loan, they could just repackage it and sell it off to another lender. Same for the FDIC—no banks were going under. Workout departments and the FDIC were like the Maytag repairman. Loans and banks almost never went bad. All they had in 2006 were good loans on their books.

As an example of just how large the private debt bubble was growing, take a look at Figure 2.6 showing the explosive growth of collateralized debt obligations, which are packaged commercial mortgages, home mortgages, consumer loans, and so forth.

Of course, the good times did end, which should not have been a surprise to anyone, yet it was a 10,000 volt electric shock to the people in the financial community who made the loans. Now the FDIC couldn't be busier, and yes, Bob's friend at the large bank is hiring like crazy to expand his workout group.

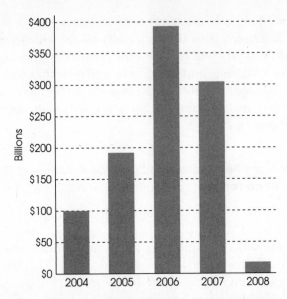

Figure 2.6   Growth in Issuance of CDOs in the United States
Issuance of Collateralized Debt Obligations in the United States exploded
from 2004–2007 and then collapsed in 2008.
Source: Securities Industry and Financial Markets Association (SIFMA).

A Nation on the Edge of Default

Consumer credit card balances and other loans were looked at the
same way. Americans never thought they would have trouble finding a job or getting more credit. Why would the good times ever
go bad? So, no one saved much for a rainy day. A study in early
2009 by Metropolitan Life Insurance showed that more than 50
percent of U.S. households do not have enough savings to cover
their monthly expenses for more than two months if a breadwinner
loses their job. And, it's not just your average Joe or Jane having
problems. Over 27 percent of those making over $100,000 a year
in household income don't have enough savings to make their
monthly expenses for more than two months.

It doesn't take a Certified Financial Planner to tell you that a
lot of people are in for the shock of their lives when they find that
rainy days can, in fact, happen. And that's one reason that the economy can turn down so quickly. Not only are a lot of our expenses
discretionary, but we are terribly vulnerable to job loss because
we have no rainy-day savings (let's not even discuss retirement

savings!). If job loss hits someone, expenses, even non-discretionary expenses, will get cut fast. This will also create a huge increase in riches-to-rags stories of people going from six-figure incomes to low-wage jobs in just a few months.

Figures 2.7 and 2.8 tell the story of a nation on the edge in terms of rapidly rising household debt and a rapidly declining personal savings rate.

One Laid Off, Three More Worried

In a high consumer-spending society like ours, layoffs of small numbers of people can have a big impact on the economy because the large number of people still employed get frightened that they might get laid off. They then cut back on their discretionary spending. In reality, it may be too late to start saving for a rainy day but people cut back on their spending anyway. And it makes sense even if it is too late. But that very fast, very deep drop in discretionary spending also means a very fast, very deep drop in economic activity, and more job losses as a result.

The Feedback Can Really Be Annoying

This feedback loop of job loss creating more job loss is ultimately what really puts the economy in a tailspin. It's not the credit crunch so much as the big downturn in people's spending. Credit is available, but there is a lack of interest in taking on more debt, combined with a lack of interest by the banks in making more bad loans to unqualified borrowers.

If banks were more willing to make the kind of reckless loans they made in 2004 and 2005, the economy would be better off—for a while. But with so many banks being burned by bad loans, they are losing their appetite and ability to make bad loans. And, of course, making more bad loans would only be a short-term cure that would ultimately harm the banks even worse. And in any case, people who fear losing their jobs are simply less willing to take on new debt for discretionary items even if their credit is good.

A good example of the unwillingness to buy because of layoff and financial fear is the auto industry. Interest rates for auto loans are at record lows right now. When combined with the incentives being offered by the automakers, there has probably never been a better time to buy a car in the last 20 years. But, sales are still down

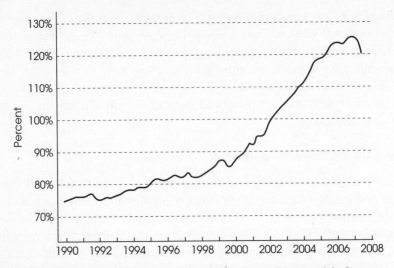

Figure 2.7 Household Debt as a Percentage of Disposable Income
Consumers are having to service an increasing amount of debt relative
to their income, making defaults much more likely as the economy
goes down.
Sources: Federal Reserve and U.S. Bureau of Economic Analysis.

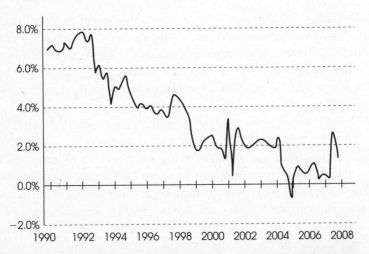

Figure 2.8 Personal Savings as a Percentage of Disposable Income
"Save less and spend more" has been our motto, but that leaves many
people with very little financial cushion and highly susceptible to credit
defaults when good times go bad.
Sources: Federal Reserve and U.S. Bureau of Economic Analysis.

almost 40 percent. It's not a lack of credit, it's primarily a lack of buyer interest and also a lack qualified borrowers. With more layoffs, the lack of interest in buying and the lack of qualifications to borrow are growing daily. So the lack of interest in buying due to fear of job loss continues to keep pounding the economy down, further adding to that annoying feedback.

Key Drivers of the Private Debt Bubble Collapse

The current thinking in financial and government circles is that we need to clear the *toxic assets* (their term for bad loans going south) out of the banking system. They are wrongly assuming that this group of toxic assets isn't growing much and can simply be flushed away. Of course, nothing could be further from the truth. As we have discussed, the number of toxic assets is growing, not staying the same. But wait, it gets worse. Not only is the number of bad loans growing, these bad loans are becoming increasingly toxic because they are *losing value every day*. As commercial real estate prices continue to go down, and housing prices continue to go down, and businesses increasingly come under severe financial pressure and even go bankrupt, the value of the assets behind these loans is decreasing constantly. So the idea that these bad loans will someday recover and become more valuable (less toxic), is based on the same kind of thinking that says, don't worry, real estate will start increasing in price again in the next few years, and the stock market will inevitably turn around from the current bear market.

Again, this kind of cheerleading analysis isn't based on solid economic drivers of growth, but mostly on wishful thinking. Analysts don't want to see the real situation. Otherwise, if toxic assets are instead growing rapidly, how can they be flushed away, and if they can't be flushed away, what will happen to the banking system? That sort of fear is impeding rational analysis and hence, the view that the toxic assets are limited mostly to subprime mortgages and the real estate bubble in states like Florida and California.

So, as an alternative to simple optimistic conjecturing and cheerleading, we did for private debt what we did for real estate and stocks, and put a more detailed analysis of the drivers of the private debt bubble in Appendix A.

All of These Problems Happen in a Relatively Good Economy, but Phase II (the Aftershock) Will Be Far Less Gentle on the Banking System

Let's not forget that Bear Stearns went bankrupt when the economy had low unemployment, low interest rates, and low inflation. None of those were much higher when Fannie Mae and Freddie Mac had to be bailed out. Again, they weren't much higher when Citibank, Bank of America and other big banks had to be bailed out. The same was true when Lehman Brothers, Merrill Lynch and AIG were bailed out. The economy really wasn't all that bad in October 2008.

But, as we said before, the good times won't last forever. The economy will start to get worse in 2009, with unemployment topping 10 percent, and even worse in 2010 with unemployment continuing in the double digits. Bad loans, along with many good loans, will default at a higher rate than today.

And all that will still be far better than when the dollar bubble pops in Phase II. At that point, sky-high inflation and interest rates will put the banks under tremendous pressure. They are simply not designed to handle interest rates and inflation of 50 to 70 percent. After the dollar bubble pops, even the very good loans will go bad. More about Phase II in the next chapter and Phase III in the last chapter of the book.

Don't Worry, Not a Single Penny of Your Tax Dollars Will Fund the Bailouts

That's right. The bank and corporate bailout money is not coming from our taxes. Instead, we're just borrowing it from foreign investors! We're also printing some of it, too. So the next time you hear about another multi-hundred billion-dollar bailout, don't get mad; it's not *your* money. Of course, we will never, ever have to pay it all back, because even if we tried (and we won't), we never could. So just sit back and relax, and enjoy the free ride—for as long as it lasts. You're never going to hear about a bailout *tax* package, we promise you that.

When Will the Private Debt Bubble Turn Around and Go Back Up Again?

Because we had a bubble in private debt, there are only two ways to go back to where we were before: Either re-inflate the bubble, which is not possible at this point (the previous drivers of the private debt bubble are now gone), or have real, underlying economic reasons for a rise in private debt, which currently do not exist. So, the private debt bubble—just like the housing bubble and the stock market bubble—will continue to fall, along with all the other bubbles in our multi-bubble economy. Why? Because, just like real estate and stocks, private debt has been a bubble, too.

Pop Goes the Discretionary Spending Bubble

A disproportionably large share of the U.S. economy is "Discretionary Spending," meaning a good deal of what people have been buying in this country has been optional. Easy money from a rising multi-bubble economy made big-time discretionary spending possible and fun. Abundant credit cards and plenty of home equity loans fed the buying party at every income level, from luxury jet-set buyers to everyday Wal-Mart consumers.

Now, as the bubbles are falling, jobs are disappearing and credit is getting harder and harder to come by. In fact, home equity withdrawals declined rapidly from their peak of $144 billion in the second quarter of 2006 to $24 billion in the first quarter of 2008 according to the Federal Reserve.

As an incredible example of just how much money home equity withdrawal gave consumers, a study by Alan Greenspan and James Kennedy found that between 2001 and 2005 homeowners gained an average of $1 trillion per year in extra spending money! Now that's a little extra spending change in your pocket.

However, now Americans at every level are no longer rushing out to buy things they don't really need at the same levels they did before. Who's going to run out and buy new granite countertops for their kitchen, for example, when they've lost their job or house? And even if you still have income and a home, the old kitchen will probably do just fine for a while longer. Food, basic utilities, and other essentials, yes. New granite countertops, not so much.

Plus, consumers' credit cards are starting to pop. Fitch's Prime Credit Card Delinquency Index of credit card debt more than 60 days late surged 23 percent in the fourth quarter of 2008. Large credit card companies, such as American Express and Capital One, are seeing their delinquency rates rapidly rising above 10 percent. So, consumers are losing the ability to borrow money from home equity and credit cards at a rapid rate. Even if they wanted to spend, it's getting harder and harder to do so.

And it will likely get much worse since much of the credit card debt held by credit card companies is subprime. Almost 31 percent of Bank of America's credit card loans are subprime, 30 percent of Capital One's credit card loans are subprime and 27 percent of Citibank's credit card loans are subprime according to Keefe, Bruyette & Woods, Inc., a financial firm that specializes in the financial services industry. Add to the basic problem of massive defaults, the huge reduction in penalties and other fees forced on the credit card companies by Congress in spring 2009, and the credit card subprime crisis could soon look like the housing bubble subprime crisis. It will also force a lot less credit card-based discretionary spending.

And most importantly, there will be no easy home equity loan bailouts for credit card holders. In the past a lot of home equity loans were used to retire high-interest credit card debt. So, home equity loans were a shadow support to the credit card boom that is no longer there, which puts more downward pressure on discretionary spending.

If the other bubbles were not popping, or if discretionary spending was a much smaller slice of the U.S. economy, a decline in discretionary spending would not pose so much of a problem. But our economy is so deeply dependent on discretionary spending that there is simply no way we can return to business as usual when more and more businesses just don't have the buyers they had in the past. How can we easily go back to the level of spending we once enjoyed when we no longer have the other big bubbles (housing, stock, credit) to push us back up? And how can the other falling bubbles possibly turn around and go back up unless we have lots of discretionary spending? They can't.

In a multi-bubble economy, co-linked bubbles rise and fall together. With the huge pink cloud of good-times discretionary spending being replaced by pink slips, our other falling bubbles have no viable way to re-inflate themselves. And without the other bubbles, especially the private debt bubble and the real estate bubble, discretionary spending has no "bubble fuel" to keep it going at previous levels. The American consumer—that Energizer Bunny of bubble maintenance here and around the globe—is finally running out of bubble steam.

What can turn all these falling bubbles around and force them back up again? The economic cheerleaders, now in the "market cycles" stage of denial (see Chapter 3), just say, "wait a while and everything will get better soon." But they never tell us *how* that is supposed to happen. With the housing bubble, the stock market bubble, the private debt bubble, and the discretionary spending bubble all popping and falling together, what will re-inflate

This Is No Ordinary Recession

Back when we were doing presentations about *America's Bubble Economy* in spring 2008, we said the watchwords for 2009 would be "Job Loss." Long before the housing and stock bubbles popped, we knew significant unemployment would be hard to prevent in 2009, as home construction, consumer spending (related to rapidly declining home prices), and commercial construction began to rapidly decline. All that came true. Next, for 2010, we predict the mantra will be "This Is No Ordinary Recession." By then, more people will realize that we are not in a down economic cycle that we can cycle out of soon. Instead, as the economy continues to decline through 2010, it will become increasingly obvious that we are not in a typical recession. In fact, it's a multi-bubble pop. There will be no automatic recovery—not U-shaped, not V-shaped, not L-shaped, not any shaped!

The feeling that this is no ordinary recession will have a chilling effect on investors and consumers who will become more cautious just when everyone will be hoping for more investment demand and more spending. As one person put it, the realization that this is no ordinary recession will slowly dawn on people the same way that you might slowly realize you have married the wrong person. It's not a problem that's simply going to disappear.

us? Certainly not a rebound in big discretionary spending by the American consumer.

Without something to turn this falling multi-bubble economy around, what do you suppose will happen next? Follow us now to the next chapter where the current Bubblequake will become the Aftershock few people recognize we are about to face.

Won't the Government Stimulus Packages Save Us?

In all of our discussions up to this point, we have ignored the potential impact of the stimulus package of early 2009. That's primarily because we don't see much economic impact from this stimulus package. It's simply too small to be of much consequence. On a monthly spending basis it comes to about the same stimulus as the spring 2008 stimulus package, which put roughly $40 billion a month into the economy over a 4-month period. That stimulus package had no noticeable effect on the economy. So even though the current stimulus package will last much longer than four months, at $40 billion a month it won't have much more impact on the economy. Also, some months we haven't even spent $40 billion.

Most importantly, just like the impact of the stimulus package of spring 2008 was overrun by the economic problems of late 2008, the stimulus package of early 2009 will be completely negated by further deterioration of the economy in 2010. So, even though the stimulus package may have some effect, it will hardly be noticed because the other factors already mentioned (collapsing home prices, collapsing consumer spending, collapsing business spending, falling stocks, etc.) will easily wipe out any positive impact it might have. By the middle of 2010 it will be like it never even happened.

Will there be more stimulus packages passed by Congress? Most likely, yes. But there is a limit. We can only do so many of these big spending packages funded by foreign investors before we really start to scare off the foreign investors who are lending us the money.

Remember, all this stimulus money and bank bailout money (including the AIG bailouts) is not coming from taxpayers, even though the media keeps saying it is. Actually, we are borrowing (or printing) *all* of it. So taxpayers should be a little less upset when they think their hard earned taxes are being wasted on lavish bonuses or worthless investments in failed banks and brokerage firms. Instead, we are *borrowing* this money. Don't spend any time worrying about how we will pay it back, because we will never pay back any of that money—just as we haven't paid back any of the money the government has ever borrowed before. In fact, we even borrow money to pay the interest due on our federal debts.

But here's the rub. Once foreigners start to realize this, they will become increasingly nervous about continuing to lend to us (especially when the dollar bubble starts popping). At that point, our ability to borrow money for lavish stimulus packages or massive bank bailouts will quickly collapse. Hence, excessive stimulus packages funded by foreign investment are, by their very nature, short-term solutions.

The Biggest, Baddest, Bad Loan of Them All

As bad as the financial judgment of private sector bankers and investment bankers is, even worse is the incredible irresponsibility and bad judgment of the public sector—the U.S. government. They have been involved in the biggest bad loan of them all: the monstrous government debt bubble. We can't possibly pay it off. Our tax base in a good year is only $2.5 trillion. In a bad year, it's less. The total government debt bubble will soon be over $11 trillion and rising rapidly to $15 trillion. Even if we directed 100 percent of our taxes to paying it off, it would take at least six years, assuming interest rates stay at their current incredibly low level. What if interest rates rose to 10 or 15 percent? We would have a hard time just paying the interest!

Our track record of repayment is not too good, either. Except for some token payments in the best years of the last couple of decades, we have *never* made any payments to reduce the debt. It's clearly a bad loan, the biggest bad loan in world history. A technical default on our huge government debt will have history-making consequences. Just when most people think things will improve and the Bubblequake is ending in Phase I, the next shoe will drop in Phase II, the Aftershock, as described in the next chapter.

Now What?

The economic cheerleaders say recovery is on the way. All we have to do is sit back and be patient. Sooner or later, a reliable "up-market cycle" is going to come along and turn this frown upside down. It's just a matter of time.

Of course, they never explain exactly *what* is supposed to bring about this magical up cycle. And even more telling, they never, *ever* said anything about a future *down cycle* back when the economy was doing well. Oh, no. As long as the economy was booming, no one said a word about a possible down cycle ahead. They only pull out the "market cycles" theory when they want people to think everything is going to be okay.

We say it is a bubble pop, not a cycle or a normal recession. However, big gains in real productivity could pull us out. But, we haven't made big improvements in real productivity in more than three decades and there isn't much hope of pulling a quick, economy-saving productivity rabbit out of the hat now. Very large real productivity improvements, such as moving from a nation of 90 percent farmers to less than 3 percent is, by its very nature, a slow process. Equally unlikely is a big jump in demand right now. The recovery of strong demand and the possibility of real productivity gains in the future are going to take some time, considerable resources, and of course, the political will (more on this in Chapters 8 and 10). So we can't count on productivity improvements or strong demand to help us right now.

How about more rising bubbles? Would that help us? Sure they would, at least for a while. The trouble is, four of our six bubbles have already begun to burst. So it is hard for a new bubble to be created.

How about big government spending on stimulus packages and bailouts? Won't that save us? At another time, they may have, but not now that we have a multi-bubble economy on the way down. No amount of stimulus spending can possibly re-inflate all these big falling bubbles. And even if it could, how long would that last? Bubbles, by nature, do eventually fall. Big stimulus spending will not be able to bring back a strong non-bubble economy. Stimulus spending isn't how a strong non-bubble economy is created in the first place.

Even if you believe in the "market cycles" idea, you still need *something* to get a new up-cycle going. We may throw all kinds of the value of the dollar is declining, despite all kinds of government efforts to keep this from happening. While not a sharp, quick rise, the value of the euro, compared to the dollar, has risen pretty steadily from a low of around 87 cents in 2000 to around $1.40 in 2009.

The Hardest Bubble to See Is the One You're In

Back in 2007, everyone we spoke to at presentations about our 2006 book could see the housing bubble. Housing prices had stopped growing and were heading down substantially in some parts of the country. However, they had a hard time seeing the stock market bubble because the market was still moving steadily upward. And they had a really hard time seeing the dollar bubble because, at that point, the dollar looked fine.

Then, starting in spring 2008 and especially in spring 2009, few people had any trouble seeing the stock market bubble after the Dow had fallen 40 percent from its peak. The housing bubble was also easy to see because home prices had fallen substantially in every part of the country and in some parts by 50 percent from their peak. But they had a hard time seeing the dollar bubble, which still looks fine, like a safe haven in stormy times.

In a few years—after it starts to fall—the dollar bubble will no longer be so hard to see. What we have seen with a vengeance in the past few years is the fact that the hardest bubble to see is the bubble you are in. No matter what the price is, as long as your bubble is moving upward, that is the right price. A stock market that slowly moves from 10,000 to 11,000 is thought to be priced properly, and so is a market that very rapidly goes from 11,000 to 14,000. As long as it is moving up, it's priced right.

The dollar is the same. As long as it is relatively stable and not causing big problems, people assume it is priced just right. And the forces that might push it down in the future, like huge government borrowing with no hope of paying it back, don't really affect people's thinking about the value of the dollar because the government *must* be borrowing the right amount—certainly not enough to negatively affect the dollar in any significant way! Whether it's $100 billion a year, or $1 trillion a year, or $2 trillion a year, it's always fine because the dollar isn't falling *too* much, so it *must* not be in a bubble, just like housing and stocks were not in a bubble—until they popped. As long as a bubble is heading in the right direction (up), they can't be in a bubble. That's why, like Alan Greenspan said, it's hard to see a bubble until it bursts.

spending and bailouts at it, and we may even have periods in which people swear a recovery is just around the corner, but in truth, without rising bubbles, or real productivity gains, or a rebound in strong demand, or a previously strong non-bubble economy to revive, we are out of ammo.

To keep up with the continuing collapse of these bubbles, please refer to www.aftershockeconomy.com/chapter2.

CHAPTER

3

Phase II: The Aftershock

POP GO THE DOLLAR AND GOVERNMENT DEBT BUBBLES

In our presentations, we often tell people that the real impact of the bursting housing, stock, private debt, and discretionary spending bubbles is not the immediate problems caused by the popping itself—although it has been very upsetting and very costly to the economy—that is not the worst of it. The real impact of these four bursting bubbles is the terrible *downward pressure* they are now exerting on the two remaining bubbles: the dollar bubble and the government debt bubble.

It won't be hard to convince you that we have an enormous government debt bubble, so we'll get back to that in a few pages. Right now, we'd like you to keep an open mind and consider the possibility that we have a vulnerable dollar bubble. We know this is hard to believe. All we ask is that you read on a bit more before coming to your own reasonable conclusions. If we are right (and based on our first book in 2006, we have an excellent track record), you cannot afford to ignore this. We know it feels fundamentally wrong, but please let logic be your guide.

The Dollar Bubble: It's Hard to See Without Bubble-Vision Glasses

Remember how hard it was to see the Internet stock bubble *before* it popped in early 2000? Remember when buying real estate was considered a great quick-flip investment before the housing bubble

began to burst in 2007? Unpopped bubbles really can be very deceiving. Of course, *after* they pop, hindsight is 20/20. But before they pop, you need special glasses in order to see an unburst bubble.

Here are your bubble-vision glasses for the dollar. Once you look at the dollar this way, you'll see for yourself that this bubble has no choice but to pop.

The key is to understand that the value of the dollar is set by the same forces that determine the value of many assets, which are *supply and demand*. Of these, demand is clearly in the driver's seat. Supply matters too, but unless there is significant *demand*, an asset simply cannot retain value. Therefore, the future of the U.S. dollar has nothing to do with what a great country we are or the proud history of the greatest economic power the world has ever seen. The future value of the U.S. dollar depends entirely on *future demand*.

Clearly, past demand has been spectacular. Prior to the bubble economy, demand for dollars was strong and growing stronger due to our growing economy and rising productivity. But once we started to inflate our bubbles, beginning in the 1980s, the rising demand for dollars was driven mostly by our growing asset bubbles. Rising stocks, bonds, real estate, and other dollar-denominated assets were very, very profitable, which naturally attracted many investors from around the world. Foreign investors bought up so many U.S. assets over the years, not because they wanted to help us out, but because their investment returns were stellar. The tremendous and growing demand for U.S. assets made the dollar increasingly more valuable. Foreign investors wanted more and more U.S. assets and needed more and more U.S. dollars to buy them—lots of demand for dollars.

Sounds great. So what's the problem?

The trouble is, all this up-up-up was driven mostly by rising financial and asset bubbles, which created rising returns on investments. In a multi-bubble economy, the value of a currency has no choice but to rise and fall with the rising and falling bubbles.

Why? Because the value of any currency is set by supply and demand, and when a multi-bubble economy is no longer rising and is, in fact, falling, so falls demand for those assets, including demand for the currency needed to buy them. This makes perfect sense. For many years, our rising bubbles created rising demand for dollars, and therefore the value of the dollar rose. Now the falling bubbles are creating falling demand for dollars, and therefore

Unlike the stock market bubble or the real estate bubble, the dollar is an unusual bubble because it did not rise to enormous heights. It is not a bubble because it went up too high, too fast; it's a bubble because it is so vulnerable to decline. The dollar has already lost significant value over the last decade. However, the dollar is still vulnerable to further decline.

What could make the dollar decline further?

Since the 1980s, the rising bubble economy has become increasingly dependent on foreign investment for its capital, and that foreign investment can easily pull out when the excellent returns investors used to receive become not so excellent anymore, or worse, they turn into losses. As we said in *America's Bubble Economy*, foreign investors did not invest in our dollar-denominated assets because they love us; they did it for the fabulous profits. And foreign investors will not slow their purchases of dollar-denominated assets because they hate us; they'll do it because our investments aren't very good anymore, and they'll do it to protect their assets from losses, especially foreign exchange losses.

But, what could possibly give foreign investors the idea that they may not be able to make as much profit on their U.S. assets in the future as they did in the past?

How about four big falling bubbles?

Falling Stocks, Real Estate, Credit, and Spending in the United States Create "No Gain, Lots of Pain" for Foreign Investors

When U.S. real estate was going up, stocks were going up, easy credit was flowing like joy juice, and everything about investing in the United States was oh-so-good, there was no reason not to invest here. It was safe, it was easy, and it produced high returns. What more could any investor ask?

In the reverse, however, falling real estate and stock values, along with declining consumer spending and evaporating credit, make the United States a far less attractive place to invest. Separately, each popping bubble makes investors—including foreign investors—lose a lot of money. On top of that, the combined effect of these falling bubbles is negatively impacting the broader U.S. economy, including driving up unemployment and threatening our banking system. As you can imagine, that isn't too attractive, either.

But all that will not be enough to drive foreign investors away. After such a wonderful party, it's hard to imagine that the good times could really end, and most investors will stick around for a while and hope for the best. In the short term, many foreign investors will simply move from riskier U.S. investments, such as stocks, to less-risky U.S. investments, such as government bonds. Also, for a while, U.S. Treasurys will be viewed as a safe haven in a world of turmoil.

Many foreign investors, just like domestic investors and economists, believe (or want to believe) that the U.S. economy will turn around soon, maybe as early as the end of 2009, and they naturally want to be ready when their U.S. investments start to pick up. However, because there is nothing that will magically re-inflate these bubbles or quickly bring us huge productivity gains or skyrocketing demand in the next few months, we know that the recession will have no option other than to continue into 2010. But even so, foreign investors still will not run away.

However, as 2010 wears on and the expected rebound of the economy doesn't happen, and a very unexpected decline does happen, foreign investors' behavior will begin a small shift. This small shift will be further encouraged by increasing concerns over the government's massive deficit and growing debt. That next small shift in 2010, after foreign investors shift their investments to less-risky choices, will simply be to buy a little less U.S. stocks, bonds, and other dollar-denominated assets. Buying a little less is perfectly reasonable. Of course, buying a little less means a little less demand for these assets. As demand for U.S. assets falls a bit more, their price will decline, and the demand for dollars falls a bit more with it, as will its price. Hence, foreign investors will put a little more of their investment resources into their own countries, thinking they can always invest in the United States after things improve.

But, as we've said, falling bubbles have no viable way to re-inflate themselves, and therefore, falling bubble economies cannot possibly recover very fast. Instead, they keep falling until there are some real economic reasons for solid economic stability and sustainable growth. Until then, foreign investors will continue to adopt a very reasonable "wait-and-see" approach.

Unfortunately, there's nothing like a very reasonable wait-and-see investment approach to really kill a falling bubble economy that is so deeply dependent on foreign investors. How can things possibly turn around when not enough of the people responsible for our past growth are willing to stay in the market or buy more?

Although it's too early to see much of a change in foreign investment sentiment right now, we are starting to detect the beginnings of a change. Net capital inflows to the United States went negative at the beginning of 2009, with a net outflow of $143 billion in January and $91 billion in February. Monthly inflows have recently been turning negative more often, with four negative months in 2008 vs. only one negative month in 2006, according to the U.S. Treasury.

As our bubble economy continues to fall (and we know it will because there is nothing to stop it), more and more investors will lose interest in buying U.S. assets. Dropping demand for these assets will put increasing downward pressure on the value of the dollar, creating a negative feedback loop of falling demand leading to falling prices leading to falling demand. At first, just a few foreign investors will decide to end their wait-and-see approach and will want to sell some of their U.S. holdings. Some of that early selling is by foreign pension funds and life insurance companies that have to be somewhat risk-averse in their investments because of the nature of their fiduciary responsibility to protect the assets of their retirees and beneficiaries. This early selling will lower demand even further and prices will drop even more, motivating more investors to flee. Fairly quickly, the number of investors selling their U.S. assets will hit critical mass, and a perfectly rational panic will kick in, bringing down the already bursting asset bubbles, including the dollar. It's all about falling demand.

One way to look at this is to think of the United States as a big mutual fund. When our performance is good, foreign investors throw their money at us, but when performance is not so good, they throw less money at us. And when performance becomes bad enough, they are going to want to take their money and go home.

Based on our analysis, we foresee foreign investors beginning to significantly lose confidence in their U.S. holdings sometime in 2010 to 2011, and increasing over time, with the likelihood of a mass exit by 2012 to 2014 becoming very high.

Needless to say, not too many U.S. investors will want to stick around at that point, either. And some of them will move their money out of the United States along with the foreign investors, making enormous profits in the process. Fear *and* greed will drive the process of pushing the dollar down: Foreign investors' fear of losing money and U.S. investors' greed to make money by moving money into the rapidly rising yen and euro.

We believe 2010 is a critical year because that is when investors will start to realize that things really aren't getting any better. Instead, they will see the U.S. economy moving toward what we call the "triple double-digit scenario," meaning double-digit unemployment, double-digit inflation, and double-digit interest rates. More on this shortly.

Right now, we need to answer a question that is probably on your mind: If the United States is no longer a good investment, where else will foreign investors go? Won't the United States still be the best place to invest, relative to other countries whose economies will be in even worse shape than ours?

The Biggest Myth About the Dollar Is that Foreign Investors Have No Place Else to Go

Lots of people we talk to find it difficult to believe that foreign investors will ever significantly pull out of their U.S. investments because many Americans believe that most foreign investors have no other profitable place to go. Bob has found in his presentations to financial analysts and asset managers that there is rather strong agreement that U.S. investments are not performing as well as they did in the past. There is also pretty strong agreement that the trade deficit is putting downward pressure on the dollar. And people don't argue with the fact that the value of the dollar has already declined. In fact, it's down almost 60 percent from its peak value in 2000, relative to the euro.

What people do not agree with, is the idea that foreign investors have profitable non-U.S. choices about where to put their money. The most common question Bob gets about a potential fall in the value of the dollar is "Where else would foreign investors put their money except in the United States?" We've heard this from individual investors, senior Wall Street asset managers, and even senior Federal Reserve officials.

Apparently, many otherwise intelligent Americans simply don't realize that foreign investors *already* put most of their money in other places! It's a bit arrogant on our part to think that foreign investors have to invest *all* of their money in the United States. In fact, they often keep most of their investment capital in their own local or regional investments. Think about it. If foreign investors actually did put all of their money in the United States, how would other countries get any capital at all? This idea is really very silly.

As the U.S. bubbles continue to fall, foreign investors will simply decide to reduce their dollar-based investment exposure and keep a little more money at home. Wouldn't you? There is always some foreign exchange risk in any investment outside your own country. Certainly U.S. investors think about this when considering investments in another country, and foreign investors do the same when they weigh the costs and benefits of investing in the United States. This is perfectly reasonable. Fluctuating foreign exchange rates can make foreign investments less attractive.

This is especially true over the long term with low yield investments, such as government bonds. For example, a euro bond may yield 3 percent and a U.S. bond may give a more attractive 3.5 percent, but if the exchange rates move even 1 percent, the advantage of owning the more profitable U.S. bond instead of the euro bond is entirely wiped out and there is a 0.5 percent loss. When exchange rates become volatile, this risk only increases and is a big consideration for foreign investors when deciding to buy U.S. bonds and other U.S. assets or to buy their own countries' bonds and other assets.

Money Does Not Have to Flow Out of the United States for the Dollar to Decline; It Just Has to Flow In Less Rapidly

Foreign investors don't have to take their money out of the United States for the dollar bubble to fall; they just have to reduce the enormous amounts they are now putting in. We currently receive about $2 billion of foreign capital *every day*. Even if not a penny is taken out of the United States and the only thing that happens is that this big inflow of foreign capital drops to, say, $1 billion or $500 million a day, the value of the dollar would fall.

People forget how much money we take in from foreign investors. It is a key part of creating and maintaining our multi-bubble economy. Pushing down the dollar will not require a major withdrawal. All it will take is a slowdown of foreign capital flowing in. No money has to actually flow out in order to pop the dollar bubble.

Maybe the United States Is Too Big To Fail?

Some people think that since the dollar and U.S. government bonds are so important to the world economy, the rest of the world won't let the dollar fall or the government debt bubble burst. This is often used as a reason why China will want to maintain the dollar's value—because it is already so heavily invested in dollars. The reality is that China does not control the market. In fact, no one group comes anywhere close to controlling the market. Because of that, it is in everyone's individual interest to protect himself by ultimately getting out of dollars even if it is not in the group's interest. As we have said many times before, last one out's a rotten egg, and no one will want to be the rotten egg.

Most Foreign-Held Investments in Dollars Won't Flow Out of the United States—They Will Go to "Money Heaven"

Remember Bear Stearns? In early 2008, the value of its stock went from about $28 billion to just $2 billion, practically overnight, but not because $26 billion was actually moved out of Bear Stearns stock. In fact, only a small portion of stock was sold before the stock price collapsed. Where did that $26 billion in wealth go? We like to say it went to "Money Heaven," meaning it simply disappeared.

When the dollar bubble falls, most foreign-held investments in dollar-denominated assets will not have a chance to run out of the United States. Instead, that capital will go to the same place your home equity went when the housing bubble popped. It will go to the same place your 401(k) and other retirement account funds went when the stock bubble dropped to half its peak value (so far). It will go to the same place that all bubble money goes when a bubble pops: it's all going to Money Heaven. See the sidebar on page 69 for more details on Money Heaven.

A Small Change in Demand Can Create a Big Change in Value

You only need a relatively small change in demand to very significantly impact value. For example, if the last person at the end of the day buys GE stock for $100 per share, then all GE stock is worth $100 a share even though almost none of the people holding that stock paid $100 a share. Conversely, if the last share of GE stock sells for $50 at the end of the day, all GE stock is worth $50 a share, regardless of what you bought or sold it for before. Asset values can go up and down very quickly because they are priced at the margin.

The same thing will happen to the dollar. It won't take the sale of a lot of dollars in order for the value of the dollar to drop significantly. Like stock, dollars are priced at the margin. Once it starts to seriously decline, the value of the dollar can and will fall very rapidly—so rapidly that most foreign investors won't have time to sell (just like you may not have had time to sell a given stock before the price went way down). Only those who sell early will escape Money Heaven, which is a big motivating factor in the sell-off as the dollar starts to fall—no one will want to be stuck holding dollars or dollar-denominated assets after the dollar collapses. This early selling will only accelerate the fall.

Once the dollar bubble falls significantly, foreign and U.S. investors together will start moving their money out of the United States in hot pursuit of the enormous profits to be made by selling falling dollars and buying rising assets elsewhere, such as the euro and gold (see Chapter 6).

The Second Biggest Dollar Myth: In a Worldwide Recession, the Relatively Good U.S. Economy Will Always Make the Dollar More Valuable Than the Euro and the Yen

First of all, the dollar is already worth 60 percent less than it was in 2000, relative to the euro. More importantly, the value of the dollar is *not* a function of the relative strength of the U.S. economy

All Dogs Go to Heaven, and So Will a Whole Lot of Money!

People often ask where the massive amount of investment capital in stocks, bonds, and real estate will go in the future. The answer is Money Heaven. Most investment money will go to Money Heaven in the future because most people won't pull their money out of falling stocks, real estate, and bonds soon enough. Anyone who doesn't move money out early won't be able to move it out at all. That's because some other people will have moved their money out of those investments before them and, most importantly, there will be little demand for those investments afterwards. Hence, the values of most people's investments will decline dramatically.

At that point most people will realize they should have moved their money out, but it will be too late. Their portfolios will have been automatically rebalanced for them, heavily weighted toward Money Heaven. For the money managers and financial advisors who will preside over this re-weighting of investors' portfolios into Money Heaven, it's going to feel a lot less like heaven and a lot more like hell.

compared to economies of other countries. Even if the United States has a stronger economy than Europe and Japan in the coming years (and it will), the value of the dollar will still be determined entirely by *supply and demand*. Demand for dollars always depends on how attractive our investments are. So if U.S. investments do poorly, even if they do better than European and Asian investments, the dollar will still go down because the foreign investors will go back to investments in their own countries where there is no foreign exchange risk.

Why would foreign investors consider investments in economies doing worse than ours as safer than U.S. investments? Because, as we mentioned before, investments in their own countries will carry no foreign exchange risk. Foreign investors will prefer their own countries' government bonds over U.S. bonds because there is no foreign exchange risk involved in buying government bonds in their home countries. This has nothing to do with the relative strength of economies; it's all about investor profits.

The Real Reason Most People Don't Think the Dollar Can Collapse Is That the Consequences Are Too Terrible to Think About

The debate over the future of the dollar is not an academic one. If it falls, it will deeply and negatively affect everyone in the United States and most people around the world. That is pretty scary. Unfortunately, this fear colors the debate about what is ahead, with most people carrying a strong bias against the possibility that the dollar could actually ever fall. This makes open and honest discussion about the future value of the dollar much more difficult, especially for financial journalists, financial analysts, and economists, most of whom would be deeply and negatively affected personally and professionally by a collapse.

Some people avoid the debate entirely because they assume the collapse of the dollar will mean the end of the world. It won't! We've added a chapter at the end of the book describing what life will be like in a post-dollar bubble world. We will rise from these economic ashes.

All we ask is that you not let fear stop you from absorbing the facts. Based entirely on logic and the evidence at hand, there simply is no other plausible scenario. The dollar can and will fall. Again, if we didn't have a falling *bubble* economy, things would be very different.

And if we weren't so heavily dependent on a constant inflow of foreign capital, things would be very different. Unfortunately, falling bubbles are exactly what we have, and a decline in the massive inflow of foreign capital to the United States is all it will take to start bringing the dollar (and all the other bubbles) down.

Hasn't the Dollar Been a Safe Haven Currency Recently?

Yes it has and it will continue to be until the US economy declines further in late 2010 and 2011. Also, international investor psychology has to change to catch up with the new reality of the dollar. In the past, the US dollar has always been the strongest and most reliable currency in the world. Many international investors still view it as such.

But that view was created before the new conditions of the dollar were created with a massive government debt of $12 trillion and rising due to a massive deficit of nearly $1.5 trillion per year. The view of the safe haven dollar was also created long before we had the massive inflow of foreign capital into our country chasing and aiding our economic bubbles.

Although the economic conditions surrounding the dollar have been changing for many years, international investor perceptions have not been as quick to change. They are similar to US investors. They don't really see the fundamental economic bubble until it begins to pop and then they see it all too quickly.

Also, the speed with which those fundamental economic conditions are changing for the worse has increased rapidly in the last year. In fact, the stress can be seen in the need for the Federal Reserve to buy nearly $1 trillion worth of government bonds, Freddie Mac bonds, and Fannie Mae bonds this year. Clearly, the world's appetite for our dollar denominated debt is limited or the Fed wouldn't have to buy the bonds.

The Federal Reserve is acting as an enormous buyer of last resort. This will help boost international investors' confidence in the dollar in 2009 and 2010 since it guarantees there will be no confidence-shaking failed Treasury auctions. Right now a failed auction would be highly damaging to investors' confidence in the dollar. But in the long run, the purchase of these bonds damages investors' confidence since it runs the high risk of creating dollar damaging inflation. It's a short term move that boosts the dollar with very bad long term consequences. Sound familiar?

In the Bursting of Japan's Bubble Economy, the Yen Didn't Collapse

You wouldn't expect it to collapse. Japan's bubble economy only had two major bubbles—stock and real estate. It didn't have a yen bubble, a private debt bubble or a public debt bubble that was anything like the United States. It didn't have to massively increase its money supply to handle a massive collapse in the private credit markets. It didn't have to further increase its money supply to buy its own government bonds to help finance a massive public debt bubble. Hence, there was little threat of inflation. Also, Japan had high internal savings rates, relative to the U.S. recently, and it did not have a huge inflow of foreign capital over decades chasing its economic bubbles.

It was a very different and much milder bubble economy. In fact, it was less of a bubble economy and more like an economy that had experienced very high real growth rates due to rapidly increasing productivity that simply saw its high productivity growth, and hence, economic growth, come to an end.

The Fierce Fight to Save the Dollar

As you might expect, the United States and other countries will make all sorts of heroic efforts to save the dollar. Keeping the dollar bubble pumped up is now and will continue to be a major focus of central banks around the globe, especially the Chinese central bank, which now has bought over $1 trillion to prop up the dollar's price. Japan has over $700 billion but is no longer accumulating a significant number of dollars. This might seem a little surprising but you can actually track the Japanese government's purchases of dollars on their Ministry of Finance web site showing foreign exchange intervention operations: www.mof.go.jp/english/e1c021.htm.

China's primary motivation in buying dollars is to keep the price of their currency, the yuan, lower relative to the dollar, and thus keep the price of their goods low for their number-one customer, the United States. The more goods they sell to us, the more jobs they create at home, and with more jobs comes more political stability. If China stops producing jobs, political instability will rise and Chinese political leaders fear that another Tiananmen Square, or worse, would not be far off.

Of course, China exports to other countries, as well, but no other customer base comes close to matching U.S. consumers. In large part because of our voracious rising-bubble appetite for their low-labor-cost goods (clothing, furniture, kitchen gadgets, tools, lamps, towels, pens, shoes, and so much more), China's economy has been growing at an astounding rate of around 10 percent annually. Even now, during the global Bubblequake recession, China is still growing at a fast, but more modest 6.5 percent, at least as of the first quarter of 2009, although a part of that growth is due to the government's enormous stimulus program. But as the U.S. bubbles continue to fall and the world's bubble economy slows, China's economy will also continue to slow. At some point, the Chinese central bank will no longer be willing—or for that matter, able—to keep buying our dollars in order to support its price.

Government Manipulations to Hold Up the Value of the Dollar Will Ultimately Fail

The U.S. Federal Reserve and the central banks of other governments, such as China, will work hard to hold up the value of the dollar. Other central banks can also borrow money to buy dollars, further supporting its value.

There is not much the U.S. Federal Reserve can do to directly manipulate the value of the dollar because it normally does not buy dollars, but it can encourage other central banks to buy dollars. And it can take other indirect actions, like changing interest rates to help support the U.S. economy, which hopefully will encourage investors to buy dollar-denominated investments. However, there is one thing the Fed could do to directly support the dollar that it has never done before. If necessary, the Fed could borrow currencies from other countries and use them to buy dollars. So, short of that, we are really quite dependent on the kindness of strangers—in this case, foreign central banks—to support the dollar.

Manipulations of the value of the dollar by foreign central banks make it difficult to predict movements in the dollar's value in the short term. But we must emphasize *short term*. In the long term, market forces, meaning the commercial supply and demand for dollars by investors, will ultimately determine the value of the dollar in the next two or three years. In the meantime, expect governments to manipulate the value of the dollar the best they can, for as long as they can, by buying dollars (lowering supply) and supporting its price.

Why are they helping us? They do it because the value of the U.S. dollar is not only our concern; the whole world is impacted by it. No one wants to see the dollar fall and all major governments will work hard to keep it up because the international losses and global financial instability caused by its fall will hurt everyone.

However, wanting a strong and stable dollar is not the same thing as being able to keep buying dollars indefinitely in order to hold up its value. So expect a lot more talk than action, and even some of the talk will not be entirely positive because many people and governments will get increasingly angry that the dollar and the U.S. economy are falling and hurting them.

Ultimately, good investor psychology and active government manipulation will not be able to overcome fundamentally bad investment performance. As the financial bubbles that were so attractive and profitable for foreign investors continue to fall and pop, no one is going to be very interested in supporting (buying) the dollar, supply will rise, demand will drop, and the dollar bubble will pop.

"It's just a flesh wound. I got it defending the dollar."

The Huge Government Debt Bubble Is Also Putting Downward Pressure on the Dollar Bubble

Expected to exceed *$11 trillion* by the end of 2009, the U.S. government debt bubble is certainly the biggest, scariest bubble of all. As we mentioned earlier, debt, even big debt, is not intrinsically bad. But debt only makes sense when it is in reasonable proportion to the debtor's ability to pay it back within a reasonable amount of time. Our $11 trillion debt is over *five times* our government's current annual income (taxes). That's very hard to pay back. How many banks would lend money to a company like that, with no plan to pay it off, and projections of further huge increases in its debt?

But that's comparing our debt to income. It is much more common to compare the government's debt to GDP. Looking at it that way, our debt isn't even one times our income. But we don't pay our government debt with GDP, we pay it with taxes and, again, our debt is five times our tax income. People use the comparison to GDP partly as a way of making the debt look smaller and more manageable than it really is.

As Figure 3.1 indicates, our annual federal deficit has been on a high growth track since 2001, but it has gone into overdrive in the

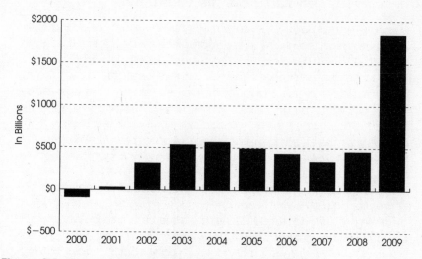

Figure 3.1   Recent Rise in Annual Government Deficit
Our annual government deficit is exploding, which is shining a very bright spotlight on our already enormous government debt (our accumulated annual deficits).
Source: Federal Reserve.

current fiscal year where it is on track to reach almost $2 trillion. As of May 2009, 46 cents out of every dollar spent by the U.S. government is being borrowed.

Who is lending us all this money?

Much of this debt has been funded by foreign investors, primarily from Europe and Asia, who have been buying over 40 percent of our recently issued debt. Yep, those same foreign investors who we know for a fact are going to slow their buying of U.S. assets, such as U.S. stocks and dollars, are also going to lose their appetite for buying U.S. government Treasurys.

What do you suppose all the big bailouts and stimulus packages, on top of already huge and rapidly growing budget deficits, are doing to the image of the credit-worthiness of the United States in the eyes of foreign investors? Sure, they're glad our economy is not going under due to a collapse of Fannie Mae, Freddie Mac, and other financial institutions, and they're happy to see the U.S. government coming to the rescue. But our current policy

Why Not a 100 Percent Tax Cut to Stimulate the Economy?

Even better than our "triple-zero" plan for reviving the housing market (in that plan the government guarantees mortgages at 0 percent interest, $0 down payment, and zero credit check) is our 100 percent tax cut stimulus package! Now this will really get the old economy going. No more arguing about who pays what taxes; let everybody get a complete tax cut! It surely will get very broad bipartisan support. Instead of collecting taxes, we can just borrow all the money from foreign investors! If we can borrow $2 trillion a year to stimulate the economy and never worry about paying it off, why don't we borrow more and really stimulate the economy?

Of course, no one would ever do this because it uncovers a big unmentionable problem: Eventually we'll have to pay the money back, or inflate our currency, or default on our government debt. Whether it's $12 trillion going up at a rate of $2 trillion a year, or $12 trillion going up at a rate of $4 trillion a year, it really doesn't matter, but it certainly looks a lot worse if we fund 100 percent of our expenses with borrowed money rather than 50 percent. It also makes it more obvious how irresponsible we really are—whether we borrow $2 trillion a year, or $4 trillion—in an attempt to stimulate the economy.

of "no bad loan left behind" means we are piling an incredible amount of new debt on top of the incredible amount of debt we already have, and the rate of that pileup is growing at a frightening pace.

As Figure 3.2 shows, the Federal Reserve is increasing its balance sheet mightily by buying up bad loans left and right. Their "no bad loan left behind" policy has made their balance sheet explode with toxic assets potentially worth much less than the value at which they carry them on their balance sheet. And those toxic assets are losing value and becoming more toxic every day.

How will we possibly pay off these debts when we can't even pay our bills? Would you keep lending money to a guy with five times as much credit card debt as he has income while he is adding to that debt at the rate of about 15 to 20 percent per year? Would you call that a good credit risk?

The Fed's bailouts are also contributing mightily to the growth of the money supply and hence, future inflation. That doesn't make

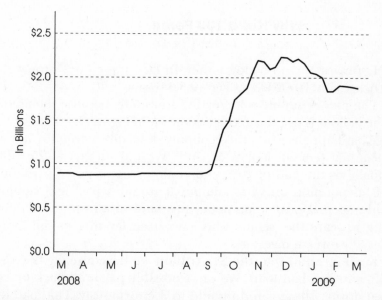

Figure 3.2   No Bad Loan Left Behind—The Federal Reserve's Growing Balance Sheet
As a buyer of last resort, the Federal Reserve has been mighty active buying bad loans, going form $1 trillion to $2.3 trillion.
Source: Federal Reserve.

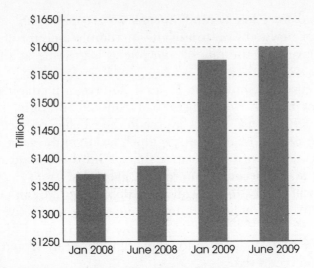

Figure 3.3 The Recent Rapid Rise in the Money Supply
Bank bailouts not only balloon balance sheets, they boost the money
supply as well paving the way for higher inflation.
Source: Federal Reserve.

foreign investors too happy, either. In fact, the money supply (M_1)
skyrocketed in late 2008, as Figure 3.3 shows.

The money supply is increasing so rapidly because the amount
of the bailout is just staggering, as shown in Figure 3.4.

What happens when the economy slows down even further and
our annual federal deficits expand? We will surpass $1.75 trillion
annually by the end of 2009 and could easily surpass $2 trillion in
2010, depending on what additional stimulus packages Congress
decides to make. At some point, this kind of astronomical debt is
going to scare the people who have been lending us the money,
especially foreign investors.

Keep in mind that the $11 trillion we have already borrowed
is effectively a bad loan. We can't possibly pay it all back or even
pay it down. All we can do is add to it enormously. That bad loan
is going to scare foreign investors from investing more money
into the world's biggest bad loan. They don't think of it as a bad
loan now, but that perception can and will change dramatically
over time.

Direct Investments by the Government in Financial Institutions, Corporate Debt, and Mortage-Backed Securities	S7.7 Trillion
Government Lending to Banks	S2.3 Trillion
Government Insurance of Bank and Fannie Mae and Freddie Mac Assets	S2.1 Trillion
Total	**S12.1 Trillion**

Figure 3.4   The Current Bailout Bill
The money supply is increasing because the bailout bill is big and will be getting bigger.
Source: Federal Reserve.

What Is the Government's Credit Limit?

Anyone with a credit card understands what a credit limit is. Does the U.S. government have a credit limit? Most people, including investment bankers and government leaders, don't even ask the question. They seem to implicitly assume that there is no credit limit and the government can just keep borrowing forever at record low interest rates. They probably know this can't possibly be true, but like so many other false assumptions underlying the bubble economy, they don't really think about it.

However, this is probably the most important question of all in determining when Phase I (the Bubblequake) will become Phase II (the Aftershock) and the bubble economy will finally fully pop. We will reach our credit limit when foreign investors stop or dramatically reduce their lending to the U.S. government because they are concerned about the risk of not being repaid with dollars that have the same value as the dollars they are lending.

As we get closer to our credit limit, the interest that the U.S. government will have to pay in order to borrow money will rise to compensate for greater perceived risk. Increased rates will solve the problem in the short-term by attracting more capital. But as perception of risk grows with the increasing size of the government's debt, the declining economy, and the continued fall of the stock and real estate markets, investor interest in lending us money will also decline—eventually

(Continued)

so dramatically that failed Treasury auctions result. At that point, the U.S. government will no longer be able to sell its bonds. Multiple failed Treasury auctions will mark the beginning of the government debt bubble collapse.

We asked, during a presentation at the World Bank, what participants thought the U.S. government's actual credit limit might be. Surprisingly, most said about $15 to $25 trillion in total debt—just what our own analysis indicates. Of course, the exact number depends on the state of the U.S. economy and the psychology of foreign investors. We do know that by the end of 2009, our government debt will be almost $12 trillion and will be growing at a rate of about $2 trillion per year.

But don't worry. We'll probably never reach an actual credit limit because, like housing prices, the value of the dollar can never fall significantly, right?

Think Like a Foreign Investor: How Much More of This Can They Take?

We know that as 2009 comes to a close there will be nothing that can significantly re-inflate the falling stock market, real estate, private debt, and discretionary spending bubbles that we described in the last chapter. Nonetheless, many people—including foreign investors—are expecting a recovery soon. Even the Chairman of the Council of Economic Advisors said in the spring of 2009 that the economy would be growing again by 2010. So as we move deeper into 2010 and nothing significantly improves, many investors, including many foreign investors, will get increasingly nervous. As demand drops and asset values continue to fall, this will eventually be a terrible blow to the psyche of investors, including foreign investors.

Time makes all the difference. The more time we continue on a downward trend, the more disillusioned investors, including foreign investors, will become. So, hope may well spring eternal through 2009, but in 2010, hope will begin to fade, and by 2011 or 2012, hope will start to seriously evaporate and a significant minority of foreign investors will begin to reduce their U.S. dollar exposure. What looks okay now will look much worse a year or two from now.

What Is the Repayment Plan for the National Debt? 10 Years? 15 Years? 20 Years?

Well, as everyone knows, there is no repayment plan. What a country! Borrow all the money you want and you don't even need a repayment plan.

This question is like asking what our credit limit is. It's very useful for understanding our national debt. So, since we don't have a payment plan, let's create one. If we assume our debt is $15 trillion at very low interest rates and our annual payment is $500 billion, then it would take about 40 years to pay it off, assuming we don't do anything sneaky like borrowing more money during these 40 years. Hmmm; not likely. And are we really going to go from an economy-stimulating annual deficit of $2 trillion to a very recession-causing surplus of $500 billion, and maintain that discipline for 40 more years? Also unlikely.

Of course, none of our lenders care if we can't afford to pay back our debt. But if anyone did care, they would say we're sunk and they'd be right. At some point, foreign investors who are supplying all this capital are going to say enough is enough. Most people like to say this will be our grandchildren's problem. But why? In reality, foreign investors do not have to wait that long to stop lending us the money. It can happen at any time.

Any loan you cannot afford to pay off or successfully refinance is guaranteed to eventually default. That will happen just as soon as foreign investors see the reality of the situation, and that perception of true reality starts to affect the value of the dollar. In the end, it will be like a giant Ponzi scheme that's destined to fail. As Bernie Madoff so accurately put it, "I knew this day would come eventually." The same will be true for our monstrous national debt with no repayment plan.

A Scary Sight for Investors in 2010 and 2011: "The Triple Double-Digit"

Beginning in 2010 and continuing forward, we see movement toward what we call the "triple double-digit" economy. By that we mean:

- Double-digit unemployment
- Double-digit inflation
- Double-digit interest rates

"We were wondering if <u>now</u> would be a good time to panic?"

Double-Digit Unemployment.   It's not hard to see this as a real possibility since as of July 2009 the unemployment rate stood at 9.4 percent. Even with the small decline in July from 9.5 percent to 9.4 percent the trend is clearly up. Also, that decline in the unemployment rate occurred at the same time that we lost almost a quarter million jobs. Clearly a lot of people had to leave the work force for the unemployment rate to go down. So, the standard unemployment rate is not always a perfect measure of employee health.

The government does produce another statistic that includes discouraged unemployed and underemployed and that figure shows unemployment at over 16 percent. However it is measured, the key point is that unemployment, discouraged workers and underemployment will likely be increasing in the near future. With credit not flowing like it did at the height of the private debt bubble, home equity not available like it was at the height of the real estate bubble, stock values much lower than their peak values, and consumer spending down from its bubble peak, it is understandable that businesses across the country are suffering and will continue to lay off workers and slow or eliminate hiring. In fact, many people now believe double-digit unemployment is inevitable.

But most people really cannot imagine that we will also have to face double-digit inflation and interest rates, as well.

Double-Digit Inflation. There are strong incentives to increase the money supply to deal with the banking and credit crises. Normally it takes about 6 to 18 months for an increase in the money supply to create inflation, but many factors can affect that timing. However, we expect to see the first significant increases in inflation in 2010. It will likely hit 10 percent by 2011 or be on an obvious trajectory toward 10 percent by then. We usually look at core CPI as the best available indicator of inflation.

With the money supply (M_1) having increased 15 percent from August 2008 to April 2009 to help fund the bailout, and being likely to increase further, inflation is a near certainty. However, it will be tempered by the fact that many banks are not lending out the money that they are receiving. So, it could take a while before we see a big increase in inflation and it will likely be moderate when it hits—heading toward 10 percent. The direct connection and timing of money supply and inflation is tricky and depends on many factors. Without digressing into a long academic discussion of the variables that impact the relationship between inflation and the money supply, we can certainly say with confidence that if we keep increasing the money supply rapidly, an inflation rate of 10 percent is almost inevitable.

Why would we continue to grow our money supply? For the same reasons we did before, only more so. Bank bailouts are hardly finished because toxic bank assets are growing more toxic every day. Continued declines in home prices, the sagging economy, and rising unemployment will all lead to more defaults on commercial real estate loans, credit card loans, auto loans, and "good" home loans, among many other types of debt going bad. Increasing the money supply to cover bank bailouts and other problems will eventually drive up inflation.

Also, in spring of 2009 the Federal Reserve began buying U.S. government bonds, Freddie Mac bonds, and Fannie Mae bonds.

As of early summer, they had bought almost $1 trillion worth of these bonds and were expressing their willingness to buy even more over the remainder of the year. Ostensibly, these bonds are being bought to hold down mortgage rates, which it is doing. But, we think the more likely reason is that the government would have a hard time finding buyers for all this debt. Essentially, the Fed is playing the buyer of last resort, which is not a good sign. More on that later.

The key for this discussion is that these bonds are all being bought with printed money—not taxes or borrowed money. That's a lot of money to print. In fact, it is almost equivalent to our money supply as measured by M_1, which is about $1 trillion. Although most financial and economic experts are expressing great confidence that this will have little or no effect on our inflation rate, it is hard to see how it couldn't increase the rate substantially at some point. You wonder what they think *will* cause inflation.

An often cited counter argument is that the lower velocity of money that we have during a recession will counteract the effect of printing all this money. Without getting too technical, in a very simple form you can think of the velocity of money as how fast monetary transactions take place. It's kind of like how fast you pay your bills. In a recession, these transactions become slower. Velocity is also slower with low interest rates. The combination of low interest rates and a slow economy is reducing monetary velocity. However, like product price deflation, changes in velocity tend to be relatively mild compared to the massive changes in the money supply that the Fed is now making.

There is also a natural limit to how slow velocity can go since people and banks want to hold as little as possible in non-interest bearing accounts or reserves. If the money is in interest bearing accounts, then it is being loaned out and is part of the money supply. If it's not being loaned out and is not receiving any interest from that money, then someone is losing a lot of money. It's not a sustainable situation in the long term. Banks may increase their reserves, but their lending would have to go down as a consequence. Higher reserves also hurt bank profits.

Double-Digit Interest Rates.   Double-digit inflation will cause double-digit interest rates because interest rates always have to be above the inflation rate in order to get anyone to lend money. So as soon as we have double-digit inflation, we have even higher interest rates.

The Important Difference Between Inflation and a Real Price Increase

Too often people refer to a price increase as inflation. Just because the price of goods, such as oil, increases, doesn't mean the price increase is inflation. As Nobel Prize winning economist Milton Friedman said, "inflation is always and everywhere a monetary phenomenon," meaning it can only be created by a central bank, such as the Federal Reserve. The price of oil could be going up because we are running out of easy-to-find oil, or demand has gone up because China's rapidly growing economy is demanding more oil. That's not inflation; that's a real price increase due to supply and demand for a good. True inflation occurs when the Fed increases the money supply at a faster rate than the economy needs it. Think of the Fed as simply a money factory. Increase the money supply very fast, and you get inflation. Slow or stop the increase in the money supply, and you get almost no inflation.

Often, inflation is created by governments to avoid raising taxes or cutting spending—"printing money." This is also why deflation will not be a significant problem in the future. Any real decrease in the prices of goods or services due to a depressed economy will be more than offset by the Fed printing money to try to stimulate the economy and deal with declining tax revenues.

Progressing toward a triple double-digit scenario (double-digit unemployment, inflation, and interest rates) will only make foreign investors even more leery of continuing their purchases of dollar-denominated assets, moving us closer to the crash of the dollar.

The Hidden Dollar Bubble Won't Fall Until the End, Then It Will Pop Very Quickly

The dollar bubble will remain relatively hidden until the end, but when it starts to blow up, it will look a lot like the financial crisis of October 2008, meaning it will come on very quickly. Unfortunately, the financial crisis of late 2008 was relatively small compared to the coming dollar crisis. When it hits, it will be too large for central banks to solve, as just explained. The reason it is stealthy is that prior to the final dollar bubble pop, much effort will have already been taken to

The U.S. Government Is the Largest Holder of Adjustable-Rate Debt in the World

One of the biggest problems with rising interest rates is that interest costs for the U.S. government start to go up. The United States is the largest holder of adjustable-rate debt in the world. It's not technically adjustable-rate debt, but it functions as such because it is short-term. According to the U.S. Treasury, almost 40 percent of its debt has a maturity of less than one year. As interest rates rise, the government is forced to pay out more and more interest on its debt every time it has to refinance this short-term debt. It is the same problem that hits homeowners when their adjustable-rate mortgages rise. If interest rates go up significantly, as they will when foreign investors begin to drastically reduce new investments in the United States, debt service could fairly quickly consume a large part of our government's income.

For example, if interest rates rise to 15 percent, even on just the 40 percent of our $12 trillion in debt that is short-term, with the other 60 percent averaging 5 percent interest, our annual *interest-only* payment would be *more than $1 trillion dollars*. In a very good economy, the U.S. government brings in approximately $2.5 trillion in taxes according to the Budget of the United States Government. That could easily go down to $2 trillion or less in a slow economy like what we are experiencing in 2009 (in fact, tax receipts dropped 17 percent in February 2009 vs. February 2008, according to the U.S. Treasury Department). Hence, at a 15-percent interest rate we could be spending approximately *half* our taxes on interest payments alone!

prop up the dollar, and much is currently being done. So it will take a long time for big problems to appear on the surface, but when they do, it will be like a fire that firefighters can no longer control. It is not uncommon for foreign currency crises to come on quickly and dramatically. What is very uncommon is for it to happen to the United States. In fact, it will be a once-in-history event.

The Government Debt Bubble Pops

The most obvious and immediate effect of the dollar bubble pop will be a sharp reduction in capital availability. This may or may not immediately increase interest rates since a huge increase in the money supply could temporarily offset the capital availability problem and temporarily keep interest rates low. This decrease in capital availability will be caused by an interaction of two factors related to the dollar bubble burst:

1. The massive capital outflow from the United States caused by the dollar bubble collapse will greatly reduce capital availability in the United States.
2. Lack of capital and potentially high interest rates will also wreak havoc on the other bubbles, especially the stock and real estate markets. Sharp declines in these markets will create a greater sense of perceived risk among lenders, which will further reduce capital availability. The negative impact of a lack of capital on the economy will also increase the riskiness of lending, eventually driving up interest rates. Real interest rates—the difference between the inflation rate and the interest rate—will eventually soar, since the perceived and real risks of lending in such an economy are increasing rapidly.

As we just mentioned, the Federal Reserve will try to help lower interest rates and calm the market with a burst of liquidity (printing money) as it has done in the past, but to a much, much higher degree. It will be trying to stimulate the economy and keep it alive. Not an easy task, and a lot of liquidity (printed money) will be required. This will cause the initial burst of inflation, which, based on our analysis, indicates it will be in the mid double-digit range. This analysis includes our expectations about what the government will need for stimulus, bailouts, and loan guarantees.

The exact inflation rates will be changing constantly and will not stay at one level for any length of time. Fortunately for the investor, the exact numbers at any given time are not relevant. If you are looking for a specific number, then you are focusing on the wrong issue. What is relevant is to recognize how the government debt bubble pop will happen and the general level of inflation that accompanies each time period as the government debt bubble pop evolves.

This attempt to stabilize the economy will be one of the final factors that lead to the next stage of the government debt bubble collapse. That's because the combination of high inflation, rapidly rising interest rates, and rapidly rising perceived risk of any lending will quickly put the U.S. government, the world's biggest borrower, in the crosshairs. Unlike in the past where the government could ride to the rescue of a Bear Stearns or an AIG that has lost the confidence of its investors, lenders, and counter-parties, the U.S. government will increasingly find itself in the position of those who it has rescued—the one who is in trouble.

That's because, as the world's biggest borrower, it is trying to borrow a bigger slice of a smaller pie. It came into the dollar bubble already stretched. The world has less capital and other governments are borrowing heavily. Against the backdrop of less capital (a smaller pie) it is borrowing more and more heavily and hoping against hope that there aren't any problems that push it over the precipice—and then the dollar bubble pops with the rapid rise in interest rates and inflation just described.

This puts into motion a rapid chain of events. The most noticeable link in the chain will be failed Treasury auctions. This doesn't mean the government can't sell any of the bonds it needs to finance its operations, but it means that it can't sell all of them. To help out, the Federal Reserve may come in and buy what others don't buy, as it already has. But this is a short-term solution to a bigger underlying problem. The bigger underlying problem is that, at this point, the world is starting to perceive greater risk in U.S. government bonds. Even if the government pays much higher interest rates, as it will have to because interest rates and inflation are rising rapidly, there is an even faster increase in perceived risk for government bonds. Government bonds are supposed to be AAA. Just like AIG or mortgage-backed securities, government bonds are quickly becoming viewed as toxic assets. All the issues we have described earlier regarding the fundamental problems with massive and rapidly growing government debt start to become very clear in such a difficult economic environment.

Refinancing of past government debt will start becoming difficult since they are increasingly being viewed as toxic assets. As we have seen in 2008, assets can go from being AAA to XXX in a relatively short period of time. Just like with AIG and mortgage-backed securities, once these assets go toxic, they start to freeze very quickly and can't be traded, and new issues cannot be sold. At that point, Treasury auctions will begin to fail completely, meaning no one will buy our debt. If no one will buy our future debt, we will have no way to make payments on our past debt. The U.S. government will be in default on its debt, and the big government debt bubble will fully pop.

When Treasury auctions fail completely, the government will have no way of funding the $2 to $3 trillion that it will need to borrow to cover its rapidly rising deficits. Also, it will have no way to fund the short-term government debt (less-than-one-year securities that comprise 40 percent of what will be our $15 trillion plus debt) that is continuously coming due.

Hence, it will have to resort to its most powerful tool, the Federal Reserve's printing press, to make up the difference. The problem is that the kind of inflation needed to fund multibillion dollar deficits is massive. Since M_1 is only about $1 trillion, 100 percent inflation can only create about $1 trillion dollars. The exact math for inflation creation is much, much more complex than that, but to give the reader an idea of the broad magnitude of the problem, that is a sufficient calculation. Hence, the United States will have to start printing at a rate that pushes inflation into the multi-hundred percent range.

Clearly, in a modern industrial economy this is not a long-term solution. But, like so many solutions to problems in the bubble economy, it is a very short-term solution that creates much more long-term harm and only postpones the real solution. The real solution is similar to what many governments that successfully fight high inflation have to do: spending cuts and tax increases. These massive spending cuts and tax increases, as outlined in Chapter 10, will ultimately help the government bring inflation back into the mid- to high-double digits. Although that is high by current standards, it is more acceptable long term and certainly much better than the devastating multi hundred percent inflation being incurred prior to the massive spending cuts and tax increases.

Despite concerns about a collapse of the financial system, it will definitely be able to maintain enough liquidity to maintain the payments mechanism. This will allow normal payment processing to occur within the United States and outside the United States, but it will not be enough liquidity to allow for significant long-term credit.

All the Bubbles Fully Collapse

With the dollar and government debt bubbles fully popped, interest rates will skyrocket, inflation will be very high, unemployment will soar, the U.S. stock market will crash but still be open, the real

The Cracks in the Dollar and Government Debt Bubbles are Already Appearing

When Standard & Poor's cut the outlook for the United Kingdom's debt to negative from stable in May 2009, a crack in the dollar bubble began to appear. Yes, it was England and not the United States getting hit, but everyone knew that the United States also has a lot of debt and the potential for inflation, and the United States might face a similar ratings downgrade later. Reflecting the fear that the dollar may be headed for trouble due to inflation, interest rates on 10-year Treasury bonds doubled from 2 percent to almost 4 percent in the first half of 2009. That is still an incredibly low interest rate, but at that rate of negative change it is an early warning sign of problems to come. And that is despite the fact that the Federal Reserve has been trying massively to keep long-term interest rates down by buying over $700 billion in Treasurys and mortgage-backed securities from Freddie Mac and Fannie Mae in the first half of 2009 (according to the Federal Reserve). That's up from almost no purchases in 2008. They are only cracks at this stage, but they are warning signs of significant longer term problems.

estate market will crash, consumer discretionary spending will dry up, and the number of banks will be greatly reduced.

The dollar will be worth a fraction of its peak value relative to the euro, and gold will be a stellar investment for many years (see Chapter 6). Most Americans (who don't follow our advice in Chapter 5) will lose most of their money, but we won't starve in the streets. In fact, because we have so much wealth to begin with, the United States will be in better shape than other countries (see Chapter 4), although life in the post-dollar-bubble world will be quite different than it is today (see Chapter 10).

One of the most striking differences will be the dollar itself, which will no longer buy nearly as much in imported goods. Like all the other bubbles, once the dollar bubble pops, it will not re-inflate any time soon. The only way to make it go up again is to increase its demand, and that simply will not be possible. Remember Lehman Brothers? Being big and powerful is not enough; you also have to be a good investment.

Dead dollars, we are sorry to say, don't bounce.

Where Did All This Begin? When Could It Have Been Stopped?

With so many interacting bubbles first driving up and then pushing down the U.S. and world multi-bubble economies, it may seem impossible to know what caused what. But based on our analysis, we believe there was one critical moment that got everything started. That critical moment came back in 1981 when the U.S. government decided to start running large federal budget deficits. This big deficit spending sowed the early seeds for the coming asset bubbles in real estate and stocks. Big deficit spending boomed the economy, attracting U.S. and foreign investors to jump on the surging investment returns of a blue-chip (normally slow growing and secure) stock market on its way to 1,400-percent growth. The dollar soared, stocks kept climbing, private debt and discretionary spending rose tremendously, and real estate prices went intergalactic before plummeting back to Earth and, well, the rest is history.

When could we have stopped it? We've had a lot of internal discussion about the increasing deficit spending and at what stage we passed the point of no return. Our best estimate is that by the time we surpassed $100 billion in our annual federal deficit it became politically infeasible to turn back. The economic pain that would have come from halting this level of deficit spending and moving instead to a budget surplus to pay down the accumulated federal debt, would have been simply too enormous to sell to voter And honestly, given all the positive effects of easy, high-deficit spending induced economic growth, it would have been politically challenging to change our course even at $200 billion in deficit spending. It was just too tempting, too easy, and too profitable to walk away from the chance to grow our way out of our economic problems with deficit spending, especially when the eventual negative consequences would not be felt for decades. Like mall-happy teenagers with someone else's credit cards, it was just too irresistible. Yes, for two years during the Clinton administration we did run a surplus, but it was insignificant in reducing the total debt and quickly became a large annual deficit again when the dot-com boom went bust and large increases in spending for defense and the Iraq war were added to the budget.

Of course, credit-crazy teenagers can't get too far without outside support. In this case, we had plenty of help from foreign investors who were more than willing to help finance the government debt. If they hadn't done so, the "crowding-out effect" from the government borrowing so much money would have pushed interest rates up too high for us to be able to easily finance our deficit spending domestically. This would have forced us to deal with our underlying economic problems sooner. Instead, foreign investors loved lending us money and buying U.S. assets. Without these investors, popping our relatively small bubbles back then would have involved a whole lot less pain than what we are about to face.

Not that we are blaming foreign investors. Investment money always flows toward opportunity. But, once you decide to borrow so much from foreign investors, you have made a game changing decision in the way you manage your country's economy. The enormous negative consequences of this decision for the U.S. dollar will kick in fully in perhaps as little as two or three more years. Just like when home prices rose higher and then fell harder than anyone ever saw before, we are about to witness the same thing for the dollar. We've never seen this before because we've never borrowed so much money from foreign investors to fund our government deficits and to help inflate our asset bubbles before. And hence, the consequences for the dollar will also be like nothing we've ever witnessed before in history.

The Six Psychological Stages of Denying the Bubbles Are Bursting

As the dollar and government debt bubbles pop in Phase II (the Aftershock), people will naturally be very upset. We believe there will be six distinct psychological stages in which individuals, businesses, and governments will first ignore, then react to, and ultimately solve the economic problems. Each of these psychological stages performs the function of keeping people feeling as comfortable as possible while avoiding making any more changes than are absolutely unavoidable at that point in time. Change is threatening, inaction equals safety, and comfort comes from avoiding any changes that might threaten the benefits of the status quo. But the consequences of inaction also create pain, so eventually some actions are taken.

Over time, as the U.S. and world economies worsen, complete denial and inaction will not be entirely possible. Still, people will strive to ignore what is happening and do the least they can because the many benefits of the old multi-bubble economy are hard to give up. Our understanding of the underlying *psychology* of coping with and resisting change is one more thing that sets us apart from all the other bearish analysts. We know that at each stage of the falling economy, there will be a deep longing to return to the past and get back to the good times. Actually, the really good times are still ahead, but first we will pass through six psychological stages of coping with the current Bubblequake and coming Aftershock.

Although these stages are distinctly different, there will be some overlap between them so we may be experiencing multiple stages at the same time.

The stages are:

- Denial
- Market Cycles
- Fantasized Great Depression
- Back to Basics
- Imagined Armageddon
- Revolutionary Action

The first stage is *Denial*, where the United States has been firmly planted for quite some time. This is the "Don't worry, just go shopping" phase of dealing with (or more correctly, not dealing with) the reality of our vulnerable multi-bubble economy. Regardless of the facts, in the Denial stage people firmly believe that home prices cannot drop any further, the stock market has already hit bottom, and the mighty U.S. dollar will always be king.

The big advantage of the Denial stage is that people do not have to take any unpleasant actions at all. We don't have a problem and therefore we don't have to change. But this stage involves more than simply ignoring the problem. In the Denial stage, we actively keep our multi-bubble economy pumped up and expanding. Governments, businesses, and individuals continue to borrow their way to prosperity, regardless of the future price tag. And even when things start going bad, the Denial stage just won't let the party quit. We continue to buy homes we can't afford until we can no longer get mortgages, and run up more and more debts we can't easily repay until we can get no more loans,. And we continue to entrust our retirements and other investments to Wall Street even when stock prices have far outstripped an economic basis because we want to believe in Tinkerbell.

In a big, multi-bubble economy that has only begun to fall, denial can be a very comfortable place to live. In the Land of Denial, there's no need to recognize economic bubbles before they grow too large. After all, this is the United States of America, the biggest, most powerful economy in history. *Everything is fine.* And besides, if things really start to look bad, we can always turn to our next stage of dealing with our economic problems, which is to rely on our abiding faith in repeating market cycles.

In the *Market Cycles* stage, an increasing number of individuals, businesses, and financial analysts come out of denial and begin to notice that something is wrong. They can see home sales falling, consumer spending slowing, jobs being lost, credit drying up, and stocks on the decline. They may even be able to recognize an individual falling asset bubble, like the declining real estate bubble. But few people at this stage will recognize any yet-unpopped economic bubbles, let alone be able to see an entire multi-bubble economy. Instead, they will explain the falling stock market, the failing real estate market, and the overall economic downturn in terms of historical up and down market cycles. While not as cozy as the Denial stage, the Market Cycle stage provides some significant comfort, too, because every "down" cycle is guaranteed to be followed by an "up" cycle.

The key comfort advantage of the Market Cycles stage as the multi-bubble economy begins to fall, is that we don't have to take any scary new actions. We can take similar actions as before, even much bolder actions, but nothing fundamentally different that would deeply change the status quo. In fact, the actions are taken to preserve the status quo to the extent possible. Many individuals and businesses will just wait passively and tough it out thinking that, sooner or later, the economy will automatically improve. It always did before, right? Even world-class economists hold tightly to this outdated faith in repeating market cycles. The current recession may be deeper than we hoped, but just hang in there—it's bound to turn around soon.

When the unrecognized multi-bubble economy does not turn around soon but continues to fall, the next stage in how people react to the unfolding Bubblequake is to worry that maybe things really are different this time; maybe (can we even say it out loud?) the economy is heading into another, full-fledged Great Depression!

During the *Fantasized Great Depression* stage, considerable fear starts setting in. Consumers and businesses significantly cut spending, more jobs are lost, banks further restrict lending, and the federal government ramps up spending money like there's no tomorrow. The words "another Great Depression" increasingly work their way into the national conversation, and the government begins actions we don't normally take, like massive government spending to stimulate the economy. The psychological advantage of this stage is the comfort we get from seeing the government run big deficit spending—supposedly it worked in the past and we can sit back passively and wait for it to work again.

But in fact, there is no Great Depression on the way. What we have instead is something new; a multi-bubble economy on its way down, so all the government spending to stimulate the economy does not have the intended positive effects that it would have in an actual depression. Instead, massive federal deficit spending just sets us up for an even bigger fall down the road, when both the dollar bubble and the government debt bubble eventually burst in Phase II, and no one wants to lend us any more money. At that point, printing dollars will be our only option, creating significant future inflation. (The differences between today's Bubblequake and the Great Depression are discussed in Chapter 10.)

With everything getting significantly worse and worse, the next stage in the ongoing process of dealing with our failing multi-bubble economy will be the urge to get *Back to Basics*. The impulse in this stage is to figure out what went wrong in the past and try to set it right in the present. If we can just rectify our previous mistakes, we will be OK and the way to rectify those mistakes isn't to create a whole new financial and economic structure, but go back to where we were before all this mess happened—go back to basics. In the Back to Basics stage we will see federal and state governments beginning to enact tough regulations that would have helped protect us *in the past* from some of the problems we now face, such as defaults on subprime mortgages and the dangers of credit default swaps.

But at this late date, these measures will do little, if any, good to undo our current problems. Such attempts will be the equivalent of installing highly sensitive smoke detectors and fancy sprinkler systems, *after* the house has already burned down. Certainly none of that will help us rebuild. Instead of protecting the current economy in any meaningful way, going Back to Basics with tough backward-looking regulations will do little to reverse the damage that has already been done, and it won't put us on a course toward future recovery. The psychological advantage of this stage is the comfort people get from returning to the past and making as little fundamental change as possible so they can feel safe.

These backward-looking actions won't help us in a falling multi-bubble economy. With the dollar bubble popping, more and more people out of work, and the economy continuing to deteriorate, we are likely to next enter the stage of *Imagined Armageddon*, in which many people may come to think everything is hopelessly going to hell. Feeling angry, helpless, and scared, some people may imagine horrible scenarios of unlikely wars, long breadlines, sharply rising crime, and other calamities that simply will not occur. The invalid analogy to this stage was the earlier rise of fascism and World War II. The psychological advantage of this unpleasant stage is the opportunity to feel like passive victims in order to avoid the discomfort of having to make real decisions that bring about real change. It's hard to know how long this non-productive stage could last or what short-term consequences it may create. Politically and socially, it's bound to be a difficult time.

Finally, after other actions have been tried and failed, the nation will enter into the final stage of dealing with the collapse of the multi-bubble economy, in which we will give up the last vestiges of comfort in the past and take major steps toward *Revolutionary Action*. This will include big changes to improve global financial stabilization, increase economic productivity, prevent asset bubble formation, provide targeted stimulation, and create sustainable capital generation.

The truth is, we could potentially make any and all of these changes at an earlier stage, including right now (see Appendix B). But politically, such radical changes will be impossible to implement until we absolutely have to. Eventually, people and governments will face reality and figure out the changes necessary to get us out of this mess. We'll certainly be there to help. It will be a very exciting time.

Is There Any Scenario for a Soft Landing?

Yes, but it would have had to occur many years ago, back when the government debt bubble was still under $1 trillion, and before the real estate bubble, the private debt bubble and the stock market bubble. In other words, we could have created a softer landing for America's multi-bubble economy back when the mother of all bubbles, the government debt bubble, was still manageable. Even when the bubbles grew larger, we still could have ended the problem, but with a not so soft landing. At this point, now that the bubbles have grown so large and are so interconnected, the fall will be far and the eventual landing will be anything but soft. For updated information on the bubbles described in Chapter 3, go to www .aftershockeconomy.com/chapter 3.

The Hamptons Effect

Rising bubbles created a rising bubble economy and plenty of bubble-money wealth. If you have a big, expensive house in the Hamptons, and a grand lifestyle to go with it, you are keenly aware that a collapse in the stock market, real estate market, and the other asset bubbles would mean an end to the good times you have come to think of as permanent. Naturally, that isn't too appealing. Therefore, you have a powerful incentive not to see the bubbles or the bubble economy, and instead to believe in wishful thinking that assures you everything is, and will continue to be, all right.

We call this The Hamptons Effect. Wealthy people, stockbrokers, and asset managers have a deep need to keep believing we don't have any bubbles and to keep investing in the stock market. The Hamptons Effect is part of the reason for the stock market rallies over the past year and it drives plenty of other irrational decision making, as well. It is part of the Denial Stage we told you about. The bigger your house, the more denial you need to sleep at night.

CHAPTER 4

Global Mega-Money Meltdown

IT'S NOT JUST AMERICA'S BUBBLE ECONOMY, IT'S THE WORLD'S BUBBLE ECONOMY

A popular fairy tale gained favor in early 2008 proposing that the rest of the world, especially China, had magically "de-coupled" from the naughty U.S. economy. Regardless of whatever foolishness and financial problems we happen to get ourselves into here, China (and to a lesser extent, the other emerging markets) would continue to be a reliable hotspot for investment profits. Even more magical, these burgeoning economies might actually help buffer the rest of the world, and even the United States, from the full impact of the U.S.-led recession.

Unfortunately, by the end of 2008 it became fully evident that this de-coupling myth could not be further from the truth. It was just another failed attempt at wishful thinking and economic cheerleading. In fact, when the U.S. housing bubble, stock market bubble, private debt bubble, and discretionary spending bubble all began to burst in late 2008 and 2009, the speed at which the rest of the world fell into deep recession was staggering. In the fourth quarter of 2008, GDP in the United States declined by 6.2 percent on an annual basis; in the UK it declined by 5.9 percent, Germany declined by 8.2 percent, Japan declined by 12.7 percent and South Korea declined by a staggering 20.8 percent (during the Great Depression, U.S. GDP fell by about 25 percent). Both Germany and Japan had accelerating declines in the first quarter of 2009 with Germany falling at an annual rate of 14.4 percent and Japan falling 15.2 percent. Mexico actually topped the list in the first quarter 2009 with a 22 percent decline. As the U.S. economy reduced its imports of goods from overseas, particularly in the fourth quarter of 2008, the rest of the world's economies, joined at the hip to ours and each other's, simply fell off a cliff.

The U.S. and other economies are so tightly linked, and the impact of the U.S. Bubblequake and Aftershock will be felt so deeply around the world, that we almost titled our first book *The World's Bubble Economy*. But such a broad title would have reduced interest among our readers in the United States, which is most of our audience, so we went with the less accurate title. Nonetheless, just as we predicted in *America's Bubble Economy,* when the U.S. multi-bubble economy started to fall, the world's multi-bubble economy had little choice but to fall, too. And as we continue to fall, the rest of the world will end up in even worse shape than us.

The United States Will Suffer the Least

The U.S. economy is by far the most flexible, diverse, and stable economy in the world. We have the biggest, strongest economy, and we are less dependent on exports than most of the rest of the world. Therefore, the United States will naturally suffer the least in the current Bubblequake and coming Aftershock. This may seem unfair because we started most of these problems by inflating so many bubbles in the first place. On the other hand, many economies around the world benefited handsomely from our seemingly virtuous upward bubble spiral. They also actively supported it by lending us the money and not complaining when the many bubbles began to rise. So it's only logical that now, during our vicious downward bubble spiral, the rest of the world will suffer as well. And, fair or unfair, because other economies were never as strong as our own, even at the height of the bubble party, the rest of the world will do more poorly than we will during each stage of the multi-bubble bust.

After the United States, Western Europe will suffer the second least, followed by Japan and Eastern Europe, which will fare more poorly. Developing nations, such as China, India, and Brazil, will suffer even worse. And it doesn't take a lot of deep analysis to realize that the poorest, most underdeveloped countries in Africa and elsewhere will do quite badly indeed.

Think of the World's Bubble Economy in Two Groups: Manufacturing and Resource Extraction

We can better understand why and how the world economy will suffer so badly if we analyze the economy in terms of two broad categories: manufacturing and resource extraction. Manufacturing can be further divided into two sub-groups: (1) High-end manufacturers, primarily Germany and Japan, and (2) Low-end manufacturers, primarily China and other Asian Tiger nations. India is similar to low-end manufacturers because it provides low-end service exports.

Low-end manufacturers are directly affected by America's multi-bubble economy, both on the way up and on the way down, for the simple reason that we are the world's largest importer of low-end manufactured goods. There is no debate that American consumers and businesses drive the Chinese and Asian economies.

The key to the expansion of these economies is the multiplier effect from their export jobs. For each job created to produce exports sold to the United States, roughly two more jobs are created in support of those jobs. This is true not only of nations, but of cities and regions, as well, although to a lesser extent. Any job that produces a good or service that is exported from a region also produces secondary jobs to support those people in the export industry, such as jobs in medicine, government, and housing.

These multiplier effects are extremely important to the export-driven economies of China and the other Asian Tigers, like Korea, Taiwan, Hong Kong, and Singapore. Because of the multiplier effect, a large increase in exports can create a massive economic boom in an export-driven economy. Of course, the very same thing is true in reverse: a big export decline can cause a massive decline in an export-driven economy.

The United States also drives the economies of the second sub-group of manufacturers, which produce high-end manufactured goods, especially Germany and Japan. The United States imports both consumer goods, such as electronics and automobiles, as well as industrial goods, such as machine tools and construction equipment. This provides a big boost to the Japanese and German economies, not only because of the exports themselves, but also because of the same job-multiplier effect described above.

In addition, it is important to realize that the low-end manufacturing countries such as China, import enormous amounts of high-end machinery from Germany and Japan to produce their manufactured goods and to build their economies. This demand helped Germany become the world's largest exporter in 2008 at $1.53 trillion in exports according to the CIA World Factbook. Obviously, this helped further boost the German and Japanese economies.

What happens when all this goes into reverse? As the U.S. demand for low-end manufactured goods declines, so does the demand for German and Japanese high-end goods from China and the Asian Tigers. When the lack of demand from low-end manufacturers like China is combined with the lack of demand for high-end German and Japanese goods from the United States, Germany and Japan will see their economies truly devastated. What's worse, it will happen quite rapidly because most of these items imported by the United States are not really needed by us. They are part of that Discretionary Spending sector that was discussed in the last chapter. U.S. spending on imported non-essential items, from luxury 600-thread-count bed sheets to entertainment electronics, will collapse as we move deeper into the global mega-recession.

The other big group in the world's bubble economy includes countries that have large resource extraction industries. This group benefits nicely from growth in both the low-end and high-end manufacturing nations and also from America's multi-bubble economy. Nations within the resource extraction group include both poor and wealthy counties, such as Australia, Russia, Canada, and nations in the Middle East, Africa and South America. Interestingly, this group also includes China, which is now heavily involved in both low-end manufacturing and resource extraction.

Naturally, economies that rely on resource extraction are especially impacted by the rising and falling demands for their various minerals, oil, lumber, grains, and other resources by the booming manufacturing economies of the world's bubble economy. The benefits to these resource-producing nations get double-boosted by both greater quantities of exports and much higher prices for their resources as demand rises. These higher prices can propel a normal economic boom into a hyper-drive boom, creating enormous job growth, highly valued companies, and billionaires just about everywhere there is a mining shovel operating.

What do you think will happen to these resource-extraction economies when demand drastically declines? The double-boost of growing exports at higher and higher prices will easily turn into a double-downer of falling exports and falling prices. Think global mega-recession, squared.

The United States produces quite a few resources itself. However, the United States has a very diverse economy and will not feel the effects of either the resource boom or bust to the same extent as other countries.

America's Bursting Bubble Economy Will Bring Down Both Groups of Exporting Nations

On the way up, America's multi-bubble economy fueled the expansion of the world's bubble economy. As each economy expanded, it stimulated and expanded other economies, not only because the United States imported many goods and services from around the world, but also because many other nations have been trading back and forth in a positive feedback loop of economic stimulus. Europe and the more developed economies bought from the underdeveloped and developing countries, and those countries, in turn, bought from other countries.

The popping of America's bubble economy will rapidly pull the plug on every exporting nation in this complex web of interdependence. Given that America's bubble economy has a heavy discretionary spending component and given that we already have quite a lot of big capital goods already in place that will keep us going for a while (like cars and refrigerators), it will be relatively easy for American consumers to drastically reduce their purchases of imported goods as the U.S. economy heads deeper into recession. And in any case, after the dollar bubble pops, the costs of imports into the United States will soar astronomically.

Salt in the Wound: Not Only Will Foreign Investors Suffer as Their Domestic Economies Fall, They Will Also Lose Their Huge Profits from U.S. Investments

While the U.S. multi-bubble economy was booming, domestic and foreign investors from around the world made tremendous profits on their U.S. holdings, including their investments in U.S. stocks, bonds, Treasurys, real estate, and other dollar denominated assets.

As the bubbles pop and these assets lose value, the once-rising profit tide will rapidly flow in reverse, leaving foreign investors with tremendous losses. The economic consequences of this worldwide evaporation of wealth cannot be overstated.

More Salt: Other Governments Have Large Debts As Well

In addition to being hit hard by a huge downturn in exports, many of these export-dependent countries, like Germany and Japan, have built up large government debts of their own during the last two decades. And, just like the United States, they are now rapidly adding to those deficits with big stimulus packages in the hope of savingtheir economies. These growing government deficits in the exporting countries will only add to their economic problems later. When their economies hit the Aftershock, their people and economies will be hit harder because their governments are strapped for cash with huge debts to deal with and they will not be able to fund social welfare programs at anywhere near the current levels that these countries have become accustomed to. It will be a real shock, especially to Europe, but also to Japan, to have governments that move from being perhaps overly lavish in their benefits to being extremely stingy.

How the Bursting Bubbles Will Impact the World

Although all the economies of the world will suffer as the current Bubblequake recession deepens into the coming Aftershock, some regions will do better than others. Just like during flu season, those who are healthier and stronger before trouble hits tend to hold up better under stress. Here's what we see ahead.

Europe and Japan

As mentioned earlier, the U.S. economy will fare the best in the Bubblequake and Aftershock, followed by the countries of Europe and Japan, which have larger shares of their economies devoted to exports than we do, and so will be hit harder when their exports radically decline. These countries will eventually provide some subsidies to keep some of their export industries alive, like autos, aviation, and electronics.

At the same time, Europe and Japan will have to continue to import some goods from other countries, although far less than before. Much more so than the United States, Europe, and Japan will continue to need to import food and energy. To keep manufactured imports to a minimum, the risk is that these countries will enact protectionist tariffs to protect what remains of their manufacturing industries, and higher taxes on food and energy, slowing the flow of imports into their countries. This will naturally decrease other countries' exports to Europe and Japan even further than they will have already fallen, adding to the already negative downward spiral for the overall world economy.

Because their export industries will be so hard hit across the board, Europe and Japan will suffer very high unemployment. Stocks will do quite badly, and real estate values will crash. The European welfare system and many labor protections, currently far more generous than ours, will become increasingly difficult for their governments to afford.

But despite this grim picture, most governments in Europe will not see their governments' need to default on their debts, as will the U.S. government. Japan will not need to default either. This is because these governments didn't run large foreign funded government deficits. Like the United States, these countries will print money out of necessity and suffer extremely high inflation, just as we will. But the value of the euro and the yen will hold up relative to the dollar because they won't have the massive outflow of capital like we will experience as investment money pulls out of the United States and flows back to their home countries.

Massive outflows of capital from the United States into Europe will cause the dollar bubble to pop and the U.S. government to default on its debt. Most governments in Europe will avoid having to default on their debt for three reasons. First, massive inflows of new capital into Europe as U.S. and foreign investors sell their U.S. assets and buy euro-denominated assets will keep more capital available for European governments. Second, as many governments seek stimulus spending to save their economies, there will be a smaller and smaller money pie. The U.S. government will gobble up a big share of this smaller money pie, going into debt further and faster than Europe, which will help keep the European governments from running up massive increases in their debt. Third, investors who buy European government bonds will encourage European governments not to go too far into debt because they will be worried about a possible bankruptcy.

China

China has had unbelievable growth in the last several years, and under other circumstances you might expect China to do fairly well despite a global economic downturn—but not in a global *bubble* economy. Much of China's recent growth has been driven by America's and the world's bubble economies. While the economies of some of the poorest countries, such as in Africa, will be in far worse shape, none will suffer the pain of crushed expectations more than China.

In addition to tremendous decreases in their exports and the resulting collapse of the part of their domestic economy that was supported by those exports, China will be hit again because it has been actively supporting the U.S. dollar for many years, a position that will prove to be particularly devastating to its own finances when the dollar bubble finally pops.

On top of the massive decline in Chinese exports, as well as China's losses due to holding so many falling U.S. dollars, China will also endure a bursting bubble economy of its own. The rapid growth of the Chinese economy created a series of co-linked Chinese bubbles that will have no choice but to burst with devastating force. Their falling bubbles in real estate, stocks, and banking will be particularly dramatic. Construction and related industries, which have grown so rapidly in the past decade, will see huge declines. This will contribute to massive unemployment in China and inflation as the government is forced to print more currency.

These economic shocks will cut into China's economy deeply. When the United States, Europe, and Japan drastically cut their imports from China, China will experience their great boom in reverse. Unlike in the United States, Chinese citizens are not so used to prosperity that they can't easily return to lower consumption, like eating less meat, for example. And when the Chinese consumer does pull back, their still-fragile economy will collapse. In fact, after a while, the Chinese stock market and banking system could actually suffer a semi-shutdown for a period of time.

Now That's Stimulus!

The Chinese government encouraged their banks to do more lending in 2009. In response, banks in the first quarter of 2009 lent out $640 billion. That's almost the same amount they lent in all of 2008! That's a whole lot more than our stimulus package, which by the second quarter of 2009 was still not spending much more than $30 billion a month on construction and similar types of stimulus initiatives. China must be really rich. But, given that their economy is only one-fourth the size of the U.S. economy you have to wonder where all that money is coming from and how long such a stimulus can last.

We suspect that a lot of the bubbles in China are being pumped up a whole lot more predictably causing China enormous pain down the road. The popping of these internal Chinese bubbles will massively magnify the misery caused by the collapse of their export economy. Right now, it might seem all is well with China, but China has a bubble economy and, like all bubbles, most people won't be able to see them until they, too, finally pop.

All of these difficulties will create a populace that is much more supportive of political change in China. Hence, the next Tiananmen Square is likely to have more widespread support than last time and the Chinese government will have a much more difficult time controlling it.

The Middle East and Elsewhere

With the exception of Israel, which will react more like Europe and Japan, the Middle East will look a lot like China in many ways. The big problem for the Middle East is oil. The massive decline in economic activity worldwide will dramatically decrease the demand for oil. Plus, the world's largest consumer, the United States, will be faced with skyrocketing prices for imported oil because the dollar has fallen. So, demand from the United States, which is declining because of the terrible economy, will take an even bigger hit because of the high price.

Although new exploration for oil will dramatically decline, it will take many years for supply to decrease enough to catch up with rapidly falling demand. The collapsing demand will ultimately push oil down to the $20 per barrel range and, for a while, it could fluctuate even lower.

Such a dramatic decrease in income will devastate the Middle East, especially because these countries are already significantly poorer than the United States, Europe, and Japan, even before the world bubble economy bursts. Like China, the Middle East will suffer massive unemployment and inflation. And like China, the global mega-depression will likely accelerate political turmoil, especially in the Kingdom of Saudi Arabia. The monarchy there could quite possibly go the way of the monarchy of Iran since there is already considerable underlying tension in the Kingdom.

Outside of the Middle East, many other countries will also suffer. When the world's bubble economy falls, the already very poor countries of Africa and Asia will be truly devastated. With commodities and mineral exports slowing to a trickle, citizens of the poorest countries will face a real struggle for basic survival. However, it is quite likely that when localized famines and epidemics start to grow larger and larger, the richer, more developed nations, like the United States, will eventually step in and help. We won't have the money we did before, but we will still likely have the money and political will to help other countries who desperately need survival support.

The Green Economy Won't Produce a Lot of Green

Although there may be some good green technologies in the works, as the economy goes down, so will investments in the green economy. In fact, the investment climate for green tech/clean tech will turn increasingly negative as we go through Phase I, given the falling stock market and returns on investment. In such an extreme down market, good investments will be taken down along with the bad. Also, demand will fall as the economy falls, as there is less spending on capital goods and construction. A final blow will hit when the government debt bubble pops in Phase II since government subsidies will be eliminated. Subsidies are very important for a lot of green technologies.

Longer term, there will be a major movement toward clean technologies. In particular, as we move out of Phase III and need to build new electrical power plants to replace our current ones, we see a strong movement toward coal-fired plants with carbon sequestration. Coal plants that don't emit any carbon dioxide into the atmosphere are the most cost effective way to produce energy with no greenhouse gas emissions. People may like windmills because they are a comfortable technology from the past, or solar power, but the economics are simply not as powerful as coal-fired power with carbon sequestration. However, the economics of solar will become much more compelling in the long term, and could become our largest source of energy.

Whether we move fast enough to prevent major global warming is another issue entirely. There is a great deal of carbon dioxide already in the atmosphere and even in a global depression, we will still emit massive amounts of carbon dioxide for some time to come. China is and will continue to be a major source of emissions. Given the poor economies that China and other countries will face, it could be some time before they convert to minimal greenhouse emissions.

Our window for addressing global warming is not infinite. At some point, even if we cut carbon emissions by half, there simply will be too much already out there. Carbon dioxide does not come out of the atmosphere quickly and if we don't act soon, global warming will become inevitable. The primary damage would be the melting of the ice sheets covering Greenland and east Antarctica. Sea levels would rise almost 200 feet, forcing another set of political and economic challenges on the world.

If the World's Bubble Economy Is Hit Harder Than the U.S. Bubble Economy, Won't That Be Good for the Dollar?

No! This is the most common misconception about the value of the dollar. Even if the rest of the world is pretty well devastated economically, and it will be, the value of the dollar will still fall further than the euro, yen, and other major currencies. That's because the value of a currency is *not* a reflection of whose overall economy is better relative to the others, but a matter of *supply and demand.*

If people see a risk that the dollar will decline in value due to inflation or to other investors becoming disenchanted with the poor performance of their U.S. investments, they will stop buying dollar investments, thus reducing the demand for the dollar and reducing the dollar's value.

That initial concern about the dollar becomes a self-fulfilling prophecy because as a small number of investors stop buying dollars, the dollar will fall, causing other investors to become more concerned and stop buying dollars. At some point, the market can change quickly from people merely reducing their purchases of dollars to a full scale panic where they try to sell off whatever dollar denominated investments they still have, causing a traumatic collapse in the dollar's value. Unfortunately, the majority of investors will not be able to sell their dollars fast enough to get out and their investment money will go to Money Heaven (see Chapter 3). However, the dollar, even after it collapses in value, will still be one of the most widely traded currencies simply because of the size of the U.S. economy and the size of its imports and exports.

If the Rest of the World Is Collapsing, Won't That Be Good for Gold?

Yes! Gold will especially benefit from the collapse of economies around the globe because it is a favorite safe haven investment for people in Asia and the Middle East. Those countries buy most of the gold in the world. In fact only 10 percent of the world's total gold is purchased by the United States; the same amount that is purchased by Turkey. India, on the other hand, buys more than 20 percent of the world's gold and will be eager to get their hands on more as insecurity rises. So, it is important to view gold from a global perspective and not a U.S. perspective. The rest of the world looks at gold as a very viable and particularly safe investment. People at every economic level often own or want to own gold. It is much more favored culturally around the world than it is in the United States and even Europe.

Instability in Asian and Middle Eastern economies will encourage investors in those countries to buy a lot more gold, further accelerating the rising gold bubble. Yes, gold is another bubble on the ascent, and eventually it, too, will fall. But that is a very long way off and, in the meantime, you might as well learn how to profit from its coming meteoric rise (see Chapter 6).

A $100,000 Toyota Camry?

An important side effect of the dollar bubble collapse will be that the price of imported goods will soar. Imported cars, for example, will be priced so high that the United States will no longer buy a significant number. This is the market's way of restoring trade balance after so many years of imbalanced trade. Some things we will have to import, such as oil, but it will be very expensive. Hence, gasoline prices in the United States will easily reach $12 to $15 a gallon (on an inflation-adjusted basis) while the price for oil plummets around the world due to the huge economic slowdown and the drop in demand.

Other goods will need to be imported because we no longer have the facilities to make them, such as toys, clothing, and electronics. Again, they will be expensive but we will still buy them since, even with higher prices, it will be hard to beat the imported prices when the alternative is to create new factories in the United States with very high cost capital and relatively high cost of labor.

The lower dollar will make our exports much cheaper for other countries and we will do a booming business in exporting necessities, such as coal and wheat. However, most other goods will be hard to export because the demand will have collapsed and other countries will likely use import restrictions to protect the remaining companies in their countries that still produce those goods.

Coal is an especially good export for the United States because many countries don't have it, yet still need it to produce electricity, even during the depths of the economic downturn. Plus, we have an awful lot of it and it will be dirt cheap for other countries to import because of the collapsed dollar.

International Investment Recommendations

Our detailed investment suggestions are offered in the next two chapters, but for those of you who just can't wait, here's your executive summary:

Our best advice for U.S. investors looking to invest in foreign markets: Stay Away! Both the low-end manufacturing and high-end manufacturing economies and the resource-driven economies we just discussed will not recover until America's economy recovers. And since America's economy won't recover until after the dollar bubble pops, there is no reason to invest overseas for many years.

Obviously, there are always exceptions but, in general, investments will not do well because overseas economies will be in much worse shape than the U.S. economy. They are simply more dependent on exports, not as diverse, and not as flexible as we are. Plus, they invested heavily in the U.S. economy, which is about to cost them dearly.

Our best advice for foreign investors looking to invest in their own markets: If the investments in your countries are not good for U.S. investors, they certainly aren't any better for you. Again, there are always individual exceptions but, in general, with economies nosediving, normal stock and real estate investments in your home countries will lose you tons of money. Gold and euros offer easy outs for those looking for returns above normal interest rates. Shorting stocks will also be quite profitable for those willing and able to move into that arena, as many foreign stocks will be plummeting just like U.S. stocks, only faster in many cases.

Our best advice for foreign investors looking to invest in the U.S. markets: Given what will ultimately be a very low-priced dollar after the dollar bubble pops, investments in the United States will eventually become quite profitable for foreign investors. In fact, this is where a great deal of money will be made in the next couple of decades and, unlike the bubble money of the past, which will mostly disappear, the money made by smart foreign investors in the United States after the dollar bubble pops will last because it's not bubble money.

The biggest challenge is timing. Most foreign investors will think that U.S. investments have hit bottom when, in fact, they still have a long way down to go. By jumping in too soon they will lose an enormous amount of money. A simple rule for anyone interested in purchasing U.S. assets is to refrain from investing until *after* the dollar bubble pops and stabilizes.

Beyond this big-picture advice we also have much more to say about specific, complex events within various industries and countries, which exceeds the scope of this book. Please contact us directly for further information.

For more information on the international bubble economy, go to www.aftershockeconomy.com/chapter4.

PART

II

AFTERSHOCK DANGERS AND PROFITS

CHAPTER 5

Covering Your Assets: How Not to Lose Money

For most people, the advice we are about to give you on how not to lose money during the Bubblequake and Aftershock is far more important than any of our good investment ideas (offered in the next chapter) about how to cash in on it. We understand that no one likes to hear this. Most of us find *making* money far more interesting than simply not losing it. But knowing how to protect yourself is absolutely crucial to surviving and thriving in the months and years ahead, so please don't skip this part. If you only pay attention to one page in this book, this should be the one.

There are just two simple rules for where not to invest as the bubbles fall:

Rule #1: Stay away from stocks and real estate until after the dollar bubble pops.

Rule #2: Stay away from long-term bonds and all fixed-rate investments (including whole life insurance).

We said *simple* rules; we did not say easy. After years of investing in stocks, real estate, and fixed-rate investments, we know that the idea of pulling out of these bulwarks of modern wealth building may feel counterintuitive and just plain wrong. Here's why you have to bite the Bubblequake bullet and do it anyway.

This Is Not a Down Market Cycle; It's a Big Multi-Bubble Pop, Pop, Pop

As we've said many times, we are not in the middle of a down market cycle. The economy is not merely fluctuating back and forth between an "up" business cycle and a "down" business cycle. The overall U.S. and world economy is fundamentally *evolving* and therefore we are not going backward to whence we came. Instead, we are going forward to where we have never been before. At this moment in history, forward involves the bursting of a series of interconnected economic bubbles. On the way up, these expanding bubbles created tremendous wealth both here and around the globe. On the way down, these bursting bubbles will destroy a very impressive amount of wealth as well. How much of *your* wealth will be destroyed in the months and years ahead is really up to you. Ignore the problem or react as you may have in the past, and things could get away from you rather fast.

Each falling bubble will put increasing downward pressure on the others, creating a combined, cascading, multi-bubble fall. Hence, our key advice during the Bubblequake and coming Aftershock is to purge your mind right now of the false idea that if you just wait long enough, economic gravity will somehow disappear and the asset values that are currently falling (like stocks, real estate, etc.) will automatically return to an "up cycle." These popping bubbles are not going to take mercy on you and float back up!

People who tell you otherwise are simply trying to cheerlead the economy. As you may recall from the discussion in Chapter 3 about the psychology of how people react to changing economic conditions, we are currently in the "Market Cycles" stage of psychology regarding the evolving economic collapse. In the face of the evidence, people can no longer say everything is fine, so the next best way to ignore reality is to say we are experiencing a "down" market cycle. We know beyond any doubt that this is no more than cheerleading because these same experts who are now insisting we will return to an up cycle soon, never once said a word about a coming *down cycle* back when stocks and real estate were soaring high. Yet now we are supposed to believe that an automatic and reliable up cycle is inevitably on its way. It's all just part of the broader attempt to cheerlead the economy and keep investors relaxed. Just be patient, they say. Everything will get better soon. The economy (and your particular stocks, bonds, real estate, etc.) will be just fine.

Please don't fall for this! Multiple, linked, collapsing bubbles cannot and will not magically re-inflate. So let's look at these two simple (but not easy) rules more closely.

Rule Number One: Stay Away from Stocks and Real Estate Until After the Dollar Bubble Pops

In late 2008, coauthor Bob Wiedemer had dinner with a friend. After a few drinks, the man revealed that he had recently made one of the bigger financial mistakes of his life. A fan of our first book, Bob's friend admitted he only half believed our 2006 analysis about the coming Bubblequake, and therefore, he sold only about half his stocks. For sure, this guy saved himself from what could have been twice the loss by selling half his holdings near the market peak, well before the Dow had fallen so dramatically in late 2008. He only wished he had sold the other half too.

Let Bob's friend spare you his learning curve. Stocks and real estate are still mostly on their way down and have *not* hit their ultimate bottoms. As a general rule, stay clear of *all* stocks and all investments, and commercial and vacation real estate, until every one of the interconnected bubbles in our multi-bubble economy has fully popped. Are there exceptions to this rule? Yes, there are a few small exceptions (see Chapter 6), but in general, *get out* and *stay out* of your stocks and investment real estate until after the dollar bubble pops. Do not throw away your money now on what may look like bargains. Don't get lured back into stocks and real estate *until after the dollar bubble has fully popped,* if you still have any interest in investing in stocks and real estate (most people won't after seeing such devastation of stock and real estate values).

We discussed the timing of the dollar bubble pop in Chapter 3. It could happen as early as 2011 or 2012, but more likely in 2013 or 2014. It could even be later, but probably not. As mentioned earlier, it is very hard to predict exactly because it is so heavily influenced by foreign investor sentiment and the willingness/ability of governments, like China, to intervene in the foreign exchange markets. A lot of factors will influence investor psychology, but clearly the massively growing deficits and the declining U.S. economy will have increasingly negative effects on investor sentiment.

Even with the market down significantly off its highs in October 2007, you should eventually sell all your stock. You don't have to do it all at once, but you should do it over a reasonable period of time. Short-term, stock prices will go up and down, but long-term they most definitely will go down, down, down, so you should sell them with all reasonable speed. This same advice applies to the stocks in your 401K plan. Move your money out of stocks and into cash.

The next chapter offers ideas about what you can do to make money during this mess, but right now, you need to wrap your mind around this very difficult to accept idea: *Stay away from investing in stocks and real estate.* This is also true for U.S. investors looking to invest in foreign stocks and real estate and for foreign investors looking to invest in the United States or in their own countries. *Stay away!* Now is not the time.

What to Do with Owned Real Estate

Unless you have very compelling attachments to or very strong sentimental interests in any vacation homes, sell them now. You can always just rent something when you go to your favorite vacation spots. Even if selling a vacation home now will result in a financial loss, it will not be as much as you will surely lose later. Ditto for investment property and commercial real estate. *Sell them all now* before prices fall even lower. We are nowhere near a bottom in real estate values. Now is the time to get out. Later on (after the chaos period that will follow the popping of the dollar and government debt bubbles), you will be able to buy vacation homes very cheaply, but only if you don't lose all your money in the collapse.

For your primary home, the situation is trickier. Many people have a sentimental attachment to their homes and may not want to sell them to capture their values before they fall further. In addition, it may not be easy to find an equivalent rental. Strictly from a financial standpoint, you probably should sell your home now, but we understand that you probably won't. If you are planning to move or retire in the near future, by all means, speed up that process and sell your home now. Don't wait for home values to rise in the near future. They won't.

If you are going to keep your home, make sure you have a *fixed-rate* mortgage, not an adjustable-rate loan. With a fixed-rate mortgage the monthly payments on your home will be dramatically reduced by high inflation when the dollar bubble pops. Of course, so will the value of your home, but at least you will have a good, cheap place to live for as long as you wish. Just the opposite will be true for anyone holding an adjustable-rate mortgage. The rapidly increasing monthly payments will quickly make repaying the loan impossibly difficult.

Your best bet is to refinance now into a low, fixed-rate, 30-year or 40-year mortgage. Grab this opportunity, while you still can. It may seem counter-intuitive when everyone is advising us to pay off our debts as quickly as possible, but you do not want to pay off your low-interest, fixed-rate mortgage any faster than is minimally required. Remember, high inflation is going to all but wipe out this debt for you in the not-too distant future. However, you do have to be able to make enough money to pay your mortgage payment or you'll risk losing your home.

You can also be very aggressive and actually borrow money from the equity on your home, via a fixed rate home equity loan, to make other high return investments in the Aftershock which we have discussed in Chapter 6. This clearly has risks—the big one being difficulty in paying your monthly mortgage payments if you do not save and properly invest the excess proceeds on your home. But, as soon as high inflation begins to hit, the inflation adjusted cost of your fixed rate mortgage payments become much lower.

What if you can't pay your mortgage? As we already mentioned, the best plan is to refinance to a low, fixed-rate mortgage, to lower your monthly payments. If that doesn't work, cut your other expenses as much as you can and fight to keep your home. If you can't refinance, stay on the lookout for any mortgage bailout programs you may qualify for in the next couple of years.

If all else fails and you cannot refinance and don't qualify for any bailouts, do not abandon your property. Even now, it can take a year or longer from the time you stop paying your mortgage until you are evicted. After the Aftershock, it will take much longer. So keep paying your mortgage as long as you can, and if you must stop paying, you can stay in your home as a squatter. When the dollar and government debt bubbles pop, banks will be overwhelmed and foreclosures will become increasingly harder to enforce. You will probably be able to stay in your home as a squatter for longer than you think. But not forever. Eventually, squatters will lose their homes, too. But at some point you may also be able to simply rent your home from the bank or government and avoid eviction. We are moving into a very dynamic situation that we have never seen before in U.S. history, as Chapter 10 describes in more detail, in which many actions will be possible that would not be possible today.

The key is to not give up easily. You can fight foreclosure and the government is actually helping you do that. In a blatant plug for a sibling's book, if you find yourself in a foreclosure situation, you should take a look at *The Homeowner's Guide to Foreclosure: How to Protect Your Home and Your Rights, Second Edition* by James Wiedemer (Kaplan, 2008). Jim is a real estate attorney who practiced during the foreclosure crisis in Houston in the mid-1980s and knows foreclosures well. It's a good book that gives you excellent detailed information on how to fight foreclosure.

Rule Number Two: Stay Away from Long-Term Bonds and All Fixed-Rate Investments

When the dollar bubble and the government debt bubble finally pop, interest rates and inflation will soar (as explained in Chapter 3). Foreign investors will no longer lend us money and will have taken out whatever dollars that haven't already gone to Money Heaven, which constricts the supply of capital and raises the price of borrowing money (high interest rates). That will leave the government with little choice but to print more dollars (high inflation).

Sky-high interest rates and inflation will deliver a body blow to stocks and will devastate the value of all fixed-income securities. Therefore, do *not* put the cash you get from selling your stocks and real estate into long-term fixed-rate bonds, bond funds, or any long term fixed-rate investments.

Where Is the Best Place to Stash Cash?

The cash you get from selling your stocks and real estate obviously has to go someplace. Right now, you are pretty safe with just about anything short-term—money markets, short-term government bonds, and so forth. However, as we move deeper into the recession and closer to the dollar bubble pop, you will need to be much more careful where you put your cash. Keeping cash in money market funds of banks and corporations clearly is not a great idea. Your money market accounts should be heavy with treasury bills. But, when the dollar bubble pops, even short term US government debt will be problematic, which means you should be moving heavily towards gold and similar investments as pressure on the dollar and government debt increases.

You should also be considering euro government bond funds such at the T. Rowe Price International Bond Fund (RPIBX). They are relatively safe since they are only government bonds and are diversified. Even now those are a good play, but make sure that you are investing only in short term funds as the bubble problems develop.

Clearly, this is a dynamic situation, but we will keep you up to date on what to do with your cash on our web site at www.after shockeconomy.com/cash.

How Long Do I Have to Follow These Rules?

We know that as the collapsing multi-bubble economy falls, the last bubble to burst will be the government debt bubble. As we explained in Chapter 3, timing when the dollar and government debt bubbles will pop is hard to nail down and will not likely happen in 2009. It could occur as early as 2011 or 2012 but more likely in 2013 or 2014. The exact timing of the fall of the dollar and government debt bubble pop is hard to predict because these events will be heavily influenced by foreign investor sentiment and the declining willingness (and ability) of foreign governments, such as China, to intervene in the foreign exchange markets to keep the value of the dollar high. A lot of factors will be at work, but clearly the massively growing U.S. federal debt and the declining U.S. economy will have increasingly negative effects on foreign investor sentiment. Sooner or later, foreign investors will have had enough risk with not much return. Once enough foreign investors stop putting money into the United States, other investors will quickly do the same, and the dollar and government debt bubbles will fall.

Letting Go Is Hard to Do

We understand that quitting stocks, bonds, and investment real estate is not easy. It's tough to just give up on investments that we have come to know and love, investments that have provided so well for us in the past—so supportive and so comfortable. It's almost like giving up on Mom and Dad. These investments have done so well for us over the past few decades, how can we just walk away? Everybody invested in stocks, bonds, and real estate, and usually everybody did so well. The world just doesn't seem right without them. And if leaving Mom and Dad isn't bad enough, moving to alternative investments may feel like going to an orphanage. Actually, you can make much more money with alternative investments (see Chapter 6) than with stocks and real estate in the past, but that will be much harder to do than in the relatively easy glory days of the rising real estate and stock markets, and few investors will join you in the alien world of investments that go up when the economy goes down. It just won't be the same.

In most economic situations, reading what *not* to invest in is pretty useless because you probably wouldn't invest in it anyway. You would just invest in typical stock mutual funds and some basic real estate just like everyone else. However, in a bubble economy, what not to invest in can be one of the most important financial decisions you make in your life. That's because the losses on stock and real estate can be so large. At this point, especially with the dollar bubble yet to pop, you have to be very careful about what investments you hold.

There was a great line in the old television show M*A*S*H that essentially said, "In war, there are two rules. Rule #1 is that young men die. Rule #2 is that doctors can't change Rule #1." If you don't like the two rules we are presenting in this chapter, here are another two rules that you can apply to this falling multi-bubble economy. Rule #1: No matter what happens, all the bubbles will eventually pop. Rule #2: No amount of optimism can change Rule #1. Being optimistic about your stock and real estate investments will not change their future value. We have to deal with the reality we have, not the reality we want.

If you are still not convinced that we are in the middle of a bursting multi-bubble economy, please re-read the last four chapters. On the other hand, if your head says, "This book makes sense" but your heart says, "I want my bubble back!" then take a few deep breaths or have a few stiff drinks or take a nap, but whatever it takes, get over it and get on with your new life in the new economy. Don't spend too much time wishing for the good times to magically return. They won't. It's time to change your thinking.

What to Do If You Sort of Believe Us, but Not 100 Percent

You don't have to believe us entirely to start protecting yourself now. You needn't change your investments completely and all

GREGORY

" I want my bubble back. "

at once, but you do need to change and you need to continue to change as our analysis starts looking more and more correct to you. Hindsight is 20/20, but times like this call for more than hindsight. What you need is foresight. We are trying very hard to offer that to you. Listen to what we are saying and keep your eyes open for evidence that what we are predicting is in fact actually happening. In time, you will believe us partially, and then you will believe us fully. The sooner that happens, the better it will be for you.

If you think we are completely wrong, we advise you to wait until you see stock and real estate values going back up again for at least one year before you invest. Waiting at least a year before buying real estate will be easy because prices move slowly and you won't miss much by holding off for a while. With stocks, waiting a year may feel more difficult because prices move quickly and you could easily miss the bottom, but if you really think stocks are such a good investment and that we are really in a long-term rally, then missing a year won't matter much in the long run.

On the other hand, if you think we might be partially right and also partially wrong, then do what Bob's friend did and only take half our advice, or take all our advice but only follow it halfway. That would certainly be a prudent course of action for any reasonable person. For example, you could sell 20 to 30 percent of your stocks with every 1,000-point drop in the Dow. You may later end up like Bob's friend, wishing you had done more, but better to do half than nothing. More sophisticated investors can employ a hedge strategy, increasing their hedging as they see the stock market and overall economy continuing to go down.

Even if you don't believe us fully now, try to be very open to changing your mind. If it looks like what we are saying is becoming increasingly true, then increasingly move in the direction of our suggestions. This show's not over by a long shot and you have plenty of time to adjust your positions. You may take some losses, but that's okay. It's not always smart to go 100 percent with any one way of thinking. Just keep your eyes and your mind open and make sure you make adjustments along the way.

What Else Can I Do to Protect Myself?

In addition to the two big rules (stay away from stock and real estate until after the dollar bubble pops, and stay away from long-term, fixed-rate investments), there are a number of other actions you can take to avoid losing money in the current Bubblequake and coming Aftershock, including:

- Pay off all variable-rate credit cards and personal debt with adjustable interest rates
- Convert your adjustable-rate mortgage to a fixed-rate, 30- or 40-year mortgage
- If you have an adjustable-rate home equity loan, refinance it to a fixed-rate loan
- Do not pay off or make accelerated payments on your fixed-rate mortgage or home equity loan
- Reduce spending as much as possible and save it for future expenses and investments (don't wait, do it now!)
- Sell collectibles, art, jewelry, and other valuables (other than gold) that don't have sentimental value now, while they are worth more than they will be later
- Take extra care to hang onto your job and definitely don't quit without having another good job lined up (see Chapter 7 for relatively safe Bubblequake and Aftershock jobs and careers)

What about Bankruptcy?

In early 2009, we saw a personal finance article suggesting that readers not wait too long before filing for bankruptcy. It suggested declaring bankruptcy to get rid of credit card debt while you still have a job. The article also advised readers to not use up all their assets paying a mortgage that was too expensive or underwater (meaning the mortgage is greater than the value of the home). In fact, the article suggested just letting the mortgage go unpaid because the foreclosure process could take a year or more to complete. During that time, while you were no longer paying credit cards or a mortgage, but still had income from a job, you could put some money away.

At the time, we were a little surprised to see such bleak, hard-nosed advice in a personal finance column, which is usually much more upbeat. It was a sign of the changing times. Better to face reality and plan for the future, than keep running full steam ahead down the wrong track. Try not to be emotional, just realistic.

The first thing you need to know about bankruptcy is that, after all the bubbles pop and unemployment shoots up, many, many people will declare bankruptcy. It may feel lousy, but truthfully, it will be a logical course of action for many people. Also, at that point, many people won't want or be able to get more credit anyway, so bankruptcy is not that terrible.

However, after the Aftershock hits, banks will be so devastated that lenders will likely not be too aggressive about collecting debts. So, you may not want to declare bankruptcy at that point since banks may not be doing much about debts for a while anyway. Also, well in advance of filing for a bankruptcy you may want to transfer any assets out of your name and perhaps into a trust fund for your children. If this route interests you, the sooner you do it, the better. Please check with a bankruptcy attorney regarding the details of the law regarding the timing of asset transfers. If the transfer is too close to a bankruptcy filing, it can be considered a "fraudulent conveyance."

Remember, Your Net Worth Is Not Your Self Worth

It's never a good idea to equate your personal worth with your net worth, but in a booming, multi-bubble economy on the rise, it may not cause you too much harm. On the other hand, in a bursting multi-bubble economy on the way down this bad habit may come back to haunt you. Most people will see their net worth fall dramatically in the months and years ahead. Reading this book can help minimize your losses and maximize your gains, but please don't focus so much on your wallet that you forget what really makes life so worthwhile. We are not being corny when we remind you of what you already know: *It's not really about the money.* It may seem like money buys happiness, especially when the money is rolling in. But remember, the potential for happiness is actually always available to us because it comes, not from money or from things, but from other people. We need to remember this when money is flowing in our lives, and even more so when it is not.

As much as this book focuses on money, and as much as every one will be terribly focused on money over the next few years, the best advice you may get won't be financial. Be sure to focus on your family and friends. Your family will need your support and your friends may need you now more than ever—and you may need them more as well. Mutual support is the key to a good life in both the best of times and the worst of times.

Look for what makes you happy and find your glass half full. You don't have to ignore reality, just be sure to see what is real and what is not.

In the Bubblequake and Aftershock, do your part to help by making sure you don't judge a person by the size of their wallet, but by the size of their heart and quality of their character.

For more current information on protecting your assets, please go to www.aftershockeconomy.com/chapter5.

Cashing in on Chaos

BEST AFTERSHOCK INVESTMENTS

There are enormous amounts of money to be made during the Bubblequake and Aftershock. In fact, we predict that more real (non-bubble) money will be made in the Bubblequake and Aftershock than in the last three decades combined. Of course, it won't come close to matching the total amount of *bubble money* made during the past three decades, but most of that money will soon go to Money Heaven (see Chapter 3).

Plenty of Profit Opportunities, but They Will Feel Quite Uncomfortable, Even Scary at Times

Gone are the days when you could just sit back with a glass of wine or a six pack of beer and watch TV, knowing that by the end of the year your house would be worth 10 to 20 percent more than at the start of the year even though you hadn't lifted a finger to improve it.

Gone are the days when you could just buy a set of stocks or mutual funds that everyone else buys and watch them rise 1,400 percent in 25 years, or if you chose higher-growth stocks, watch them grow 2,500 percent or more. No need to be a stock-picking genius or a high-risk, high-judgment venture capitalist to make ridiculously high returns. In fact, for most investors, it was better if you didn't use any judgment at all and just chose index funds, as John Bogle, the founder of Vanguard Funds (the second largest mutual fund company in the United States), correctly advised. Back then, you could just sit back and watch the stock market automatically take your investments to tremendous heights while you did absolutely nothing.

Those were the good old days. That's over now. Today, good judgment and taking risks are critical to making money and will be even more so in the future. In fact, good judgment and taking risks will be critical to simply holding onto your money in the future. Without smart thinking and some risk-taking, your money will go straight to Money Heaven, along with just about everyone else's money in the next several years. This journey is not for the faint of heart.

Invest Where Most People Do Not, and Be Very Smart About It

The highest returns on investment in the past have often been made by people who spotted trends or new ideas *before* everyone else. In fact, they often invested in ideas that other people roundly criticized. That's investing the old-fashioned way. Old-fashioned investing says it is important to invest in opportunities before other people see that they are good opportunities because that's when you get the best prices. But seeing something early is not enough. You could invest in a lot of things other people don't see and lose a whole lot of money because you might be seeing a bad investment. Being contrarian is necessary but not sufficient for success in the Bubblequake and Aftershock; you also have to be *smart* and see a *good* investment before others see it.

What will qualify as "smart" in the treacherous future investment environment? To our thinking, there are three key factors:

1. You have to correctly judge the macroeconomic environment. If you don't, even your most well thought out investments will be crushed. We have made a strong case in Chapters 1, 2, and 3 about what the future macroeconomic environment will be like. If you don't correctly judge the future environment, you will likely lose most of your money—as will most everyone else.

2. You have to invest for the long term. Even if your macro economic analysis is spot-on, it is hard to make correct short-term judgments (less than a year). Investor psychology, government actions or inactions, and unusual political events can have major impacts on the short-term course of the financial markets. Even more annoying is that certain events or actions may have little effect on the economy, but they will have a major effect on financial markets because investors mistakenly *think* that those actions will have a major effect on the economy, such as the stimulus package and interest rate cuts of spring 2008.

3. You have to go against the conventional wisdom in fundamental ways. There is a lot of talk in the business world about disruptive technologies or unconventional thinking. In truth, most technologies are rarely very disruptive or very unconventional. The terminology is more of a marketing gimmick than reality. It is easy to think you are being unconventional when, in fact, you are only being unconventional on the surface and not in any fundamental way.

This is true for investing, as well. You may think you were being unconventional, for example, if you jumped back into the stock market in December 2008 when almost everyone else was getting out, but in fact you were being very conventional. You may have appeared unconventional on the surface, but fundamentally you were supporting the very conventional wisdom that says stocks are always a good long-term investment. They're not. Being unconventional *in a fundamental way* means realizing that, at this stage of the evolution of our economy, stocks are a bad investment for the long term.

It's not easy going against the crowd. Bob recalls feeling this very personally when he sat on a panel of nine financial advisors at a Renaissance Weekend in December 2008. The members of the panel were asked if they would *hold* or *sell* stock that had been intended as a long-term investment of five years. Only Bob and one other person said they would sell now. Everyone else insisted they would hold on to the stock for the five-year period. Resisting the conventional wisdom by not holding on to stocks for the long-term is unconventional in a fundamental way and uncomfortable in a fundamental way.

Remember, in the future, more long-term money will be made during the Bubblequake and Aftershock than in the rising multi-bubble economy of the past. Most "bubble money" will ultimately go to Money Heaven, taking along with it a lot of hard-earned money. However, post-bubble money, which will be hard to make and very scary and will require a fair amount of skill, will not go to Money Heaven. For that reason, much more long-term money will be made in the future than in the bubble economy.

Also, be aware that the government and many financial professionals have a vested interest in spinning any news in a positive light for stock, real estate and other investments helped by the bubble economy. Keep a level head and look at the economic fundamentals of what's really going on with the economy and don't focus on the latest spin. There is plenty of news out there that gives you the real economic picture and many financial journalists who have at least some degree of skepticism of any spin. It's easy to find if you want to see it and, of course, you can always go to our website www. aftershockeconomy.com.

Best Bubblequake and Aftershock Investments

Good investments during the Bubblequake and Aftershock will come in two basic flavors:

1. Investments that take advantage of a falling stock market (Phase I: the Bubblequake, which we are in now).
2. Investments that take advantage of a falling dollar (Phase II: the Aftershock, which is still ahead).

These two areas make up the basis for the enormous opportunities to make money when others will be losing their shirts. This meets the first criteria of smart investing because it involves correct macroeconomic analysis: In the long-term, stocks and the dollar will go down.

However, in reality, investments cannot easily be divided into these two camps because there is a great deal of overlap between the two. For example, is investing in a falling stock market not also an investment in a falling dollar (since that will drive down the stock market) and vice versa? Hence, we will present our list of investment recommendations as a laundry list, rather than try to artificially divide into them in two groups. Still, it's a good idea to understand these two macroeconomic trends are occurring and serve as the rationale for every investment on the list.

Smart Investing for a Falling Stock Market:
Shorting Stocks Using LEAPS

We love LEAPS! Long-term Equity AnticiPation Securities, or LEAPS, follow Rule #2 of smart investing very well, which is to invest for the long term. In the case of shorting stocks, that means you should never short short-term, you should always short long-term.

LEAPS do this perfectly by allowing you to short stocks for one- to two-year periods. LEAPS are the name for long-term stock options. Most options are for much shorter periods of time. You buy *put* options when you want to short a stock and you buy *call* options when you want to buy (or go long) on a stock. You buy LEAPS exactly as you would buy options, only the short-term volatility risk is lower because they expire over a longer period of time. LEAPS, however, are not offered on every stock that is option-able. So don't expect to find them in the option chain on all option-able stocks.

If you are not comfortable dealing with options, then LEAPS are not for you. However, if you are comfortable with options and would like to learn more about the technical details of buying and selling LEAPS, we recommend you take a look at *Understanding LEAPS* (McGraw Hill, 2003) by Marc Allaire and Marty Kearney, which provides an excellent description of LEAPS and how to use them.

Smart Investing for a Falling Stock Market:
Shorting Stocks Using Bear Funds

Bear funds are an easier way for most people to short a falling market. They will not provide the returns of LEAPS but they are much easier to use since you can purchase them like mutual funds. These funds usually short indexes such as the S&P 500 and can use leverage to even "double short" the market. This means that if the S&P index falls 10 percent, the fund should increase in value by roughly 20 percent. However, these funds are traded on a daily basis, which means they may not track long-term trends as closely as LEAPS. In fact, some leveraged funds have done very poorly in tracking long-term trends. ProFunds offers a wide range of bear funds and is one of the best in the business. They have certainly been a pioneer in the market. For more information on bear funds and some specific funds to consider please visit our web site at www.aftershock economy.com/bearfunds.

The Future for Good Hedge Funds Is Brighter Than Ever

The opportunities for hedge funds to make money in the Bubblequake and Aftershock are enormous, but they can't do it by doing what worked in the past. Hedge funds, like individuals, will have to change. They will have to move strongly against what most hedge funds are doing. Instead of doing well by doing what everyone else does, they will have to fundamentally challenge conventional investment wisdom—just like people have always had to do to make a lot of money in business in the United States.

They will also have to become more entrepreneurial, meaning no more "2 and 20" (2 percent management fees plus 20 percent of the upside). Instead, fees will more likely be 1 (or even 0.5) and 30. They will have a much higher upside, but a minimal or limited management fee. In the future, hedge funds will have to make their money only when their investors make money. They will share in their gains and losses.

Most importantly, they will have to have, by sheer luck or by correct analysis, the *right* macroeconomic view of the global economy. They will have to be right when almost all of their competitors are wrong. This is nothing more and nothing less than what has worked so many times before in American investment management.

Smart Investing for a Falling Dollar: Buying Euros

A very obvious way to profit from the coming fall in the dollar is to buy euros. The easiest way to buy euros is through an ETF (exchange traded fund) trading under the symbol FXE (a Rydex Investments product). Each share of FXE sells for the price of 100 euros. You can buy this ETF just like a stock through your normal brokerage account.

You can also buy euro funds that are invested in euro government bonds or euro corporate bonds. These have the advantage of paying interest on your money, as well as the appreciation on the euro. We recommend going with euro government bonds, given the issues many corporations may soon face. Funds we recommend are listed on www.aftershockeconomy.com/eurofunds. Although many other currencies will rise relative to the dollar, the euro is the strongest and easiest to trade. The euro zone will likely see significant problems among its members with some countries possibly dropping out of the euro. However, despite some problems, we expect the euro to easily survive the coming Aftershock.

We should add that even though it isn't as sophisticated as investing in euros or euro bond funds, buying gold is also a way to benefit from the relative rise in euros. Gold can be easily sold for euros so it always tracks the euro price even if you buy it in dollars. Hence, buying gold with dollars is indirectly an automatic investment in euros. Gold is shunned by many sophisticated investors, but the reality is that it is a reasonable way to invest in euros while also gaining the appreciation that gold will have on its own, outside of the relative rise in the euro versus the dollar. More details about gold are offered later in this chapter.

Smart Investing for a Falling Dollar: Shorting Fixed-Rate Bonds Using ETFs

There are ETFs that short fixed-income bonds, such as Treasurys. When interest rates rise, fixed-income bonds fall in value making these ETFs an excellent investment opportunity. One option is the ETF that trades under the symbol TBT (a ProFunds Group product), which tracks two times the inverse of the daily performance of the Barclays Capital 20+ Year U.S. Treasury Index. This allows you to "double short" long-term U.S. Treasuries.

ETFs can be highly volatile so you need to be a long-term player who won't panic and sell at the wrong time. These investments are only for relatively sophisticated investors. You can find more information on short bond ETFs on www.aftershockeconomy.com/etfs.

Be Careful with Commodities (Other than Gold)

Investing profitably in commodities, such as copper and oil, will require a good macro awareness of changing trends in supply and demand. At first, the collapsing economy will put heavy downward pressure on the demand for all industrial commodities, which will naturally depress prices. But later, when the dollar bubble begins to fall significantly, commodity prices will increase dramatically *in dollar terms*.

For example, the price of oil will eventually fall as low as $10 to $20 per barrel as worldwide demand declines with the overall world economy. But in the United States oil will eventually cost $100 to $150 per barrel due to the drastic decline in the value of the dollar.

Commodities in General

In general, commodities will go down in value when the economy goes down. However, as we just mentioned, this downturn is different because of the dramatic fall in the dollar. The low-value dollar makes commodities imported into the United States more expensive. Even if the commodity is produced in the United States, it will rise to the imported price level because it could be exported. The low-value dollar makes U.S.-produced commodities low-priced in foreign currencies and hence, good exports. U.S.-produced commodities will often be much lower-cost than anything produced by other countries. So expect demand for U.S.-produced coal, grain, and beef to be very good.

Again, there is a limit on this export growth because some of these commodities, such as lumber and copper, will see demand fall precipitously worldwide because they are used in producing capital goods. However, both coal and grain will see solid demand since they are used heavily for production of necessities—food and electricity. In terms of U.S.-produced commodities, we see the brightest future for coal since many countries have a current need to import it and will need to import it in the future to produce electricity even in the Aftershock. However, even necessities will feel some downward pressure. For example, grain will be hurt since the demand for beef worldwide will fall—a lot of grain is used to feed cattle. Also, grain's price now is highly influenced by ethanol requirements in gasoline and those requirements could easily be reduced if grain prices are very high due to high exports.

Exactly how the twin forces of a cheap dollar and worldwide recession will affect exports of U.S.-produced commodities is a complex issue. One thing is certain, though; dollar prices of U.S.-produced commodities will be high. Equally certain is that world prices in non-dollar terms will be quite low due to the worldwide drop in demand due to the worldwide recession.

For investors, these twin forces will produce a great deal of volatility. Increasingly, a commodities play will become a dollar play. Commodities are always volatile and the popping of the bubbles and the impact of the falling dollar will make them even more volatile. It won't be a market for the faint of heart or the inexperienced newcomer. It's like going from Class I rapids to Class V. On page 135, we describe the specific impact of the popping of the bubbles on specific classes of commodities.

As the Bubbles Pop, Gold Will Not Be Treated as a Commodity; It Will Be in a Class by Itself

We want to point out that, as the bubbles pop, gold will not be treated as a typical commodity. This has often been true throughout human history and will remain true through the popping of the bubbles. Gold holds an unusual position in the minds of many people around the world as a store of monetary value. Even in the United States, until the twentieth century, it was the most common mode of monetary commerce. Hence, it is not really a commodity in the same sense as wheat or zinc or oil.

For this reason, long term, it will act very differently from other commodities in terms of its price. Other commodities are driven by commercial demand. Gold will be driven by demand for it as a store of monetary value. In the short run, before the bubbles pop, it may at times follow other commodities in terms of price as they go up and down. But as the bubbles start to pop, its attraction as a traditional store for monetary value will set it increasingly apart from commercial commodities. Yes, the demand for gold as jewelry will fall since jewelry is a discretionary good, but that loss of demand can be more than offset by a big increase in investment demand. Furthermore, a great deal of gold jewelry that is purchased in Asia and the Middle East is often for investment purposes since it can be easily resold if the money is needed.

Metals, Such as Copper, Platinum, and Silver

Metals, such as nickel, zinc and especially copper, have huge industrial demand. Conversely, there is little investment demand for these metals. As the bubbles begin to burst, the industrial demand for these metals will fall precipitously. This will be especially true for copper, which has seen a massive increase in price in the last few years. As we predicted in *America's Bubble Economy*, much of the demand that was driving copper's price came from China, which is seeing its demand for copper decline precipitously as its exports decline (and will continue to decline) during the popping of the bubbles. In addition, as we predicted earlier, there was clearly some speculative demand for copper that has heavily dried up even before the base industrial demand declines much more severely in the Aftershock.

The advice regarding commodity metals is simple. You can play with them for a while and, if you are a good and/or lucky trader, you can make some money; but as the bubbles start to pop, get out. When the bubbles pop worldwide, commodity metals prices will fall dramatically. Again, the falling dollar will counteract the fall in worldwide prices for commodities produced in the United States.

Let's look at a couple precious metals other than gold that are getting a lot of attention. First, let's look at silver, which is a bit of a hybrid. It has some industrial demand, although the traditional use in photography is quickly evaporating. Like gold, it also has some investment demand because it has long been used as a secondary store of monetary value next to gold. Similar to copper, when the bubbles pop, there will be a big decrease in industrial demand, and there will also be a big decrease in demand for silver in jewelry as discretionary spending declines. However, there will likely be a significant increase in investment demand. In fact, for short periods, silver has outperformed gold. Long term, silver will likely do fine, but the safe bet and likely the highest long-term return in investment metals is gold.

Another precious metal that is getting a lot of attention is platinum, which is in a similar position to silver in that it is a hybrid metal with both strong industrial demand and investment demand. However, much of the industrial demand is from catalytic converters in the automobile industry and, since autos are a capital good, it will see an unusually sharp decline in demand. Because of that, platinum is likely to be harder hit than silver, so we would recommend staying away from platinum as the bubbles begin to pop.

In dollar terms, gold benefits as well as other metals from the rise in the euro, and will perform better because of its traditional investment role. Gold—which is almost entirely for investment—simply has much more worldwide allure as an investment compared to other metals and precious commodities, such as diamonds. Given all this, why bother with the others, since they won't likely perform as well?

Oil and Gas

Oil and gas will be a tale of two cities—one where the price is very high, and one where the price is very low. In the United States, the price will be high; in the rest of the world, it will be low. This is one of the more unexpected effects of the popping of the bubbles, but it makes perfect sense. The price of oil has been driven up by the economic growth engine of the world—the U.S. economy—and as that economy hits a major downturn, so will the price of oil. This is especially so because much of the recent growth in oil prices is from Asian growth, which is highly dependent upon massive exports to the United States. When those exports drop substantially, the Asian economies will fall dramatically. And so will their consumption of oil.

However, in the United States, where we have to buy oil with dollars that have declined substantially in value, the price will be very high.

It will be strange that just across the border in Canada, the price for oil and natural gas will be low because Canadians can buy it with Canadian dollars. But if we import it into the United States, the price will be very high because we have to pay for it with U.S. dollars. It will be one of those strange but true moments of the post-bubble era and will last as long as it takes for the world's economies to balance their foreign trade and the foreign exchange markets.

Gold Is a Great Bubblequake and Aftershock Investment Because It Takes Advantage of a Falling Dollar, a Falling Stock Market, and a Falling World Economy

Let's get something clear right up front: We are not gold bugs. Like most smart, reasonable people, we don't jump on bandwagons based on wishful thinking or a habit of seeing only doom and gloom. Traditionally, the warning to "Buy gold!" has been the long-time mantra of the chronically pessimistic. More recently, however, an entirely new, much more optimistic crowd is starting to buy gold, too. And for very good reasons.

As other asset values decline, people will want to put their money somewhere. They will want to buy something, preferably something of rising value that has a long tradition of acceptance and demand during difficult times. That is gold. As demand continues to rise for gold, and then rapidly rises when the other bubbles pop, the price of gold will shoot up. The rising gold bubble is your very best bet for profits during the Bubblequake and Aftershock.

Will the gold bubble eventually fall? Of course it will; it's a bubble. But why not go for the ride? Compared to other assets, such as stocks and bonds, the amount of gold now available is relatively tiny. You can count on more gold being mined in the future to satisfy growing demand, but demand will surely outpace supply, pushing up the price. Huge and growing demand, and relatively tiny supply—you do the math.

Like we already said, we are not gold bugs. In fact, gold just might be the silliest of all investments. Think about it. People spend tons of capital, time, and effort to haul a bunch of rock out of the ground at enormous expense and smelt out tiny bits of gold from the rock, melt them together, and then do absolutely nothing with it—just put it in a vault. How much sillier can you get?

But in the coming years, silly gold will be a truly smart, truly spectacular Aftershock investment. Huge amounts of money will be made—*and lost*—in gold. Gold is a rising bubble on its way to becoming one of the biggest asset bubbles of all time. Second only to the fall of the dollar bubble, the bursting of the gold bubble will be quite impressive, as well. (More about this in our next book.)

Gold is an excellent investment for these crazy times because it takes advantage of *both* the falling stock market and the falling dollar, as well as the overall falling world economy. Gold is an investment opportunity that is custom made for the crazy times ahead. Silly times call for silly investments? Well, sort of.

Here are some not-so-silly reasons why gold will be a super-smart investment in the Bubblequake and Aftershock:

• The gold market is very, very small compared to the stock and bond markets. Even a small shift of capital out of these markets and into gold will dramatically boost its price. And a large inflow of capital into gold will have a very huge, positive effect, indeed.

• Dollar-based investors receive a double benefit by buying gold. That means if you buy gold with dollars you are taking advantage not only of the price rise in gold, but also the fall of the dollar. As an example, if gold goes up four times, and the euro goes up two times against the dollar, your net increase is eight times.

• Gold has significant potential for being an illegal tax avoidance technique. Once the bubbles collide, tax rates in the United States and around the world will increase and incomes will decline.

The combination means that interest in tax avoidance, even if illegal, will skyrocket. Holding physical gold is a very effective way to avoid taxes in the United States and around the world. We, of course, do not advocate illegal tax avoidance, but there's no denying others will find this appealing, further boosting the demand for and the price of gold.

• The gold market is much more of a world market than U.S. stocks and bonds. Foreign investors can buy stocks and bonds, but in many countries buying gold is easier. Hence, gold has a much greater world demand. For example, India is the world's biggest consumer of gold, buying 20 percent of the world's gold output annually—about twice as much as the United States. On the other hand, India is not a large consumer of stocks and bonds. There's not a stockbroker on every corner of town, but there is a gold dealer. Therefore, the ease with which worldwide investors can buy gold will also heighten its appeal.

• Gold is viewed much more positively as an investment in the Middle East and Asia than it is in the United States. Hence, for those countries, which are the biggest consumers of gold, its acceptability as a good investment will push up the price of gold when their economies tank even worse than the U.S. economy.

• It is very difficult to rapidly increase gold production. Gold mining will not be able to keep pace with demand for many years. When demand for gold goes up, so will the price.

• Rightly or wrongly (in the past it has been wrongly) gold is seen as an inflation hedge, and so high inflation often drives gold purchases. Inflation will be very high in the United States and also in major European and Asian nations.

• All of the world's stock and bond markets will be under downward pressure. Some stock and bond investors, especially in the Middle East and Asia, will move out of stocks and bonds and toward higher gold holdings over the next few years, driving up the price.

• Just as we predicted in 2006, as the world's banking system comes under increasing stress, gold is having, and will continue to have, increasing appeal.

• Gold closed out 2008 with its eighth consecutive year of increases. And that is before all the economic problems the world will face ahead, which will be the main drivers of gold's upward rise in the future.

How to Buy Gold

The Easiest Way to Invest in Gold: Buy Gold ETFs. Gold ETFs (exchange traded funds) first came on the scene in the fall of 2005 and are now traded like stock on the New York Stock Exchange with the price tracking one-tenth the price of an ounce of gold. Each share is backed by real, physical gold, and you can even have the physical gold shipped to you if you like.

There are two gold ETFs and they are very similar. One has the symbol GLD and is a product of State Street Global Advisors. The other has the symbol IAU and is a product of iShares. Both can be bought like regular stocks.

ETF funds now hold more than 700 tons of gold. Like stock, gold ETFs can also be bought on margin.

If You Like the Feel (and Security) of Physical Gold: Buy Gold Bullion Bars and Coins. The most fun, but somewhat more difficult way to buy gold, is to buy actual bullion bars or coins such as the American Eagle or the South African Krugerrand. Coins are usually one ounce in weight, but often come in smaller half-ounce and tenth-ounce sizes. You can buy these from local coin shops, but they will be a bit more expensive per ounce than buying online. However, there are no shipping and insurance charges. Some states may charge sales tax or, like Maryland, may require that you buy at least $1,000 worth of gold in order to be tax exempt. You can find local coin shops in the yellow pages or online.

Buying bullion online or by phone may be the best way to buy bullion for many people. Simply type "gold bullion" into the search bar of your favorite Internet search engine and investigate options. Online outlets and retail stores require certified checks or cash to buy gold, or will ask you to wait until your check clears your bank before they ship or let you pick up your gold.

One problem with buying gold bullion is storage. You can keep it at home, but for extra security, you might want to store it in a safe deposit box. Even a small box can hold quite a lot of gold. Another problem is that retail stores often have a much higher sales commission than a gold ETF, often ranging from $15 to $30 an ounce.

An Alternative: Buy from a Gold Depository. In addition to storage problems, and hassles and costs of buying and selling physical gold, the bigger issue with buying physical gold is that you miss out on the advantages of buying gold on margin. For leveraging gold and for ease of ownership of physical gold, you should consider depositories. Buying gold from a depository means you always keep direct legal ownership of the gold, although not necessarily physical possession. If the depository were to go bankrupt, the gold would still be yours. As soon as you buy it, they sign legal ownership over to you and deposit it with a separate legal entity. Also, at any time, you can ask for your physical gold to be shipped to you.

Depositories allow you to buy gold on margin, with the maximum percentage of the margin determined by the federal government, like margin on a brokerage account. Usually, it's between three and five times the amount of the gold paid for, depending on the volatility of the price at that time. That means you can use $10,000 to buy $30,000 worth of gold. You can also buy gold ETFs on margin, but it may be easier and more flexible with a depository. However, depositories usually have a higher commission rate (and other costs) than you would normally find on an ETF.

Do not Buy Stock in Gold Mining Companies.   Some investors would rather buy stock than gold, so why not buy stock in companies that mine gold? Before the financial crisis and when the stock market was rising rapidly, gold mining stocks had generally performed better than gold itself. However, we do not recommend gold mining stocks because they will be pulled down when the overall stock market goes down. Gold will do far better than gold stocks in the long run, and as the stock market bubble fully falls, it will take gold mining stocks with it. However, once the gold bubble begins to take off, some gold mining companies could see large increases in the price of their stock. This will be more true of pure play gold mining companies rather than large mining companies that have heavy exposure to commodities metals that will be hit hard by the huge decrease in world demand during the Aftershock. Also, by the time the gold bubble is rising rapidly, the stock bubble will have been pretty well deflated so you will be buying gold mining company stock at low prices. An exception to this recommendation is if your investment vehicle allows investments in gold mining stocks, but not directly in gold. Still, great care is needed to avoid the downward influence of a collapsing stock market on gold mining stock. For more information on how to buy gold, go to www.aftershockeconomy.com/gold.

Are Governments Manipulating the Price of Gold?

This is the favorite question among gold bugs, who often believe that there is a great deal of government manipulation of gold. While much of their concern is likely paranoia there are two ways governments can influence the price of gold.

Central Bank Sales and Purchases: Central bank sales have actually been declining, which would increase the price of gold. China has even been purchasing gold, which also increases prices. The amount of gold sold by central banks (which lowers the price of gold) is not overwhelming on an annual basis, usually between 400 and 500 tons, and is limited by the Central Bank Gold Agreement, which was extended for another five years in June 2009. Also, sales are usually spread out so they do not normally negatively affect the price too much on a given day since that is not in the best interest of the selling central bank.

Currency Manipulation: As the euro rises, gold in dollar terms often goes up with it, although not always. So the efforts by central banks to push up the dollar and push down the euro would decrease the price of gold in dollar terms.

How much these two actions are used to manipulate the price of gold is unclear, although it is clear that the primary focus of currency manipulation is usually on the currency itself, not its secondary effect on the price of gold.

The Fed does buy and sell some gold in the gold market, but it is unclear how much impact this has on gold prices. Of course, in the Aftershock this could change. If the price of gold rises dramatically, governments may become more interested in manipulating its price to keep it from becoming a highly attractive alternative to government bonds, etc. However, long-term manipulation, if any, will fail when market conditions overwhelm any attempts to manipulate the price of gold, just as any attempts to manipulate the value of the dollar will also ultimately fail in the Aftershock.

Will Gold Be Confiscated or Become Illegal, as It Was During the Great Depression?

It's unlikely in the modern global economy that making gold illegal in the United States would do any more than hurt smaller, middle class investors who can't easily buy gold globally. Also, any talk of making gold illegal would dramatically increase its price (like heroin), thus being very counter-productive. Further complicating the situation is that a great deal of gold is already in circulation, making it difficult to outlaw. A large black market for middle class gold could easily develop.

Also, people often forget that, unlike our stock market, the vast majority of the demand for gold is outside the United States. So, the price is very much determined by the international market. Whether the United States makes gold illegal or not is only one factor affecting the price of gold. Since most of the demand for gold is outside the United States, it certainly won't be the largest factor.

There's no guarantee the U.S. government wouldn't make owning gold illegal, but given the problems just mentioned and the limited positive benefits for the government, we think it is unlikely. Also, to even get to the point where the government is concerned about it, the price would have to rise very dramatically from where it is today, making it a very attractive investment.

Leveraging Gold

One thing we've seen in recent years is that leveraging (borrowing money to fund part of the purchase of an investment) can light a fire under the growth of your assets. Hedge funds and private equity funds used leverage to create astounding returns for several years. But that fire can get out of control and burn you, as the hedge funds and private equity funds certainly found out. The same goes for leveraging gold. There is no quicker way to make money in gold, and no quicker way to lose it, than by leveraging it. The greater the price volatility, the greater the risk, because even if you are right in the long term, you can be squeezed out by margin calls in the short term due to sharp short-term declines in the price. The price may jump back to its high very quickly, but you may have lost much of your money in the dip when you couldn't make the margin calls on your highly leveraged gold investment and had to sell your position at a low price.

Because we believe there will be greater volatility in the beginning of the gold bubble, we suggest you keep your leverage more limited. However, as the gold bubble begins to take off with the dollar bubble pop, you should probably increase your leverage.

Up to date information on timing of leverage is available at www
.aftershockeconomy.com/gold.

If you decide to buy on margin, the amount of margin you can
get is controlled by the government, like any brokerage account.
But, depending on the volatility of gold, you can leverage three to
five times. That means at a 3X leverage you can get $30,000 worth
of gold for $10,000 cash. There are also significant interest costs
associated with leveraging.

Gold now and in the future will likely be highly volatile, so
be careful. We can't tell you how much leverage to use since
the amount of leverage you can take on is very much a factor
of your wealth and willingness to take risks. All we can say for
sure is that for most people leverage is like alcohol: Use it in
moderation.

Not only do we write books on the evolving macroeconomic environment, our company, The Foresight Group, provides customized analysis
of how the coming economic changes will directly impact your particular investments or business. Our number is 1–800–994–0018. For those
who don't like advertising in books, we understand, but this book isn't
just an academic exercise. It can greatly help individuals and businesses survive and prosper in the coming years. We also offer a newsletter
that you can sign up for at www.aftershockeconomy.com/newsletter.
Also, feel free to just call us and share your thoughts, good or bad, on
the book. We may not always be able to take your call, but you can
always visit our web site at www.aftershockeconomy.com and give us
your feedback there.

The Gold Bubble: The Biggest, Baddest Bubble of Them All

Although gold will perform spectacularly in Phase II (the
Aftershock), it is important to recognize that, like the stock market
and the dollar, gold too will follow a classic up-down bubble trajectory. The coming gold bubble could easily last 10 or more years,
and at its height, gold prices could become truly stratospheric—so
high, in fact, we won't even mention our best guess for fear of losing

credibility. (Of course, as soon as the Aftershock hits, we will certainly tell you all about it.)

The reasons that the gold bubble will go up are actually the same reasons the gold bubble will go down, only in reverse. Gold will go up when the other bubbles (stock, dollar, real estate) go down because investors will want to buy something seemingly stable and profitable while their other assets look increasingly unstable and unprofitable.

In time, however, the instability of other assets will evolve to stability again, and their huge downside risks will transform back to normal upside gains.

However, people will be reluctant to give up on gold at that point, just as they are reluctant to give up on stock and real estate today. Gold will have been a proven winner at that point and stocks and real estate will have been proven losers. People will say the reason for gold's rise is a fundamental shift away from intangible assets, such as stock and bonds, whose value can easily evaporate depending on investor interest and government irresponsibility; and toward more tangible assets, like gold. But it's pure nonsense. Stocks, bonds, and real estate have much more intrinsic value than gold, and over time, that reality will dawn on investors, who will start selling off their gold to buy stocks and bonds again, and the gold bubble will pop—big time. Bubbles always do.

How far gold will fall depends on a couple of factors. It won't collapse completely because there is some commercial value for jewelry and industrial uses. However, for some period after the gold bubble pops, there will be a huge oversupply of gold, relative to industrial and jewelry demand. That will certainly push the price into the ground. With a huge oversupply and no investment demand, the price of gold will fall well below the cost of production, probably in the range of $50 per ounce when adjusted for inflation.

After the gold bubble has popped many years from now, private investors and central banks will eventually no longer hold gold and we will have finally completed our long evolution away from metal-based money, to the next stage of money, as we explain in Chapter 8. In the meantime, we highly suggest you join us on the wonderful ride on the gold bubble. You won't believe how high we're going to go.

How Will Other Investment Vehicles, Such as Life Insurance and Collectibles Perform?

Life Insurance

Term life insurance is fine; whole life insurance is not. Whole life or even hybrid life insurance (combination of term and whole) will do poorly simply because much of the money is often invested in real estate, stocks, or other investments that will do poorly during the Aftershock.

Term life insurance is fine since it is not really an investment. However, keep in mind that with very high inflation, the value of the pay-off amount will be greatly reduced. On the other hand, the real cost of the annual premium payments will also be reduced by inflation. Also keep in mind that once the bubbles burst, quite a few life insurance companies may go under and not be able to pay their claims. So once the value of the dollar begins to fall, keep a close eye on the health of your insurance company and increase your term life insurance to keep pace with inflation.

Art and Other Collectibles

All collectibles crash in value. In fact, if possible, postpone any collectibles purchases until after the Aftershock, when everything is at bargain basement prices. Not only will they be far cheaper due to the poor economy, but your selection becomes huge because so many people need to sell their collectibles to raise money.

If you only have an investment interest in your collectibles, you would do best to begin selling off your collectibles now before their market value drops dramatically. You would be far better off buying gold as your new "collectible."

Are Diamonds Still a Girl's Best Friend?

Investment-grade diamonds will likely do OK during the Aftershock, but non-investment diamonds will definitely fall in value due to declining demand for jewelry during the Aftershock, which is very much a discretionary purchase. Even during the current Bubblequake there has been a huge drop in demand and some decline in prices for diamonds. Much of the increase in the value of investment-grade diamonds long term will come from the rise in the euro. Diamonds can be easily sold for euros and, hence, their price will go up in dollar terms as the euro rises.

A Final Note on Investing: Dumb Luck Is Still Important

Of course, as in past moneymaking periods, much of the money in the future will be made through dumb luck. The money will be made by people who didn't really see what was coming but, for a variety of reasons, happened to take one or more of the right actions that lead to a profit.

Gold is an obvious example. Many people will hold gold because they were naturally inclined toward gold for cultural reasons, or to avoid taxes, or because they thought maybe the end of the world was near. These people will make a lot of money in the future. But gold is also a bubble. Hence, many of the people who will make money in gold through dumb good luck will also lose it through dumb bad luck because they won't know when to (or even that they should) get out before the gold bubble pops.

Other people will be lucky if they happen to live outside the United States and they have the capital to invest in the United States after the dollar bubble falls and U.S. investments become very cheap for foreign investors. It won't be that they planned it; it's just that they live outside the united States. The dumb luck of living outside the United States when the dollar pops will have to be combined with good judgment in investing in the United States, but there is still a large component of being in the right place at the right time due to plain dumb luck.

For current information on the best Aftershock investments, please go to www.aftershockeconomy.com/chapter6.

7

Aftershock Jobs and Businesses

THE GOOD, THE BAD, AND THE UGLY

One of the most surprising aspects of writing this book was looking back at this chapter in our 2006 book and seeing how very little of it needed to be changed. Our recommendations passed the test of time, and the economy evolved just as our analysis indicated it would. Basically, we nailed it. Now, three years later, we are going to tell you essentially the same things that we tried to warn you about before. This time, you may find it more relevant to your daily life. Given our unmatched track record for correctly predicting the Bubblequake, you should feel very comfortable about our advice in this chapter on how to find or hang onto relatively safe Aftershock jobs and businesses. Almost all our previous recommendations remain the same, except that we are now able to refine the timing.

As a reminder, this chapter is no different from the rest of the book in that we give you our best analysis, even if it is not what you want to hear. We don't sugarcoat the truth. Hence, this is not a typical job counseling book that lists the winner jobs and loser jobs because in reality, it's going to be pretty rough all the way around. There will be jobs and businesses that do better than others, but there won't be many winners (although there are a few). That makes reading this chapter all the more important because even small mistakes can become big problems later. The earlier you see what's coming, the better prepared you can be. This is no minor economic adjustment that we are about to face, so it is critical that you seriously consider the advice in this chapter.

148

This Ain't Your Daddy's Economic Slowdown

This is not the recession of the late 1970s and early 1980s. What we tend to think of when we hear the term "economic slowdown" is not what we are about to get. This one is going to be bigger, badder, deeper, and much longer than anything we've seen before. To understand how this will impact jobs, it helps to think of the U.S. economy in three parts:

1. **The Capital Goods Sector**—cars, construction, major industrial equipment, and so forth
2. **The Discretionary Spending Sector**—fine dining, entertainment, travel, high fashion, jewelry, art, and so forth
3. **The Necessities Sector**—basic food, shelter, clothing, energy, health care, and so forth

Typically in an economic downturn, we can expect to see the Capital Goods Sector slow significantly, the Discretionary Spending Sector decline somewhat, and the Necessities Sector to mostly be spared, under normal conditions. By this point, you've probably guessed that conditions during and after the bubbles collapse will be anything but normal. If you hope your job or business survives the current Bubblequake and coming Aftershock, or you'd like to gear up for a change, the following insights may shed some light on what to expect in each of the three economic sectors.

Keep in mind that all three sectors will suffer significant job and business losses, with the Capital Goods and Discretionary Spending sectors doing the worst and the Necessities Sector faring better but not great. Conversely, all three sectors will have some safe jobs and profitable businesses, but competition for these will be fierce.

The Capital Goods Sector (Autos, Construction, Major Industrial Equipment, and so on)

Super-high interest rates, coupled with a big economic slowdown, will be very bad news for the Capital Goods Sector. As we discussed earlier, our huge accumulation of government debt, plus our other foreign and domestic debt, will drive up interest rates to unprecedented levels when the bubbles pop. High interest rates will make borrowing money very expensive for individuals and, more importantly, for businesses. High interest rates will be nothing short of an unmiti-gated disaster for the Capital Goods Sector, which depends on cus-tomers having access to low-cost capital. And high interest rates will make recovery after the Bubblequake far longer and more difficult than in previous recessions.

Most Businesses Will Fare Poorly in the Capital Goods Sector

We won't dress it up for you. The bottom line for business owners in the Capital Goods Sector is not pretty. If you can sell now and get out, you should. No one can predict exactly when the Aftershock will hit, but even if it takes another three years, the marketplace for your business is unlikely to improve much. In fact, the value of Capital Goods Sector companies will decrease substantially as unem-ployment continues to rise and the economy falls. So if you have a business in the automotive, construction, industrial equipment, or any other Capital Goods industry, the longer you wait to get out, the more vulnerable you will be to very significant losses.

What will you do after you sell? Options include using your pro-ceeds to invest in the huge wealth-building opportunities discussed in Chapter 6 or just holding it safe and in cash for retirement. But, be care-ful. As we discussed in Chapter 3, you will have to be increasingly careful about where you hold your cash. Keep an eye on our web site regarding where to put your cash at www.aftershockeconomy.com/cash.

Very Limited Job Prospects in the Capital Goods Sector

As hard as it may be to sell one's business, it can be even harder to quit your job and train for another career. Unlike selling a business, which at least provides the possibility of getting some cash, quitting a job usually means walking away, cold turkey, from a paycheck. And in the Capital Goods Sector of the economy that paycheck may be quite a bit better than jobs elsewhere in the economy. So we are fully aware that you may have no interest in leaving a lucrative job in order to take what may be a lower-paying position.

Still, you might as well know the cold, hard facts: Jobs in Capital Goods industries will be the worst hit by the coming Bubblequake and there isn't much you can do to protect yourself other than to gear up to move on, the sooner the better. Your best bet may be to rethink your career with an eye toward joining an industry that will do far better when the bubbles burst.

Bubble Babies

We all know what Beanie Babies are, but Bubble Babies? A Bubble Baby is a celebrity CEO or businessman who has done extremely well during the Bubble Economy but won't be able to do nearly as well in the Aftershock. Their CEO skills and ability to be paid hundreds of millions of dollars have been much more related to riding rising bubbles than leading companies. They have more political skills than business skills. They know how to create the buzz and be recognized as great leaders or great businessmen.

We know who these people are, the question for the future is which of these celebrity Bubble Babies will be able to perform as well during the Aftershock as they did in the rising bubble economy. Who among them will have the real skills required to start or lead a business during the difficult times ahead? Are they Bubble Babies or are they real businessmen and businesswomen? We'll soon find out.

If a major career makeover is not your style, you may want to consider making a move to a more stable area within your current industry. For example, if you work in the construction industry—which will take a truly terrible hit—you may find that moving into repair-oriented work, rather than new construction, will keep you busy while others sit at home. Of course, many construction workers will also get this idea after the bubbles pop, so the sooner you begin your transition, the better.

The Discretionary Spending Sector (Travel, Restaurants, Entertainment, and so on)

As the economy continues to fall, Americans are not going to run out to the mall every night after work (if they have work) and squander their limited cash and very limited credit on one more high-priced designer handbag or the latest CD. Discretionary spending is, well, discretionary. And many items and activities we currently enjoy will simply be off our shopping lists after the bubbles pop. This will certainly slow many businesses to a crawl and force others completely out of the game, further driving up unemployment.

But discretionary spending will still hold up better than the Capital Goods Sector of the economy because some people will still have money and they will keep spending their money, only at a lower level than before. So, instead of discretionary spending disappearing altogether, the people who can still spend will simply buy lower-priced discretionary items. Instead of shopping for designer handbags at Saks Fifth Avenue, for example, they may downgrade to Target or Wal-mart.

The restaurant business will face this trend as well. Once the bubbles pop, far fewer people and businesses will have money for eating out. That will certainly affect all restaurants. But there will still be some people and businesses that do have money and will be quite happy to go to restaurants, as long as they don't have to spend as much as they used to. So the restaurant industry will continue to be a huge industry in the United States, but business will shift dramatically toward the lower end. Lower-cost Mexican and Chinese restaurants, for example, will continue to do okay.

To a large extent, the same thing will happen throughout the Discretionary Spending Sector. Instead of brand names, we'll buy bargains. We will still want to buy some stuff we don't absolutely need, we'll just buy a lot less of it and at lower prices.

As we said earlier in the book, the Discretionary Spending bubble is popping, and this bubble makes up a large portion of the overall U.S. economy, so when it falls, a whole lot falls with it. That means, once incomes and credit cards are in short supply, a much greater percentage of the U.S. economy is going to feel the pain than ever before. This is an entirely new situation for us. Back in the 1920s, when the nation was much less wealthy heading into the Great Depression, discretionary spending represented a much smaller portion of our overall economy. So when the stock market bubble crashed in 1929 and the economy took a major downturn, the large dip in discretionary spending had much less impact because it just didn't make up that large a part of the economy. Other industries took a big hit, but people still had to eat basic food and buy basic clothing, so most of these industries just kept on going.

It's a very different situation today. So much of what we currently buy (and that keeps our economy going), we can easily do without. We may not like forgoing a trip to Whole Foods or Wegman's, where we can select from a huge range of expensive goodies, but if we have to we certainly can and will survive on cheaper foods from low-priced stores. We may not like to skip the latest, high-priced fashions, but if we have to, we can easily shop at lower-level and discount stores. We can also survive quite nicely without $100,000 kitchen and bathroom makeovers, complete with granite countertops and stainless steel appliances. As incomes and assets evaporate, Americans are learning to manage without these pricey pleasures.

If spending on lavish food, clothing, and housing can easily be cut, and if this kind of spending represents a big chunk of America's current economy, then the impact of these changes will be very, very negative indeed. While the Discretionary Spending Sector will be hit less hard than the Capital Goods Sector, the fact that Discretionary Spending has become such a big part of the current U.S. economy means a downturn in this sector will greatly accelerate the coming Aftershock and make our post-bubble recovery quite difficult.

Businesses and Jobs in the Discretionary Spending Sector

We've already mentioned how a slowdown in the Discretionary Spending Sector will harm many businesses in the restaurant, retail, and home improvement industries. The travel industry will take an even greater hit. Leisure travel will be especially hard hit. Travel to major entertainment destinations, such as Orlando and Las Vegas, will be seriously stalled while more Americans go someplace closer and cheaper—like into their living rooms to watch TV. Leisure travel overseas will face the double whammy of minimal discretionary spending and a dollar that has fallen dramatically.

Business travel will suffer, as well. Domestic business travel will decrease due to the sharp slowdown in the economy and the cost-cutting mindset that most companies will be forced to adopt. Overseas travel will be hit by high costs and the low value of the dollar, so only the most important overseas business travel will continue. Also, with our imports way down and our exports low due to the major recession around the world, there simply won't be much need for business travel overseas.

Businesses that will survive during these leaner days will include low-end restaurants, low-end clothing stores, discount shops of every description, used clothing and household furnishing stores, and businesses that cater to local, inexpensive travel.

If you own a business in the Discretionary Spending Sector, you might want to give some very serious thought to selling your

Fierce Competition for Jobs Will Reduce Pay

Normally, when an economic downturn is relatively short or relatively mild, rising unemployment doesn't go too high or last too long. In this case, job losses will be staggering after the dollar and government debt bubbles pop, and there will be a mad scramble for those jobs that haven't been destroyed. This means, for most people it will be increasingly difficult to find a job, any job, regardless of your qualifications and experience. And for those lucky enough to be employed, keeping a job will mean putting up with less desirable working conditions, benefits, hours, and pay. In fact, as competition for jobs greatly increases, most wages will surely fall. It's not about your professional worth, but simply an issue of supply and demand. Lots of willing workers (big supply) and not too many jobs (lower demand) equals a lower price paid for your services. After all the bubbles pop, people will accept wage cuts in most jobs for one simple reason: If they don't, somebody else will.

business now or in the next couple of years. Depending on what you sell and to whom you sell it, you may be able to survive. But only the most clever, well-placed, or just plain lucky businesses in this sector will thrive in the coming Aftershock.

If you are currently employed in the Discretionary Spending Sector and are in a position to retrain for another career, this would be a good time to look elsewhere, such as the Necessities Sector.

Some Good News: The Necessities Sector (Health Care, Education, Food, Basic Clothing, Transportation, Government Services, and Utilities)

In the job market, the Necessities Sector is the place to be. Many of the jobs in this sector historically don't pay very well, and they will pay even less after the bubbles pop. But, at least you will have a job and it will be much more stable and reliable than most other jobs in the post-bubble economy. Even at lower pay, Necessities Sector jobs will be a godsend for families with a spouse who used to make more money than his or her mate, but now is unemployed. The lower-paid, still-employed spouse, working as a nurse, teacher, medical administrator, or other Necessities Sector employee, will likely retain his or her job and be able to carry the family through the worst of the downturn.

The Necessities Sector is composed primarily of health care, education, and government services, usually run by government or other non-profit entities. The private companies that supply these government and non-profit entities have the potential to survive as well. Of course, as things get increasingly negative for the rest of the economy, the Necessities Sector will also take a hit, just not as badly as the other two sectors.

Health Care Jobs and Businesses

Health care is currently a very strong element of the U.S. economy and it will continue to be the best bet in the Necessities Sector after the bubbles pop, but not without a lot of pain. Many people will lose their private medical insurance as they lose their jobs, which will dramatically reduce health care revenues. The government will step in and fill the gap with Medicaid and Medicare, but benefits will be tight.

The loss of so many privately insured people will cause some big problems for the health care industry, particularly in health care capital goods, such as radiology machines and hospital construction. However, businesses providing services and supplies to the health care industry will continue to do okay, but will still be hit hard by the large overall decline in health care revenues.

Health care jobs that will do the best include:

- Nurses
- Primary care doctors
- Psychiatrists
- Nurse Practitioners
- Physicians' Assistants
- Medical technicians, support personnel, administrative staff and others involved in primary care medicine (not specialties)

Specialists and their supporting staff and services will not do well, with surgeons taking the biggest hit due to falling demand. Elective procedures, such as cosmetic surgery, have already taken a hit since late 2008. Once the coming Aftershock hits, every type of specialist and their support staff will see very big declines.

Health Care Could Become 25 Percent of the GDP When the Bubbles Pop

Health care will be one of the safest havens for business owners and workers in the Bubblequake and Aftershock. Currently, the huge health care industry accounts for about 16 percent of the nation's GDP. As other industries decline, especially in the Discretionary Spending and Capital Goods Sectors, the more stable health care industry will naturally assume a larger percentage of our economy. We've seen this before on a smaller scale. For example, during the oil bust in the 1980s, the percentage of the Houston economy represented by non-oil industries grew dramatically.

Add to this an aging population with increasing demands for health care, and it is quite possible that health care could take over a staggering 25 percent of our economy after the bubbles pop.

That means that not only will the safest jobs and businesses be in health care during the Bubblequake, but also that the nation's hopes for regaining significant productivity growth in the post-bubble economy will lie with dramatic productivity advancements in the health care field.

Government Jobs and Businesses

After health care, the next-best positions in the Necessities Sector will be government services jobs, such as police and firefighters. In the Aftershock, as in past recessions, government services will still be needed. However, unlike past recessions, government services will have to take massive cuts when the government can no longer borrow money after the government debt bubble pops.

In particular, government spending on the defense industry will take a very deep cut. It won't be because people all of a sudden don't care about defense, but when push comes to shove and Americans have to choose between military spending and kicking Mom off Medicare, they will reluctantly cut the Defense Department before pulling the plug on Medicare and Medicaid. However, funding per capita on Medicare and Medicaid expenditures will also decline dramatically, as we discussed in Chapter 10. But we suspect that, along with massive medical benefits cuts, they will drastically cut defense spending. This will particularly hurt government contractors, especially those dependent on the Defense Department for funding.

No one will like any of this, but the days when our government could simply borrow all the money needed to buy everything it wanted will be long gone. Deficit spending, at that point, is no longer an option. And let's not forget that the government won't be able to borrow money from Social Security taxes anymore because the surplus will be entirely gone. Currently, Social Security taxes are funding more than a third of our deficit. Take that away and we are going to have huge government cuts in all areas, with defense spending up there with everyone else.

In addition to job losses related to defense, businesses and individuals who supply capital goods or construction services to the government will also be hit. Road construction and maintenance, and transportation in general, will do poorly. As new construction of both roads and buildings plummets, businesses that can make the switch to repair work and related services will fare better.

Education Jobs and Businesses

Along with health care, the demand for public education will continue, so businesses that supply education or health care products or services to the government will benefit from strengthening their marketing and business ties to these areas and increasing their percentage of sales in these sectors.

Jobs in education will be more secure than in, say, the restaurant business (Discretionary Spending Sector), but do not make the mistake of thinking that all education jobs are a lock. As many as half of all jobs in education will be lost, as tax revenues drastically drop at both the state and local levels. Jobs at primary and secondary schools will hold up better than those in higher education. Elementary, middle, and high school math and science teachers will still be in demand, while music and art teachers will get laid off in droves, along with extra curricular personnel. Seniority and union membership won't matter once all the bubbles pop. Instead, if you want to get or keep a job in education, you'll need to be very good at your job, be willing to teach more classes to more students, and be very loyal to your school's administration.

The picture for higher education will be even tougher. Strong departments in practical fields, like engineering and computer science, especially at top colleges and universities, will retain their professors far better than those in "soft" departments (sociology, English, etc.) at liberal arts schools. Don't count on tenure to save you if your department has to take big budget cuts—it won't. And if you are lucky enough to be retained in a strong department, be prepared to teach four classes a day, five days a week, for less pay. Not only will your teaching load go up, your research funding will go down, especially from internal sources.

Big Opportunities after the Bubbles Pop: Cashing in on Distressed Assets

In nearly every industry in all three sectors of the economy, there will be many opportunities to benefit from falling asset values. Just as high-priced office furniture from bankrupt dot-com companies ended up at auction sales for pennies on the dollar after the relatively small Internet bubble popped, there will be countless auctions of every description all over the planet after the biggest bubble crash the world has ever seen. Opportunities to make large profits by buying and servicing distressed businesses and other assets will actually become one of the good sectors in our post-bubble economy.

As always, timing will be key. One of the biggest mistakes many people will make is buying distressed businesses too soon. In this very unusual economic downturn, involving the fall of multiple bubbles, we will face very high interest and inflation rates that will take a lot longer to come down than anyone might imagine. It will be easy to mistakenly think the worst has passed and the time is right to start buying up distressed businesses and assets, when actually the price of these bargain properties will likely fall even lower. For maximum profits, think years, not months. *Many people in the stock and real estate markets are making this mistake right now. They think that because an asset has lost 25 to 50 percent of its peak value, it is a bargain. It emphatically is not!*

Once the Aftershock hits, the servicing of distressed assets and businesses will be an instant and long-term winner. Bankruptcy attorneys and liquidation/auction houses will obviously do quite well. And so will a whole range of other people and companies who will buy, restructure, manage, and resell distressed businesses and other assets, making huge incomes and profits along the way, including:

- Accountants and financial analysts involved with forensic accounting and distressed properties accounting.
- Consultants, bankers, managers, and others involved in the acquisition, restructuring, and management of distressed businesses and other assets.

For more current information on jobs and businesses, please go to www.aftershockecomony.com/chapter7.

PART

III

A NEW VIEW
OF THE ECONOMY

Forget Economic Cycles, This Economy Is *Evolving*

Do you know that old expression "You can't see the forest for the trees?"

While most economists and financial analysts cling to the idea of market cycles to explain the recent upheaval, our longer view of economic change shows us that the overall world economy is actually *evolving*. This bigger view is key to the success of our analysis. Without it, we could not see the fundamental trends driving the economy. All the best financial and economic analysis in the world is not going to help a bit if you get the bigger picture wrong. Countless investors, businesses, families, and leaders are doing that right now and the cost of this mistake will be devastating.

Once you understand that the economy is evolving and what forces drive that evolution, you not only better understand shorter-term movements in the economy over 2 to 5 years, but also longer-term trends across 5 to 15 years and beyond. An accurate short-term and long-term view of the economy has a great deal of value. The short-term view helps enormously in understanding how to protect yourself and profit during times of economic upheaval. The long-term view is critical for planning long-term investments and business, as well as understanding how to move the overall economy out of upheaval and back to solid, sustainable growth.

Even though people often talk about business cycles, we all sort of intuitively know that the economy is really evolving. We know, for example, that the business cycle of the 1920s never really repeated itself. Neither have the business cycles of the 1930s or the 1960s. Every era has had its own unique aspects that made it very different from the others, like different stages in a person's life. A five-year-old is not a fifteen-year-old.

What ties all these different eras together is the continuing evolution of our economy. Not just in the United States, but in the world's economy. Certainly, we would all agree that the evolving world economy is very different today than it was in, say, 1900. And it will be very different in 2100 than it is today. We can also probably agree that these changes are not entirely random. For example, we don't go from an economy based on barter to an economy based on electronic transactions overnight; nor do we go from the exploding trade of the Industrial Revolution back to the Stone Age. Economic change does not hop randomly about; the overall world economy is evolving.

Understanding what drives that evolution is key to understanding our current economy and its latest problems. It also helps point the way toward how to solve these problems and what will drive the economy forward into the future.

Although this evolution is relatively simple in concept, it is made more complex because it does not happen in a vacuum, but involves many other aspects of evolving human society. It has been said that when you look at one part of the Universe you find it is tied to every other part of the Universe. This is also true when looking at the evolution of the economy; it is tied to the evolution of the rest of society, including the evolution of science, technology, and politics (which we will tell you more about in future books). And all that is actually tied to the evolution of the rest of the Universe. For now, let's focus on the evolution of economics.

Please sit back and relax when reading this chapter because it is a very broad discussion that is wholly different from the rest of the book, which focuses so tightly on the current economy and what will drive it in the near-term future. Right now, we'd like to tell you about how we see all of that fitting into an even bigger big picture. Although we have to spend most of our lives focusing on everyday issues, like our checkbooks, it is liberating, enlightening, and even fun to occasionally experience an even deeper understanding of the broader forces that shape our checkbooks and our lives.

What follows is a brief introduction to co-author Dr. David Wiedemer's Theory of Economic Evolution. All the ideas in this book about what is ahead, and all our customized analysis for individuals and organizations, are based on this analysis. It may seem entirely theoretical, but in fact we use it in very practical ways for analyzing specific conditions that will impact a particular industry, investment, or business.

The View from 30,000 Feet: We Are Not Changing Randomly—We Are Evolving

If we could pull way back from this particular slice of time and view the bigger picture, the way an airplane flying high above the earth gives us a broader view of where we are and where we're going, we would see a fascinating landscape that few people on the ground may think about. At 30,000 feet, our current economic problems can be seen, not merely as a collection of random events, isolated from the rest of time, but as a logical progression in a much broader trend: *the evolution of our monetary system,* as shown in Figure 8.1. We didn't just land in today's world by accident. Given our overall flight path, this was just the next logical—and to some extent, even predictable—place to end up.

By "predictable," we mean in the same sense that an overall weather trend is predictable. While specific weather conditions at any one house will vary, based on many local, hard-to-predict factors, the overarching weather trend toward winter or toward summer goes beyond the random fluctuations at any one location. So too, with our economy. The exact course of local financial events is always subject to many unpredictable forces, but the *overall economic trend* (like the trend toward summer or winter) is not random. It's part of a much larger evolution—the evolution of money itself.

The overall evolution of money is the fundamental reason why the "economic cycles" argument only works for relatively narrow

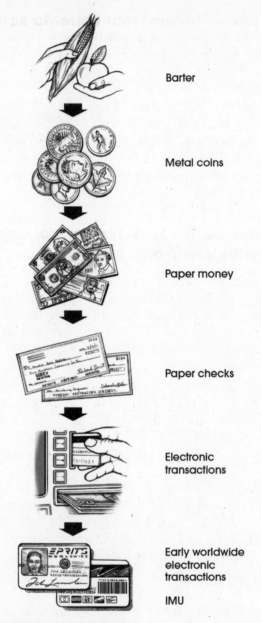

Barter

Metal coins

Paper money

Paper checks

Electronic
transactions

Early worldwide
electronic
transactions

IMU

Figure 8.1   The Evolution of Money

periods of time. Over the course of 100 years or more, and even periods as short as a few decades, economic cycles simply cannot fully explain how the economy changes. That's because we are *not* running in circles. We are evolving.

The Evolution of Money: From Barter to Barcodes

Many thousands of years ago, when the most basic trade between human beings first began, our monetary system was straightforward and simple: *You give me a chicken and I'll give you a basket of roots.* Barter was certainly direct, but not necessarily without complication: *If the chicken is big enough, you can keep the basket. But if the chicken is too skinny, I want the basket back, and you owe me one toad, which I'll pick up next week.* Sort of like a prehistoric version of *Let's Make a Deal.*

Strictly speaking, barter is really not a monetary system at all, but a way for people to directly trade back and forth, one on one. Over time, as people traded more goods and services, back and forth, sometimes between large tribes, the barter system was made a bit easier with the use of standardized units. Each item or service was assigned a value of so many cows, or shells, or bushels of wheat, facilitating multiple trades like a big Stone Age eBay.

It's interesting to note that had we not evolved into bigger, more organized tribes, the barter system would not have been *forced* to evolve to accommodate the higher, more complex level of trade. Being forced to evolve is a key point that we will return to again and again, because just as in biological evolution, economic evolution happens in reaction to changes in the broader environment, otherwise the evolution would not happen. In biological evolution of a species, the broader environment is the species' changing physical world. In economic evolution, the broader environment is the changing human world.

As we will see shortly, the evolution of money has been driven forward by the even broader evolution of society, itself—in a process we call STEP Evolution. More on that later. Right now, the point is that we developed a more organized form of barter, involving shells and other objects, in order to trade more effectively and efficiently with each other. In other words, barter evolved: At first, we didn't need shells to make barter work well; later, we did.

Evolving from Barter to Money Based on Precious Metals

As time went by (many thousands of years), trade became even more complex. Why? Because we had more stuff to trade and more contact with people who wanted to trade, especially beginning about 4000 B.C., when we figured out how to smelt metals into tools and other objects, which made it possible to more efficiently build all sorts of things, like larger and more durable houses, weapons, and ships. As societies became more organized and complex, and as people wanted to trade more and more things, we naturally used the new technology of smelting metal to create something that would replace simple shells and other fragile barter trinkets with something more durable, easier to carry, and of more uniform value: metal coins, the world's first pocket change.

Coins fashioned out of gold, silver, copper, nickel, brass, and other metals have been used for many millennia. Over time, shiny silver and gold became the standout favorites, perhaps because we liked how they looked, and more importantly because they were quite rare (smaller supply, higher value), they had high value to weight, and they resisted rust and wear. Compared to using sacks of salt or wheat for exchange, metal coins became the money of choice.

For larger transactions, the all-time favorite has been gold. The value of a gold, silver, nickel, or any other metal coin was simply set by the market price of that particular metal. A gold coin, therefore, was literally worth its weight in gold.

Gold (and to a lesser extent, silver) remained the metal money of choice as societies continued to evolve. After the movable type printing press in 1450 and the steam engine in 1775 ignited an explosion of trade around the world, more and more gold was needed to keep up with trade. After a while, great big bags of gold weighed too much to lug around all day, and large quantities of metal money were becoming too expensive to protect, transport, verify, and use. More importantly, there just wasn't enough gold available to keep up with so many potential transactions. By the 1800s in the United States, trade was simply growing too fast to dig up enough gold to keep pace with our rapidly expanding economy.

So, money was forced to evolve again.

Evolving from Metal Money to Paper Money

The solution was ingenious: create an IOU for gold or silver, and print it on lightweight pieces of paper. The limited supply of metal money was constrained by the rate at which gold and silver could be dug up out of the ground. On the other hand, paper money could easily be printed without the natural limitations of a gold or silver mine. Paper money was portable, foldable, and easy to conceal.

Plus, unlike mining silver and gold, paper money was far less expensive to produce and protect.

But the biggest advantage of paper over metal money was even better than all that, because the ability to make and manage paper money gave the U.S. economy something it could really run with: room to rapidly grow. Paper money made it possible for the nation's money supply to more easily keep pace with expanding trade.

But not without some problems.

A Run on the Bank. Today you'd get arrested for it, but back in the late 1800s, whenever private banks wanted more cash, they simply went to a back room and printed more dollars. To convince people this paper money was actually worth anything, banks guaranteed the value of their dollars by saying the paper money was "backed" by gold—meaning that for every paper dollar in circulation, there were actual piles of gold stashed away in bank vaults.

But bankers maintained only limited gold reserves, preferring to loan out a multiple of the reserves they held and risking a run on the bank if everyone attempted to redeem the paper money they had issued. Economists called this a "fractional reserve" system.

The idea that paper dollars were not 100 percent backed by gold naturally left some folks feeling a bit skittish about the true value of their paper cash, and so, not surprisingly, they weren't especially fond of using it. As late as 1890, 9 out of 10 commercial transactions in the United States were still done with gold. And when Americans did use paper dollars, insecurity ran high. Every so often, panic would send mobs of people running to their banks to try to get their money in gold, creating what economists called a run on the bank.

Backed by the Full Faith and Credit of the U. S. Government. Insecurity about the nation's currency was greatly reduced by the creation of the U.S. Federal Reserve in 1914. To prevent a run on a bank, the Fed could provide banks with additional dollars, as needed.

The creation of the Fed and a national currency backed by the reputation and power of the federal government not only put the public at ease, it helped dramatically increase domestic trade because there was enough money available for more and more financial transactions. The Fed's ability to increase and manage the nation's money supply, as needed, contributed significantly to the rapid growth of the U.S. economy in the roaring 1920s.

Taking the Metal Out of Money for Domestic Transactions Created Big Long-Term Gains, but Not Without Some Short-Term Pain

Evolving from metal money (gold) to paper money (dollars) and managing that paper money at a federal level, turned out to be a very powerful tool for building national wealth.

Unfortunately, the newly established Federal Reserve failed to understand just how powerful a tool it had. After the 1929 stock market crash, the relatively inexperienced Fed did not know how to properly manage the nation's money supply well enough to cope with the Great Depression.

With the economy temporarily struggling and the nation needing more dollars than we had in available gold, President Franklin Roosevelt decided in the 1930s to free the United States from the requirement to back paper money with piles of physical gold and the dollar's domestic evolution off the gold standard was complete. Instead of metal-based money, the country would benefit from the freedom of using dollars backed by the full faith and credit of the United States government. Instead of gold, our word would be considered as good as gold. In the long run, after the short-term pain of the Depression, taking the metal out of money for domestic transactions allowed the U.S. economy to grow enormously in the twentieth century.

Taking the Metal Out of Money for International Transactions

Although we were no longer restrained by gold for domestic transactions, it took us another 40 years to drop gold from our international transactions, as well. Prior to 1973, the value of the dollar overseas was determined by a fixed exchange rate and backed by gold. But after a while, we just didn't have enough gold available to back every dollar we wanted to trade. So in 1973, the only way the United States could continue to buy goods from foreign countries was to move off the gold standard for international transactions. Taking the metal out of money for international transactions meant the U.S. government no longer set the dollar at a fixed price, convertible into gold. Instead of the price of gold, the forces of *supply and demand* were allowed to determine the value of our dollar, with moderating control by central banks. No longer constrained by our limited gold reserves, our international trade was free to expand tremendously.

Essentially, we did for foreign trade in 1973 the same thing that we did for domestic trade earlier in the century. And, similarly, this move off the gold standard for foreign transactions was one of the reasons for the tremendous boom in foreign trade over the last 30 years.

Taking the Metal Out of Money for International Transactions Created Long-Term Gains, but Not Without Some Short-Term Pain. Just as going off gold for domestic transactions created long-term gain but also some short-term pain, going off gold for international transactions has produced long-term gains—but not without the short-term pain of massive trade deficits and related temporary bubbles. In other words, our current problems (rising and falling bubbles) are part of a painful, relatively short-term transition in the evolution of money! (We said this in our first book in 2006 and we challenge you to find any other analysis about our current economic problems that comes close to this kind of big-picture understanding.)

Going off the gold standard is not a bad thing, in and of itself. In fact, it is very good. But in these early stages, going off of gold for foreign trade is like giving a college kid a credit card with a multi-trillion dollar credit limit. It can easily be misused. In the past, if you ran a trade deficit, you would eventually run out of gold and could trade no more. Today, freed from the constraint of running out of gold, we can run very huge trade deficits—at least, for a while.

With so much freedom to spend and spend, it's no surprise that we began buying (importing) much more that were selling (exporting), creating a massive U.S. trade deficit bubble. Importing more goods than we export means huge amounts of dollars flowing out. Once these dollars are in the hands of business people in other countries, many of these investors like to use their dollars to buy U.S. stocks, bonds, and real estate, hugely increasing the amount of foreign capital invested in the United States. As long as there are profits to be made, foreign investors will continue to buy, invest, and loan dollars.

But as investor psychology begins to sour and profit expectations start to evaporate—due to stock market downturns and unfavorable exchange rates—and foreign investors will begin selling off their U.S. dollars, stocks, bonds, and other assets faster than a bookstore trying to unload last year's calendars.

At first, central banks will buy our dollars to stabilize its value. But such efforts can only go so far. Once the value of the dollar on the foreign exchange markets begins to slip enough that significant profits can be made in other currencies, the dollar bubble will crash, and nothing will stop the mad dash of foreign capital out of the United States.

It will be reminiscent, on an international level, of an old fashioned run on the bank: For a while, everyone will want their money back.

The Short-Term Pain: The Bubblequake and Aftershock

In the Bubblequake of late 2008, the stock market fell dramatically and major banking institutions collapsed. In all, four big bubbles started to pop: real estate, stock, private debt, and discretionary spending.

Next, in the Aftershock, these bubbles will fall further and two more bubbles will also burst: the dollar and the U.S. government debt bubbles. With foreign investors becoming less interested in investing in the United States and ultimately moving their capital out of their U.S. assets to protect them, the value of these assets will fall and the last of our multiple bubbles will collide and fall. Our dollar will have far less buying power than it has today, stocks will fall, the real estate bubble will be hard to remember and the nation's astronomical government debt bubble will become the equivalent of a McMansion mortgage for a family living on a McDonald's paycheck—our government will be in default and able to borrow no more.

Interest rates will climb, as will inflation. Unemployment will rise and consumer spending will be way down, including business and consumer spending on imports. The economies of other countries, especially those heavily dependent on exports, will fall. And the world's economy will be reeling with the pain of a temporary global mega-depression.

The Short-Term Solution: Adam Smith's "Invisible Hand" Smackdown

The combined problem of imbalanced international trade and an over-valued dollar is very easy to solve—in the short run—with the

"I got out of tulips after the market collapsed, but I'm slowly getting back in. Especially pink ones."

normal free-market economics of supply and demand. The bursting of the dollar bubble is key. When other governments, primarily China, Japan and Europe, are no longer able to support the dollar and foreign investors begin losing lots of money on their dollar-denominated investments, the value of the dollar will fall to the point that imports and exports, when combined with investment flows, are equal.

That means, as the buying power of the dollar falls, at some point the cost of a Toyota, for example, will be so high that people will prefer to buy GM and Ford cars. That price point may be $70,000 or it may be $100,000. Whatever the price point that equalizes imports and exports will be the price for these cars, in dollar terms.

This is Adam Smith's "Invisible Hand" of supply and demand at work automatically restoring balance to international trade by making it too expensive for us to import much from other countries. The Invisible Hand will guide the dollar to the proper level to slow imports and rebalance our foreign trade, providing a bottom point for the falling dollar bubble.

Clearly, this automatic supply-and-demand solution solves the problem of imbalanced trade, but it is not a long-term solution because it severely damages world trade. Long term, many changes will have to be made to revive world trade, including some dramatic changes in our international monetary system. More on that later in this chapter.

Slowing Productivity Growth: The Real Trouble Behind the Bubbles

When our bubbles collide and pop, the real trouble hiding behind America's bubble economy will get a whole lot harder to ignore: slowing productivity growth.

Many influential economists insist that U.S. productivity grew dramatically during the late 1990s due to heavy investment in information technology. Other economists, such as Robert Gordon and Nobel Prize winner Robert Solow, say that overall productivity has been growing, but at a much slower rate since the mid 1970s, and the only reason people keep missing this fact is because productivity measurements ignore many key factors that impact real growth.

Please understand that when we use the term "productivity growth," we are not talking about the conventional output-per-man-hour statistics that go up and down with every monthly economic report. Beyond this narrow measure, we are talking about the really *big picture* of productivity growth that has driven the overarching rise of human efficiency and production over centuries—for example, reducing the number of people required to grow our food from 75 percent to just 3 percent of the nation's population because of advances in farming technology.

How to measure productivity growth is a tricky question that will continue to be debated for years. But from a big picture perspective, this much is clear: the dramatic productivity growth of the first half of the twentieth century has fizzled out since the 1970s.

How do we know that? We know because if productivity had grown significantly, inflation-adjusted wages would have, as well. In fact, real wages have grown very little in the last three decades as shown in Figure 8.2. If productivity growth were significantly increasing over the last 30 years, we'd certainly see wages going up, too.

We used to have wonderful prosperity-creating productivity growth in the United States. From 1913 to 1972, our productivity grew at an average rate of 1.6 percent per year. That may not sound like much, but it was enough to make the United States the wealthiest nation on earth.

But by the 1970s, productivity growth in the United States and other advanced economies began to look as flabby as a Macy's Thanksgiving Parade balloon after the air has started to leak.

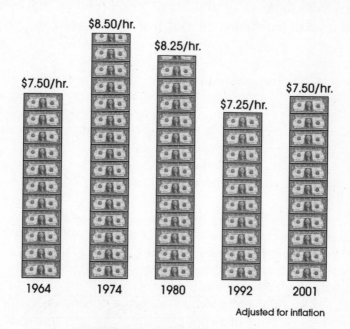

Figure 8.2   Real Wage Growth 1964–2001
When adjusted for inflation, wages have failed to grow significantly for more than three decades.
Source: Bureau of Labor Statistics.

Over the years, it's become increasingly difficult to significantly boost productivity simply by building bigger factories or using more machines. Other than the productivity improvements created by high-tech electronics, no other technology or industry has improved enough to drive significant productivity growth since the 1970s, as shown in Figure 8.3.

To get a feel for how productivity growth has leveled off, consider the flight pattern of the airline history. From 1900 to 1957, we went from not being able to fly at all to producing the powerful Boeing 707—quite an accomplishment. A half-century later, from 1957 to today, we have only managed to go from the 707 to the 777. That means, in the first half of the twentieth century, aviation achieved the productivity equivalent of going from the runway to 30,000 feet; but in the second half of the twentieth century, we've just inched up a bit higher. That's what we mean by slowing productivity growth.

With the exception of information technology, nearly every U.S. industry, from lumbering, to farming, to oil refining, has followed this same flight path: huge productivity gains during the first half

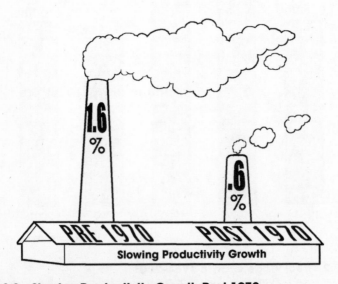

Figure 8.3   Slowing Productivity Growth Post 1970
Although U.S. productivity continues to grow, the rate of that growth has declined dramatically since 1970.
Source: Bureau of Labor Statistics.

of the twentieth century, followed by much less dramatic productivity gains in the second half of the twentieth century.

In the 1980s and 1990s, personal computers and the Internet may have seemed like the Next Big Thing. But the actual productivity growth they created pales in comparison to the earlier productivity explosions ignited by the development of the internal combustion engine, electricity, telephones, and economies of scale in production. In truth, after the mid 1980s, productivity gains from investment in information technology came primarily from declines in the prices of personal computers and related equipment.

Meanwhile, the productivity superstars of yesteryear, while still driving some current productivity growth, are beginning to run out of steam.

In our factories, assembly-line technologies and automated production of everything from mass-produced cars to machine-wrapped candy bars drove huge productivity improvements from 1910 to 1970. But other than some fine-tuning, there have been no equally dramatic productivity improvements since.

Down on the farm, as we swapped work animals, wheelbarrows, and hand tools for tractors, trucks, and fertilizers, food production skyrocketed from 1900 to 1970, while the labor required to produce that food fell like a rock. But there hasn't been anything approaching that level of productivity growth in the last 30 years.

Nevertheless, many people continue to insist that productivity growth is still going strong. Some say that the Industrial Age has given way to the Information Age. But to fantasize that the modest productivity improvements created by the Internet, or even the significant improvements created by high-tech electronics, are in the same league as the truly massive productivity explosion propelled by electricity, airplanes, telephones, powerful steam engines, internal combustion engines, electric motors, freshly laid railroads and new steel mills is like comparing a couple of fancy bicycles to a fleet of bulldozers.

Yes, the Internet has had a significant impact on the productivity of some individuals and industries. (It sure made writing this book a lot easier.) But in our high-tech excitement, let's not lose track of the really Big Picture. Yes, our nation's productivity is still growing, but the *rate of our productivity growth is slowing down.*

This is actually a complex subject and we can deal with it only briefly in this chapter. For more information, please go to our website at www.aftershockeconomy.com/productivity.

How Will We Solve These Problems in the Long Term?

Eventually, we will solve these problems the same way human beings have been forced to solve every other major monetary problem since the beginning of time: evolution!

With domestic trade we evolved from money based on metal to a monetary system governed by the Federal Reserve. This evolution allowed more sophisticated control over the domestic monetary system that helped create the rapidly expanding domestic economy of the twentieth century.

For international trade, the evolutionary pattern will be basically the same: We will go from foreign trade based on gold to a monetary system governed by an international equivalent of the Federal Reserve, which will create a more sophisticated international monetary system that will help rapidly expand world trade. (As we said at the start of the book, we don't have any political ax to grind or philosophical agenda; we are simply analyzing the evolving economy, and this is where our in-depth analysis shows us that we are going.)

For domestic trade, evolving from gold to paper money was a big step forward in growing the U.S. economy, but the transition was messy and helped create the Depression. Likewise, evolving from gold to paper money for international trade will also eventually lead to more wealth for the entire world, but the transition will be messy, and is helping to create the current Bubblequake and coming Aftershock.

Economic pain will provide the necessary pressure on governments to evolve and make the changes needed to create a much better global monetary system, the next step in the evolution of money. As always, the pain of not evolving will provide the impetus to move forward. As in our own individual lives, it sometimes takes a short-term crisis to force us to move ahead.

How Will Our Money Evolve Next?

No one knows for sure, but based on how things have gone so far, we think we have a clue. More than merely an educated guess, we think we know some general features of how money will evolve next because, as we said earlier, the evolution of money does not happen in a vacuum, but is actually part of a much broader evolution of society.

We call it STEP Evolution.

What follows is a *basic introduction* to STEP Evolution—a powerful and reliable new way of understanding how things non-randomly change, which we will tell you more about in another book. Love it or hate it, please let us know what you think about STEP Evolution and the evolution of money by visiting us at www.aftershockeconomy .com/step.

Introducing The Biggest "Big Picture" On The Block: STEP Evolution

American songwriter, Woody Guthrie, once said "Any fool can make something complex; it takes a genius to make something simple."

Simplicity certainly is our goal.

Just as we have a theory of *physical evolution* that helps explain how matter started with the Big Bang and evolved into our universe, and we have a theory of *biological evolution* that helps explain how living things evolved after the Big Bang, it is possible to imagine that a theory of *societal evolution* might help explain how human society has evolved (after a great deal of biological evolution) and how it may continue to evolve into the future.

Stated in the simplest terms, **S-T-E-P Evolution** is the co-evolution of **S**cience, **T**echnology, **E**conomics, and **P**olitics.

From the beginning of human history and continuing into our shared future, Science, Technology, Economics, and Politics are not simply changing randomly through time, but are inevitably *linked and evolving together.* At any moment in time—past, present, or future—each depends on the others, and each changes in response to the others.

In other words, it's a package deal.

That's why we didn't have cell phones in the Middle Ages when the science, economics, and politics of the day simply could not have produced that technology. That's why important advancements in science—like the idea that the world is round—simply will not be accepted until the supporting technology, economics, and politics evolves enough to handle them. And that's why once-powerful kings inevitably fade from world politics when the prevailing winds of science, technology, and economics change.

Throughout time, Science, Technology, Economics, and Politics have been linked and co-evolving together. In fact, each pushes the others forward: Science drives Technology, Technology changes Economics, and Economics shapes Politics.

<u>S</u>cience → <u>T</u>echnology → <u>E</u>conomics → <u>P</u>olitics

Science (Our Knowledge of the World) Ultimately Drives Social Change

At first blush, such a statement may seem unlikely. But when we look at the evidence over thousands of years, a clear pattern emerges. Science—that is, our collective knowledge of the world—is the driving force behind the evolution of human society. We don't say this because we love science and we want it to be true. We say it because that is what the evidence shows.

You can see this for yourself by breaking STEP Evolution down into . . . well, steps.

The first step in STEP Evolution is undeniable: Science (our collective knowledge about the world) drives Technology. You can't have TV (a technology) without knowing something about electricity and many other types of knowledge (science). So it seems perfectly plausible to say that changes in Science drive changes in Technology.

<u>S</u>cience → <u>T</u>echnology

Throughout history, advancements in <u>S</u>cience have driven the development of new <u>T</u>echnology. Clearly, over the years, advances in Science have given us all sorts of useful innovations—things like antibiotics, instant coffee, Velcro, and computers.

But here's where it gets interesting and perhaps unexpected. These new technologies aren't just fun gadgets to amuse us. They have profound effects on our lives. From the beginning of human history, new technologies have vastly transformed how we live and compete for survival, changing everything from what we eat to how we trade goods and services.

In other words, new <u>T</u>echnologies profoundly affect <u>E</u>conomics.

Think of the dramatic economic changes that followed the invention of the steam engine or the printing press, for example.

How in the world would we ever have developed an industrial economy without first having industrial technology? It just wouldn't happen. Technology changes and that forces Economics to change.

Technology → Economics

Sure, there are countless relatively small changes in the Economy that have little to do with new Technology, but that's not what we are talking about. Think BIG Big Picture. How far would global trade (economics) have advanced without Bigger, steam-powered ships (technology) that could cross an ocean? But once we have those ships, how in the world could we have stopped global trade from eventually evolving? On a big scale, new Technology forces Economics to change.

And it doesn't stop there. In time, sweeping new Economics inevitably reshapes Politics—including how people share resources and power, fight wars, follow or defeat leaders, and run governments.

Economics → Politics

This means, when Economics significantly changes, so too do our Political structures. In fact, you can't stop Politics from changing once Economics changes—eventually, the new economic conditions will topple the old system and help support a new system. That's why we don't have too many monarchies left in highly prosperous nations with large middle-class populations. That kind of economy just doesn't support kings and queens as nicely as previous economies did.

So, if Science drives Technology, and Technology changes Economics, and Economics inevitably reshapes Politics, then it is reasonable to say that Science (our collective knowledge about the world) is driving societal change.

Science → Technology → Economics → Politics

In short, Science drives new Technology, which gives us new ways to compete for survival, which reshapes Economics, which changes Politics, and over time, ultimately drives our evolving world.

Therefore, if Science (our collective knowledge of the world) is changing non-randomly and is, in fact, building on itself and evolving, then everything else is evolving, too.

But Isn't Society Changing Randomly?

No, not if you look at the truly BIG Big Picture. Certainly, lots of things do come and go randomly through time. But over the course of *thousands of years* the big general features of human society have evolved non-randomly.

This makes sense. Given that advancements in science systematically build on each other, and given that new technologies don't simply materialize out of the blue, it follows that human society—when viewed over the broad sweep of time—is also changing non-randomly, building on what came before, following an evolutionary path.

As Isaac Newton once said, when referring to his dependency on Galileo's and Kepler's work in physics and astronomy, "If I have seen further, it is by standing upon the shoulders of giants."

Of course, there are countless fits and starts, but over the long haul of history, Science (our collective knowledge about the world) advances systematically. Therefore, Technology, when viewed over the long haul of history, advances systematically. Therefore, Economics—which only changes significantly when it has to change because of new Technology—also advances systematically. And therefore, our Political structures, which only change dramatically when forced to change by new economic conditions—also advance systematically.

Science, Technology, Economics, and Politics—in other words, the basic elements of human society—evolve!

It may seem as if things are changing randomly, but if you stand far enough back and take a big enough view, we can see that a certain amount of evolutionary progress has been made. While life on planet earth is far from perfect, over the centuries, STEP Evolution has worked in our favor. We may occasionally feel nostalgic for bygone days, but do we really want to live without plumbing, have to kill what we eat with our bare hands, and perhaps die at the ripe old age of 27 from a rotten tooth because we have no antibiotics? On the whole, STEP Evolution has worked to ease our struggles to survive and prosper, greatly increasing our productivity, health, and quality of life.

History does not repeat itself, but the forces that shape history do. If we can figure out how the forces of STEP Evolution changed the past into the present, we can begin to understand how the present may evolve into the future. Why? Because the same forces that propelled the past to evolve into today, will continue to drive the present to evolve into tomorrow. Understand these forces and you can have some clue about what may happen next.

Come On, Can We REALLY Predict Future Social Evolution?

We cannot predict the details of the future, but we most certainly can predict that the future will *evolve*. And based on what we know about that evolution, we can even venture a guess about what that future might look like.

Predicting the general features of the future with STEP Evolution is sort of like trying to figure out the general features of an unknown object—say, a dinosaur—when all we have to work with are the most basic building blocks, the fossilized bones. When trying to reconstruct a dinosaur, we will never figure it *all* out down to the tiniest detail. But if we know what we're looking at, bones can tell us a lot. By putting the pieces together and applying what we know about other living creatures, we can get a pretty good picture of something no human has ever seen. True, we won't know what a dinosaur thought about or what it ate for lunch on a specific day. But with enough bones and enough science, we can confidently know that it had a long tail, big jaws, and a relatively small brain. And although we'll never get to see it in action, we can assume, based on the science of how other animals move, that it probably ran like the wind. In this same way, we can use the basic bones of evidence of how STEP Evolution has changed the world so far, to construct our best guess about how the world will evolve next. Again, we are not trying to predict the details of the future; we are predicting future evolution.

This requires that we ignore many distracting details and stand way back to get a very broad view of what has already occurred. Just as you can't stare at a mountain and watch it evolve, you can't see STEP Evolution by focusing only on today or the recent past. STEP Evolution is the evolution of Science, Technology, Economics, and Politics *over very broad sweeps of time*—not a few years or even a few decades. Just as the earth is the product of billions of years of geological evolution, human society is the culmination of thousands of years of STEP Evolution. And as long as the sun continues to shine, our future will be the continuation of it.

Sounds Interesting, But What Good Is STEP Evolution to Us Today?

Plenty! In the short term, we can use STEP Evolution to help predict emerging trends in technology and business over the next 10 to 20 years. We look forward to telling you much more about this in another book, but right now it's important you understand that

STEP Evolution is not just an interesting way to think about life, but also a highly practical and powerful tool with many, many specific applications in business, technology, personal finances, and social and economic trends.

For example, STEP Evolution tells us what specific signs to watch for as we move through the Bubblequake and into the Aftershock. In the near term, it points us in the direction of the best jobs and hottest careers just on the horizon. And it offers detailed advice on how to invest wisely and protect your assets throughout the changing times ahead, which we shared with you earlier in the book.

Well beyond the scope of this book, STEP Evolution and its many tools can help shed light on how specific industries, technologies, and business sectors will fare in the near future. It can even help make specific, very practical recommendations to individuals and companies.

Taking the long-term view, STEP Evolution helps illuminate the bigger picture of where we've been and where we're going next, putting today's headlines into the much broader context of big, evolving change. Knowing how the past evolved into the present, and how the present continues to evolve into the future, offers tremendous insights into today's world. Present-day problems like poverty, crime, racism, terrorism, and wars cannot be fully understood, nor effectively solved, until we understand how they evolved in the first place.

Rather than pushing any particular social reform or political agenda, STEP Evolution objectively analyzes the key forces that have shaped history to better explain where we are today and where we're likely to go tomorrow.

What Does All This Have to Do with the Future of Money?

Everything. Although we have left this introduction to STEP Evolution to the end of the book, we have actually been using it all along. STEP Evolution and its many powerful tools, like the STEP Evolution Matrix, can be used to analyze *any* type of big societal change, including the future of money. STEP Evolution can even analyze how a significant event—like the current Bubblequake and coming Aftershock—fits into the broader evolution of money and the even broader evolution of Science, Technology, Economics, and Politics.

If you doubt that the general future of money (or the general future of anything else) is in any way predictable, please remember that by "predictable," we mean in the sense that a general weather trend is predictable. The exact course of specific, local events is always subject to many unpredictable forces, but the *overall trend* (like the overarching trend toward summer or winter) is to a certain degree predictable and not entirely random.

Again, we will leave the specific details about STEP Evolution and its many useful tools to another book. For now, here's how the evolution of money fits into STEP Evolution, and what it means for the future of the international monetary system.

Due to the constraints of this chapter, we have had to simplify the complex relationships between the elements of STEP theory. For more information, please go to our website at www.aftershock economy.com/step.

The Future of Money

Driven forward through time by STEP Evolution the next step in the evolution of money will be the development of an international agency (the global equivalent of a international central bank) that manages a single international currency that is entirely electronic. We are not saying this will come quickly or easily, but eventually it will come. In time, old-fashioned cash stashed under the mattress will become as useless as a manual typewriter.

Why a single international currency? Because it will be necessary to avoid repeating the pain of another global Bubblequake. A single international currency will eliminate the problems with foreign currency exchange, making currency bubbles (like our current dollar bubble) impossible. It will also block us from spending our way into huge foreign trade imbalances (like our current international trade deficit bubble). And because a single international currency is the most technologically and economically efficient form of money at this stage of our societal evolution, it eventually becomes the best option.

Will nations resist it every inch of the way? Absolutely . . . for a while. But eventually, they will come around, for the same reasons evolution always occurs: because it beats the alternative. In the long view of STEP Evolution, a global economy requires a global currency.

Why an electronic currency? Because money—like every other human technology since the Stone Age—evolves through time following the STEP Evolution principles of "Material Substitution" and "Energy Substitution" (which we explain in more detail at www .aftershockeconomy.com/substitution).

Certainly we have the beginnings of an all-electronic monetary system already in place. Credit cards, debit cards, electronic checks, checks by phone, checks by fax, direct deposit, and online banking are all beginning to supplant some of our cash and check payments because they are so much more efficient. Moving cash around in a big, money bucket brigade is expensive, requiring banks, ATMs, armored cars and security personnel. The cost of cash maintenance and cash crimes drains a society's productivity.

Remember those big bags of gold coins we don't bother lugging around anymore? Remember the high cost of mining, protecting, and using gold? Sooner or later, people do prefer cheaper, easier, and better—especially when the consequences of *not* evolving become very, very painful, as they are in the Bubblequake and in the coming Aftershock.

Hard to Believe? Actually, We Are Already Almost There

It may be hard to believe we will ever have a single international currency, given how fond individual nations are of their own forms of money. But when you look at how far we've already come, it's easier to see that we're much more than half way there now.

Imagine how hard it would have been 2,000 years ago to convince hordes of Germanic tribal chiefs wrapped in bear skins that their warring tribes of 10,000 or more people would eventually come together to form a single European Union in the twentieth century, with a single European currency, the euro. Given how far we've already come, it's only a matter of time before Japan, the United States, and the European Community come together, too, to create a common international currency.

Again, we are not saying this because that is what we hope will happen. This is not about wishful thinking or pushing a political agenda. In the big picture of STEP Evolution, evolving to a single electronic currency is just a matter of time. Sooner or later, unless the sun fails to shine, all other less-efficient options will simply be eliminated.

A Likely Scenario for How an International Currency Will Evolve

The natural solution to the Bubblequake and Aftershock will feel as unnatural to many Americans as giving up baseball. But sooner or later, major social and political changes, including a single, global electronic currency, operated by a central administrative agency, are in the cards for us. After the temporary global mega-depression, an international electronic currency, operated by a central administrative agency, will eliminate foreign exchange problems. We don't know what this new currency will be named, but for convenience, let's call it "IMU" (pronounced EYE-mu), short for International Monetary Unit.

At first, the IMU will simply be a merger of the euro, the dollar and the yen. Other strong democracies, such as Canada or Australia will then join. Then use of the IMU spreads around the world since a country does not have to be a member of the governing group in order to use the IMU. IMUs will be far cheaper for society to administer than cash. There'll be no expensive bills to print or coins to mint. There'll be no cash to steal. IMUs will be inflation-free because the system that controls the supply of IMUs will be set up to avoid it. For more information on the IMU and its adoption, see www.aftershockeconomy.com/imu.

Many people, including some Americans, will oppose the coming evolutionary transition to a new form of money, but change is inevitable. When America's bubble economy fully pops, and people ride the roller coaster from denial to panic to anger to understanding, the first thing they'll do is blame the politicians. Of course, it will be too late to punish the politicians who created the problem.

Congress and the White House will become a revolving door as the party out of power blames the party in power for the country's economic woes. Government will be unable to solve the problem, at least for a while, and each election will bring in new blood. Change can happen in a number of ways. A wise, courageous, but politically suicidal president could sacrifice his party's power by instituting radical reform. The same thing could happen today if a president chose to burst the bubble early to lessen our fall.

But the possibility that any president would willingly devalue the dollar or purposely shrink stock prices is about as unlikely as the lion, having clawed his way to the top of the food chain, suddenly going vegetarian. The political system's own Darwinian process selects against leaders who harm their party's chances in the next election.

What's far more likely is that nothing fundamental will change in the next few years. The Aftershock will hit, the President will get the boot, and so will whoever comes in next. The revolving doors in Washington will scare off competent politicians and attract the most radical elements of both parties.

Eventually, after we've endured the political version of *The Beverly Hillbillies* for several election cycles, candidates will step forward who are willing to support real and responsible reforms, politicians more like Franklin Roosevelt than Herbert Hoover.

To do so, they'll have to cross political boundaries that haven't been crossed since the New Deal when FDR pushed through a number of interventionist government policies like the Social Security Administration, the Securities and Exchange Commission, the Federal Deposit Insurance Corporation, and welfare. Whether you think FDR saved the country with deposit insurance or saddled it with expensive poverty programs, you have to admit he did force politicians of all stripes to confront the problems of the day and come up with ways to deal with them.

Evolutionary changes won't come overnight but, like mice in a maze, we are going to run down every avenue until we eventually solve our problems. When the dust finally settles, the result of this financial crisis will be sweeping political and economic changes, including a far more stable monetary system and much higher incomes for the entire world.

As long as nations continue to cling to their own currencies, we will face potential difficulties in how those currencies are valued in relation to each other. Problems with foreign exchange didn't exist before we evolved enough to have so much global trade. Now that we have global trade, we need a global currency. Until we have it, we will have problems—like the coming painful Aftershock. Fortunately, pain is just the thing we need to help move this transition along.

In the meantime, like every other important societal change so far, our transition to the future will involve some resistance, followed by struggle, crisis, suffering, more struggle, and eventually, when all else fails . . . *evolution*.

Some Final Thoughts: Turning Economics into a Science

STEP Evolution is the missing link that connects economics with the rest of societal evolution. And, by connecting the evolution of society to the evolution of life, and thus to the evolution of the Universe, STEP Evolution not only makes interesting cocktail conversation, it finally links economics with science and begins to elevate it from a pseudo-science to a real science.

The actual conversion of economics into to a real science, thoroughly grounded in physics and chemistry and all the other hallmarks of a real science, will be a very complex task, indeed, and certainly not appropriate to discuss here. But making that conversion from pseudo-science to real science begins with a most important conceptual leap: If our current economy is part of a long evolution of society, life, and the universe—starting with the Big Bang—then there are certain predictable forces that drive that economic evolution. Understanding these forces is critical to deciphering how we arrived at today's world and where we are going next. And it is absolutely essential for understanding how our future economy will evolve.

ABE Award for Intellectual Courage

Lee Smolin is one of those unusual academics and intellectuals who can spot a major problem and write very coherently about it. His book, "The Trouble with Physics" is one of the best critiques of the current physics communities that has been written. He points out, very convincingly, that the physics community, after decades of very impressive breakthroughs, has come to a virtual standstill since the early 1980s. In his many years teaching and researching at major academic institutions, such as Princeton, Yale, and the Fermi Institute at the University of Chicago, he has seen the physics community become overly focused on String theory as the theoretical basis for breakthroughs in our understanding of physics.

More importantly, the physics community has not allowed or encouraged much discussion on other theories that might bring
(Continued)

greater insight into the problems physicists are having such trouble solving. And, String theory hasn't gotten physicists anywhere in almost 30 years. The inability of this academic community to encourage and create alternative theories that may answer their questions is a serious problem.

What does this have to do with the Bubble Economy? Not much directly, but it has a lot to do with the current state of economics. In many ways it is facing a similar problem. Although there was much progress made in the decades prior to the 1970s in a variety of areas including Milton Friedman's work on monetary policy and John Maynard Keynes' work on fiscal policy as well as advancements in econometrics, very little has been accomplished since. The economics community has not been very encouraging or creative about major new approaches to understanding our economy. These failings are much more apparent to us than those of the physics community since they affect our pocketbook, but the failings of both communities are very similar.

Most importantly, any movement to make economics a real science, as opposed to a social science, has ground to a halt. In the end, for economics to be a real science, it has to be directly tied to the mother of all sciences, physics. If physics is having a problem, all sciences will have a problem, including economics, which needs to become a science. We should all share Mr. Smolin's concern about physics because it affects all the sciences and, ultimately the same problems affecting the mentality of the physics community are likely affecting other sciences as well, just as we see similar patterns in economics. Hats off to Lee Smolin for his important insights and his enormous courage.

For more information on the topics discussed in this chapter, go to www.aftershockeconomy.com/chapter 8 or visit our blog site at www.aftershockeconomy.com/blogs.

9

The New View of the Economy Helped Us Predict the Current Bubblequake, So Why Don't Some People Like It?

This new way of understanding the economy based on the Theory of Economic Evolution, which is part of the broader STEP Evolution, made it possible for us to see what others were (and still are) missing. It made it possible for us to accurately predict, in 2006, Phase I of the Bubblequake of 2008 and 2009 (we also predicted Phase II and Phase III in that book, but they're still in the future). And it is directly responsible for our current prediction about the coming Phase II, the Aftershock, in this book. In fact, we even know what Phase III will look like (see next chapter) and Phase IV (see next book).

However, many other economists and financial analysts didn't see and still don't see these phases coming and most of them will not agree with this book. How come? Why will some people not see what seems pretty straightforward and obvious to us?

The reason is the six psychological stages of dealing with the Bubblequake and Aftershock that we first told you about in Chapter 3. We have been in the first stage (Denial) for a long time, and now we are entering the second stage (Market Cycles), in which most experts believe things will get better soon.

Understanding why some people react badly to our book is important for understanding why the bubble economy occurred in the first place and for seeing where we are in the progression of those six psychological stages. The roots of the antagonism to our ideas are grounded in the need to deny these problems until we have absolutely no other choice but to face them and solve them. Until then, most people want to maintain the comforts and benefits of the status quo.

So, it's not only important that we be able to analyze and predict what happens with the economy, it is also important for us to be able to analyze and predict the reactions people will have to our predictions. It's somewhat unusual for most books to do this, but quite essential to a good understanding of what is happening with the economy and how it is evolving. It is also important for the reader to understand where other people are coming from so that the reader can better understand why so many other people might not be agreeing with us and why you should be listening to us.

Here are what we predict will be some of the main reactions people will have to the book and why some people won't like it.

It's Not a Cheerleading Book

Most people want a highly plausible cheerleading book. They don't want to understand what's really going on with the economy; they just want to hear that the economy will improve, even if we hit some rough patches along the way. They want good news, but it has to be plausible, meaning that it is based on some kind of seemingly rigorous analysis. The analysis itself can be terrible, but as long as it supports the idea that things will get better, that's what they want to hear.

Ideally, this analysis should also square with conventional wisdom, for example, the idea of market cycles. But it can't be too optimistic or it will sound like fantasy. It has to be very cognizant of current problems while being fundamentally optimistic that the economy, stocks, and real estate will inevitably turn up.

Alan Greenspan was a master at this. He was the perfect cheerleader because he was optimistic, but always quite plausible. Greenspan never talked too much about any fundamental economic problems, except with very long-term issues, such as the long-term cost of Social

Security and Medicare. However, he always brought up some negative issues that made his overall optimism seem well considered. Even when his views didn't square with reality, people still loved to hear them.

As of this writing in mid-2009, people love to hear the view that the economy will turn around in the second half of the year. Even if it takes three more quarters or even as long as another year, people still want to hear about a turnaround. There are often no good reasons behind these views, or if they are based on any analysis, it is very biased or outright misleading, but that's what most people want and that is what they get. In fact, the National Association of Business Economics released a report in late May 2009 saying that a panel of 45 economists they interviewed expects that economic growth will rebound in the second half of 2009. Nearly 75 percent of those who responded to the survey said that the recession would end next quarter. No economists thought the recession would move beyond the first quarter of 2010.

Even when analysts and economists are proven wrong, time and again (for example, when the housing market did not bottom out in 2006, or in 2007, or in 2008, and when the economy didn't turn around in the second half of 2008, or in the second quarter of 2009, etc.), these people still retain a lot of credibility because at least they are trying to be optimistic. Of course, they clearly have no idea of what they are talking about and are constantly proven wrong, again and again, but that doesn't matter—at least they are trying to be plausibly optimistic. The audience that wants cheerleaders still likes what cheerleaders are saying. In this group, nobody likes a bear, least of all when the bear is right.

It's Not a Complex Book (although It Is Based on a Complex Analysis)

For some readers, a really complicated book is best. It makes the reader and the author feel like they know something that very few people can understand. This makes the author and their readers feel really smart. It also obscures the upsetting truth about the economy. This group may not want a cheerleading book, but they also don't want to be too fundamentally critical of the economy or its future prospects. This group might like a detailed analysis of complicated Credit Default Swaps (CDS) and the intricate ways they might threaten the economy, even though the real threats to the economy are simpler and much more fundamental.

Many people in this group are very threatened by the real economy since many of them will lose their jobs in the Aftershock, including many economists and financial analysts and other professionals. But here's a question: If these people could not predict or even talk about something as big and important as the Bubblequake that just hit us in 2008, exactly what value to society do these economists and financial analysts serve? What good does their analysis do if it couldn't tell us so many banks would fail and the stock market would lose half its value?

Once the Aftershock hits, these folks will finally lose their credibility. At that point, we won't need any more inaccurate cheerleaders; we will need some accurate thinkers!

These analysts and economists often don't want to see the reality of the economy because they want to believe something else. At this point, they *really* don't want to see it, because if they see it now, they will have to ask, "How did so many smart people make such terrible mistakes?" Maybe because they weren't so smart? But if that is the case, then what will happen to Wall Street and what does that say about economists and politicians and their super-smart advisers? It says that they are quite likely to fail, and take the economy down along with them. That is really painful for all of us.

For example, the biggest mistake made in the run-up to the recent financial crisis was that people on Wall Street *and* Main Street *and* in Washington all thought that it was perfectly fine for housing prices to go up 100 percent or more while people's incomes only went up a few percent. That was a pretty basic economic mistake to make, but that was their fundamental error. It wasn't Wall Street gods gone bad, or greed overtaking people. It was just plain bad investment judgment at a very fundamental level, and this very bad investment judgment was made by just about everyone, from the least financially sophisticated people in America to the most financially sophisticated people in America.

Our analysis in America's Bubble Economy was quite different. We looked at the fundamentals driving the housing market rather than hoping that huge price gains were well justified and would keep on coming. The analysis was spot on and even televised nationally when Bob Wiedemer said in February 2008 on CNBC's Squawk Box that homebuilding stocks would go down even when almost every other financial analyst felt that, for some reason, they had already gone down enough and were certainly at the bottom of the cycle and would naturally go up. Of course, that's about the same thing people were saying in spring 2009. Same song, second verse, one year later.

Even at the very top of the financial world, the people were not very smart about their investments that they theoretically should have been extremely smart about. Instead, they bankrupted (or effectively bankrupted) very impressive banks and investment banks that had previously survived the greatest of our nation's financial difficulties. It's absolutely amazing that these people had such poor investment judgment that they couldn't even survive in an economy with some of the lowest unemployment levels, lowest inflation rates, and lowest interest rates in our nation's history. It was absolutely phenomenal misjudgment in the face of easy-to-see facts. Clearly, this shows that these people weren't very smart at what they should have known best.

In the more distant past, Wall Street has shown great skill and innovation due to the fine efforts of some very impressive people, such as J.P. Morgan and Charlie Merrill. But, these great skills were not on display by the Wall Street of the past decade. That these supposedly impressive financial managers had such terrible judgment inevitably raises the question of how well the economy will do in the future. And it makes a very uncomfortable statement about the way our society is structured and the people who are running it. It's not just bad or evil individuals that are causing us problems; it's something much more profound that is affecting our economy.

One dramatic example of how people in power can prefer complexity to cover up fundamental problems is the terrible Challenger Space Shuttle disaster. When the space shuttle Challenger blew up shortly after takeoff in 1986 hundreds of NASA scientists could have done enormous amounts of research into the problem and produced voluminous papers on the subject, and even then, maybe would not have figured out exactly what went wrong. Physicist Richard Feynman, on the other hand, did a simple experiment of putting the rubber seals from the shuttle's booster tank into ice water to simulate conditions on the day of the launch. When Feynman pulled the seal out of the ice water, it was brittle and broke easily, thus solving the mystery of why the shuttle exploded. It was an excellent example of simple and straightforward analysis, but in some ways, it made hundreds of NASA scientists look bad and in doing so, made the whole NASA organization look pretty bad.

This made a lot of people inside and outside NASA feel pretty uncomfortable. Of course, at least they were willing to bring Feynman in to look at the problem, which was a good step. Today's NASA might be far less willing to do so.

The ideas in our book make people uncomfortable in the same way. If it's really that simple to understand our economic problems, then a lot of people in positions of power are not doing their jobs and cannot be very smart. That's painful.

It's Not a Crazy Book

Crazy books are just cheerleading books in disguise. They propose crazy economic or financial theories that aren't real. Some of these books are far more critical and radical, and more "doom and gloom" than we are. They might say much more critical things about our country. They might be far more critical of individuals such as Alan Greenspan or Wall Street Titans. But, they are so silly that they aren't very threatening. Hence, they are effectively cheerleading for the status quo.

Examples of books that are not crazy and took on important issues are *Uncle Tom's Cabin* and *Silent Spring*. Both of these books were well written and were very honest about the issues they were taking on. They weren't crazy, but in being very realistic they were also very upsetting and many people didn't like them at all. Fortunately, many people did like them even if they were highly critical of the status quo, as they were the right books at the right time for a nation that was already changing its attitudes in the direction the books were advocating.

Still, many people don't like that kind of book and prefer crazy books, as they are far less threatening. Our book is not a crazy book and lays out a very reasonable and rational analysis of our current economic situation, including how it started and where it is headed. For that reason many people will not like it.

It's Not an Academic Book

In most academic circles, an author has to be published in a refereed journal to have any credibility; otherwise academics aren't going to be very interested in the book. That actually makes a lot of sense in some ways because there are plenty of crackpots out there and this is a good way of filtering them out. However, a problem arises when the academics are fundamentally wrong in their analyses. Then the policy becomes a real negative because academics are not exposed to different viewpoints (in part because they don't want to be).

In addition, academics often have the problem of a narrow focus. A narrow focus is good—in fact absolutely necessary for good analysis—but only if you have a good understanding and theory of what is going on in the broader context. For example, if you don't understand continental drift, trying to study minute changes in the Appalachians isn't going to improve your understanding of how they were formed. You have to have a good overall theory, or a narrow focus is just a way of avoiding the hard work of developing a theory that really explains what is going on with the economy.

Many economists today are looking very closely at a specific area and aren't able to understand the broader economic issues. U.S. economists made this complaint about Soviet economists during the Cold War. A Soviet economist might be an expert researcher on grain production in the Ukraine, but that economist would be very careful not to research the much broader economic issues facing the Soviet Union. By keeping his focus narrow, he would not upset other Soviet economists with potentially fundamental criticisms of the Soviet economy.

As a personal example, after writing our first book in 2006 and before the Bubblequake hit in late 2008, Bob spoke one time to a highly respected economist who had written with much insight on the stock market and real estate. Bob asked him about his thoughts on the dollar, because Bob felt the dollar would be one of the key issues affecting the value of both stocks and real estate in the future. This respected man replied that he hadn't thought about the dollar too much because it was outside his area of interest and expertise, but his general feeling was that the dollar was likely overvalued. Wow! He hadn't thought about the dollar much? This is a good example of how too much focus on one area leads to a lack of insight about the overall economy, as well as a lack of insight into one's specific area of focus—in this case, stocks and real estate.

Bottom line is that academics aren't going to like this book, even though one of the authors has good academic credentials—a PhD from one of the leading economics departments in the United States, the University of Wisconsin-Madison. It is a book that is just not going to get a lot of academic respect at this point in time, even if it is right.

To admit that a non-academic economist could be doing more insightful work in economics than many academics would be a fundamental criticism of the economics profession. For most economists, that would be a very painful admission. For a few who realize that it is true, it might be a good thing, but the economic analyses in the book will have to be more proven over a longer period of time before academics take this book and the previous one more seriously. Fortunately for us, we do have one big thing in our favor: The Bubblequake (and its Aftershock) we predicted will help change that by severely discrediting the current group of economists, thus opening the door for a new group of economists to bring in fresh ideas on how the economy really works.

It's Not Suggesting Armageddon

One of the most common themes we see in some financial books that attract people is that, rather than present an honest assessment of the problems we will face, they instead say that our financial problems will result in financial Armageddon. That might be combined with another Armageddon theme that says that a financial collapse will result in violent unrest across the world. Another lighter version would be the "end of capitalism" or the rise of dictatorships in the United States and/or other currently democratic countries. Some people prefer reading this because it is much more comfortable than facing the reality of a fundamental change in their economic, social, and political lives. They retreat to the fantasy of Armageddon because they know it's not really true and is a good way to avoid changes in society or the economy that they would rather not see. *Pretend Armageddon* is simply a more comfortable alternative for some people than what our book predicts.

It's Not a Status Quo Book

All of the above reasons why people don't like our book come down to this one common denominator: it's not a status quo book. Other books, in one way or another, more strongly support the status quo by saying so directly or by being so off base or by adding so much meaningless complexity that they offer no real threat to the status quo. This book threatens the status quo in a fundamental way.

The inevitable future consequences of the current Bubblequake and coming Aftershock will force big changes on our businesses, our government, and our society. Like the aftermath of the Revolutionary War in the United States or World War I in Europe, the status quo cannot last. Fundamental changes to our current property rights system are inevitable after the dollar bubble bursts and that is far scarier to most people than the Terminator fantasies or other pretend end-of-the-world scenarios.

We are daring to say that we have made big economic mistakes in the past and the final result of all the chaos created by those mistakes will be a much, much better and wealthier society than we have today, but one that will be fundamentally very different from today.

How Our Book Stacks Up Against the Rest

On the surface, the book you are now holding in your hand may seem (to people who haven't read it) like just another "doom-and-gloom" economics book. In fact, *Aftershock* is substantially different from any other book currently available.

Some books have correctly predicted that our economy is heading for trouble. To varying degrees, each has contained some partially correct insights, forecasts, and advice. Many have offered some truly bad investment ideas. And many others have provided some very good investment advice, but for wrong or incomplete reasons.

Obviously, we don't have the space here to analyze the details of all the more bearish economics and finance books in the marketplace today. Instead, we'd like to take a closer look at two popular books, *Empire of Debt* (John Wiley & Sons, 2005) by Bill Bonner, and *Crash Proof* (John Wiley & Sons, 2007) by Peter Schiff. We chose these two, not because they are the worst or the best of the bunch, but because these well-received books have attracted a lot of attention and therefore, serve as good models against which we can compare our predictions and our entirely unique perspective.

Empire of Debt spends a good deal of time trying to make the case that the United States (like the indulgent and ultimately doomed Roman Empire) has been greedy and self-centered, that debt is intrinsically immoral and financially unsound, and that our economy is about to pay a well-deserved high price for our wicked ways. Sounds pretty convincing to some. But let's break this down into its parts.

First, the United States is not the Roman Empire or anything like it. For one thing, our country was founded on the ideals of democracy and the rule of law. We have a constitution, public elections, and a more or less free-market economy—not exactly the ingredients for an evil empire. The author's general point about our culture being greedy and self-serving is a matter of personal opinion and to us it's really not relevant to the economic problems we are about to face. Perhaps the fact that we have been the most successful economy in history makes the author want to hold us to a higher standard—one that he feels we are falling short of—but that hardly makes us an empire. So let's just move on.

The key word in Bill Bonner's *Empire of Debt* is "debt." Here is where we differ dramatically. Like Bonner, we also think that the tremendous U.S. government debt will help bring the economy down, but for very different reasons. Bonner sees debt (both government debt and consumer debt) as intrinsically bad, both for moral reasons and for economic reasons. Let's bypass the morality question and just say we disagree. More relevant is the question of whether or not debt is, by nature, always bad for an economy or a society.

Clearly the answer is No. As we pointed out earlier in this book, *debt is not the problem, stupidity is.* Smart debt can be very good for individuals, businesses, and governments. Smart debt allows you to go to medical school so you can earn a good income later. Smart debt can help start a company or grow a government in many significant and beneficial ways. For example, in the 1870s and 1880s, super-smart debt made it possible to build transcontinental railroads that accelerated our country's economic growth far faster than staying out of debt would have done. And there are countless more examples. Big government debt is *not* always bad, as long as it's smart debt.

Dumb debt, on the other hand, well, that's a different story. Dumb debt buys you nothing but trouble down the road after you've painted yourself into a corner. Dumb debt is what a teenager gets into after three hours at the mall with Daddy's credit card. Dumb debt is what got Freddie Mac, Fannie Mae, and Wall Street into big trouble in 2008. And dumb debt is what our federal government started back in the 1980s and is now into up to its eyeballs. Bonner's *Empire of Debt*, along with every other contrarian book out here that says big government debt will eventually be our downfall, completely misses this important distinction. Debt is not the problem, *stupidity is.*

How about Bonner's investment advice? We fully agree that the U.S. economy is about to crash and we need to be prepared. And we also agree with his advice to buy gold. But we do not believe, as he says, that gold is a "good store of value." If gold was such a good store of value, we certainly would not have seen gold swing from as low as $250 an ounce in 1978 to more than $1,000 an ounce in early 2008, and then back down under $800 in 2008, and so on. The price of gold is extremely volatile, which by definition disqualifies it as being a "good store of value."

On the other hand, we know beyond any doubt that gold is an excellent investment opportunity right now. Why? Because our analysis shows us that gold is a bubble on the way up (see Chapter 6), and we can ride that bubble for many years before it, too, will fall. Unlike the many other books that tell you to buy gold, we do so for the right reasons, based on the right analysis of the much larger economic changes that are occurring. No other book looks at bubbles in this way and no other book understands how our multi-bubble economy has been and will continue evolving (see Chapter 8).

The second book we've chosen to look at is *Crash Proof* by Peter Schiff, which we actually like more than most others. But again, just like the other authors, Schiff tells us that big government deficits are always bad. Not true. He also says the United States is close to being tapped out on debt, and very soon we will no longer be able to get any further loans, when in fact we will see our current $10+ trillion debt expand to $15 or even $25 trillion before the U.S. government falls into default and can borrow no more.

In addition to blaming debt, Schiff also says our economic problems are due to a lack of domestic manufacturing, which we know is not the reason for our troubles (the falling bubbles are). Most industrial nations have seen the percentage of their GDP related to manufacturing decline substantially in the last 50 years.

In terms of his advice for wealth preservation we agree that U.S. stocks are no place to put your money. But we also know that Schiff's recommendations to move out of U.S. stocks and into foreign stocks is the equivalent of moving from the proverbial frying pan into the fire. We know for a fact that foreign stocks will crash for the same reasons we know U.S. stocks will crash, because we have an understanding of the larger forces that are driving this global multi-bubble collapse. Schiff, like everyone else, is missing this because he doesn't have the bigger picture.

Additionally, Schiff says oil will be a good investment. We say demand for oil will continue to fall, making it a lousy investment except in the United States, where the falling dollar will push the price up. He says gold is now in a bull market; we say gold hasn't begun to hit its bubble heights. He says stay liquid and keep your cash handy to pick up bargains in real estate and other distressed assets; we say it's far too soon for that, please avoid all bargain hunting until *after* the dollar bubble pops. Again, we are basing all this, not on our intuition or lucky guesses, but on our detailed analysis of how the overall economy is evolving.

Actually, we are a lot more respectful of these successful authors than we sound here, but our point is that our book—and *only* our book—comes close to being right *for the right reasons*.

What Good Are Economists Anyway?

Hey, we didn't say that. *BusinessWeek* said it on the cover of their April 15, 2009 issue. The story pointed out that economists did a pretty poor job of predicting the current downturn. We'd call that an understatement! Economists were way too busy being cheerleaders and not very interested in doing real economic analysis. So, we agree with *BusinessWeek*—who needs economists who are cheerleaders? We don't. They are useless.

But in a sense, who can blame them? They're doing what the market demands. Most people want economic cheerleaders, not real economists, and the economic community is more than happy to oblige. But is this really good academic work? What if people wanted the earth to be flat? Should physicists crawl all over themselves trying to come up with the latest ideas on why they are right? What if people didn't like the theory of evolution and biologists responded by desperately trying to prove evolution wrong? We all know this would not be good academic work, although it might be a good way to get and keep a job and bring some physicists and biologists much fame and public support. Good for the pocketbook and the ego, but not good for the academic study of biology or physics. The same is true for many economists today. They are meeting a rigorous market test, but not a very rigorous academic or intellectual test.

Economists come in two basic varieties. The first group (the majority) knows better than to make any significant economic predictions, especially in print, that will later come back to haunt them. Instead, these economists spend most of their lives studying the past and reviewing the literature. If they do venture forth into a forecast, they are careful to keep it vague and short-term, and it's always just an extension of the past. Certainly, nothing that involves fundamental change.

The second, smaller group of economists is willing to make some future predictions, but they are often busy "fighting the last war" in the sense that they try to apply the lessons of the past to the present and future. U.S. Federal Reserve Chairman Ben Bernanke is a prime example of this. A longtime student of the Great Depression, Bernanke is approaching our current problems like a replay of the past, not an evolution into the future. His perspective (and that of others like him) is that what worked (or could have worked) before should work now; we just have to avoid past mistakes. Like the first group of economists, this group of bolder economists is also dedicated to nonthreatening predictions that don't rock the status quo, regardless of the facts on the ground.

Some economists have tried to at least be creative and interesting, as with *Freakonomics*, but that book didn't predict much about the current economic downturn. It was an interesting read and wildly popular (certainly for an economics book), but if it didn't predict much or even focus on the most important economic problem of our time, how good and how relevant is the economic analysis in it?

Over time, as economists are shown to be increasingly off the mark and increasingly more like cheerleaders than economists (or are simply irrelevant to the current economic problems), we see increasingly difficult job prospects for bad economists both in academia and in think-tanks or research institutions. Funding for these institutions is highly dependent upon donations and government support that will be extremely hard to come by once the dollar bubble bursts.

Although we never like to see anyone lose a job, career prospects for cheerleader economists will become increasingly bleak and, in some ways, maybe that is an important part of the turnaround. Getting rid of bad economic analysis and replacing it with good economic analysis is the kind of solid foundation we need to have for future growth. Future growth isn't going to be as easy as blowing bubbles, like in the past. We will really need to know what we are doing economically to move forward. Losing the bad economists will be beneficial to almost everyone and

is certainly one of the silver linings of the Bubblequake and its Aftershock.

Financial analysts are even more frightened of change. Sector and company analysts, especially those employed by big brokerage firms trying to sell stocks, naturally want everything to turn out well and for the stock market party to keep going (or get going again). Most financial analysts are big proponents of "buy-and-hold" investing, meaning you get in and you stay in for the long haul, no matter what happens to the value of your investments in stocks, bonds, and other assets. Buy-and-hold investing is a no-brainer winner in a rising asset bubble, like the rising stock bubble. And even when the stock bubble fails to continue to rise, or even declines a bit, the buy-and-hold approach is easy: just wait until the market turns around. Financial analysts typically ignore the macro view of the economy because what difference does it make? Whatever happens, just keep your cool and wait it out. Bull markets always follow bear markets; it's just a matter of time.

But in the fall of 2008, even the very best financial analysts took a beating. They expected financial stocks (which in the past, had driven the stock market bubble higher) to continue to perform. But they didn't—in a big way. By early 2009, financial stocks were down 50 percent or more. It turns out if you don't have an accurate macro view, all the best financial analysis in the world won't keep you from getting hit by a freight train.

ABE Award for Intellectual Courage

As we were preparing to finalize this manuscript we noticed an article by Simon Johnson and Peter Boone. It began by saying "Euphoria returns! Who could have guessed that Bank of America stock would rally 70 percent the week it learns that the Feds are demanding new capital equal to nearly half the bank's market capitalization." That caught our eye. It went on to question the ongoing stock rally by pointing out that 22 percent of Americans have houses worth less than their mortgages and that there are parallel problems for commercial property. We don't agree that we are heading into a situation similar to Japan's lost decade in the 1990s as they suggested (we think the current falling bubble economy will not turn into a malaise but will continue to fall until the dollar pops, at which point, it will be a very different situation than in Japan in the 1990s). But we were pleased that they were willing to point out that large budget deficits and trillions of dollars of new loans to the banks "are recipes for hyperinflation and, if the Fed and Treasury don't pull away from the punch bowl soon, sharply increasing inflation is very much in the cards."

Although this may not seem like a radical position, and there are certainly others who hold similar views, it is unusual that mainstream economists are beginning to speak out so boldly on these issues. Clearly, Paul Krugman of Princeton University and Nouriel Roubini of New York University and Robert Shiller of Yale University have been the leading advocates of intelligent skepticism about our current economy from the mainstream economics community. They've done a good job. But hats off to Mr. Boone and Mr. Johnson, as well! Simon Johnson is a Professor at MIT's Sloan School of Management and a senior fellow at the Peterson Institute for International Economics. The Peterson Institute is one of the best of the economic think tanks and, pound for pound, does more good work than any of them. However, given their strong expertise in global economics, we would have hoped to see more sharp criticism and analysis of the current bubble economy from their staff and their director, Fred Bergsten. That Mr. Johnson is stepping out more boldly on these issues now is truly a step in the right direction.

We also want to recognize a few other people for their courage. In the field of business journalism, on the print side, *Newsweek* columnist

(Continued)

Robert Samuelson and Washington Post syndicated columnist Steve Pearlstein have consistently been courageous in their willingness to give a very honest appraisal of the economy and to point out cheerleader mentality. They're the best in the print business.

On the electronic side of business journalism, few have hit the mark more accurately or more frequently than Paul Farrell, senior columnist at Dow Jones MarketWatch. Paul was simply born with intelligent skepticism in his genes.

Finally, we have to give one of our highest awards to bubble expert Eric Janszen, whose web site iTulip was one of the first to call the Internet bubble. He has also been at the forefront of poking holes in the current bubble economy in his articles and his books. We might add that in the Internet bubble days, no one had a more accurate book than Tony and Michael Perkins, whose *The Internet Bubble* was the best book written on those crazy days. Needless to say, Tony and Eric have been long-time friends and we owe Tony a great debt for introducing us to Eric.

For updates on recent literature and discussions of the Bubble Economy, go to www.aftershockeconomy.com/chapter 9 or visit our blog site at www.aftershockeconomy.com/blogs.

10

Phase III: A Look Ahead to the Post-Dollar-Bubble World

We'd love to say that after Phase I (the Bubblequake) and Phase II (the coming Aftershock), the worst will be behind us. Unfortunately, our analysis does not bear that out. In fact, there will be no way to avoid the miseries of Phase III: the post-dollar-bubble world.

Preparing for Phase III will be the subject of our next book, but we thought you might like a bit of a look now to see what we're in for. It isn't pretty. There won't be much to like about the post-dollar-bubble world (other than the wild profits you can make if you follow our advice now in Chapter 6). Once the dollar has fallen in Phase II, life in these United States and around the world will be profoundly changed in Phase III. Before you get too depressed, it's good to know that we will surely pull ourselves out of this mess in Phase IV when we start to make some of the changes that will lead us to real prosperity; even more than we had before.

But first, Phase III.

Before we go on, we have to say, like a disclaimer before a disturbing television program, "Reader discretion is advised." This is scary stuff: massive unemployment well above Great Depression levels, skyrocketing home foreclosures, bank failures, bankrupt businesses, and swelling welfare rolls. On the other hand, we are not about to face Armageddon, either. There will be no terrible wars, no dictators rising to power, no mass violence in the streets. That stuff is purely for the movies and will not happen (unless you are watching

The Terminator.) The post-dollar-bubble world is quite real and that is what makes it so bad. It is real and we will have to deal with it. It's a lot like going bankrupt—really terrible, but hardly the end of the world.

So if you want more cheerleading and someone telling you that everything will be fine as we quickly pull out of the current recession, this chapter is not for you. It's for people who really want to understand where the economy is headed. Part of the reason for including this chapter here, rather than saving it for our next book, is to test publicly our predictive analysis. Our first book hit the mark two years ahead of the validation. Now we are going out on a limb again by putting this on paper so we can be held accountable. We're very interested to see how closely the results of our predictive analysis will match future reality.

Although we might avoid Phase III, we don't think it is very likely. At this point, there simply aren't many other plausible ways for the economy to go. Once you give up the need to think the status quo cannot change, it frees your mind to see basic facts. There simply is no reasonable scenario in which the dollar bubble will not eventually fall (see Chapter 3 to understand why). We know this last chapter of the book won't make us many friends right now. However, to the extent we are right in the next few years, our future credibility

should increase. To the extent we are wrong, our future credibility should decrease. You be the judge.

The Most Striking Change in a Post-Dollar-Bubble World: The U.S. Government Can't Borrow More Money

When the dollar bubble collapses, the huge government debt bubble will fall, too. That means the falling value of the dollar will have caused enough foreign investors to become concerned enough about the value of their dollar-denominated investments that they will no longer be willing to buy U.S. government bonds at a reasonable price. This means the government will not be able to refinance its debt (just like a company that loses the faith of its creditors) and instead the government will have to resort to inflation, tax increases, and budget cuts to deal with the situation.

Like a family without their credit cards, the U.S. government will be forced to live within the constraints of its actual income, which at this point will be a rapidly declining tax base, much like what California is now facing, but far worse because the U.S. government became very comfortable receiving so much income from deficit financing. Inflation would normally be an additional tool for the government to raise money, but inflation can only be raised so far without destroying a modern industrial economy, such as that in the United States. The amount of inflation the government can feasibly run was discussed in Chapter 3 (about 50 to 100 percent in the long term and far higher for a short period).

That means the government will not be able to create any big stimulus packages or tax cuts or anything of the sort. It will have to cut, cut, cut spending so it can live on its income. Some may see this as a refreshing change—a government that lives within its means. But it will not feel very refreshing. Many things we take for granted, like large pensions, will have to be curtailed. We have gotten very comfortable with a government that always has money and never has to worry about running out; a government that never has to raise taxes to fund wars or stimulus packages; a government with unlimited credit. That's over.

Even during the Great Depression the government's finances were rock solid and it could certainly borrow money, if needed. But, in the post-dollar-bubble world, the government will be like the rest of us, only worse. It will have its credit cards cut off and a much lower income while still having a massive debt that it can't possibly make payments on or even pay interest on (and eventually it won't make principal or interest payments as we discussed in Chapter 3). So, it will have to live within its means.

With No Ability to Borrow, the United States Will Have to Make Massive Spending Cuts

When the U.S. government can no longer borrow and has a rapidly declining tax base, the first action will be to make up the difference by massively increasing the money supply and creating horrendous multi-hundred percent inflation. However, this will be a short-term solution as the devastating effects of that level of inflation on our economy will fairly quickly force the government to make massive cuts in spending (just like the rest of us). These will be very unpopular to say the least, but when the alternative is raising taxes on a populace that is reeling under the pressures of the falling economy, the government will be forced to make lots of unpopular cuts.

Key cuts will hit both the "guns and butter" of the government budget. On the guns side, the military budget will be reduced over several years by 50 to 70 percent with a disproportionate share of the cuts falling on the Navy and Air Force (more details in our next book about where that will be).

On the "butter" side, the most important cut will be to make Social Security means tested, making Social Security essentially a welfare program. For those who have little or no income or assets, Social Security will definitely be there to help. However, for those who have income or assets, forget it.

In addition, Medicare (medical care for older people) reimbursements to doctors and hospitals will be reduced. Since huge numbers of unemployed people and retirees with no more retirement money will qualify for Medicaid (medical care for poor people), Medicaid will explode in size so reimbursements to doctors and hospitals will have to be cut from their already abysmally low levels, and there will be tougher rules on what gets reimbursed. A large percentage of doctors today won't even accept Medicaid payments because the reimbursements are too low. But Medicaid will grow to be so important that doctors won't have any choice but to accept its payments. Essentially, in a post-dollar-bubble world, Medicaid will become our national health care program.

High inflation will do much of the dirty work in cutting budgets. Remember, when inflation is high, budget cuts are accomplished simply by not raising budgets to match inflation. So, inflation will be blamed for much of the government budget cutting.

The cuts to the military, Social Security, Medicare, and Medicaid will produce a large share of the cuts needed to make the U.S. government budget match its greatly lowered income and inability to borrow. But the biggest cut will be the elimination of interest payments. Like the automakers' restructuring, a key part of the government's restructuring of its cost structure will be the elimination of debt payments. Other cuts will be made to programs such as Agriculture and Commerce. User fees will increasingly fund programs in these and similar areas in government. Whatever can't be funded by user fees will likely be cut. Any subsidy programs in the government will be gone almost completely.

Federal and military pensions will also be cut, primarily through lack of increases large enough to offset inflation. Fairly quickly, pensions will not be very valuable. Of course, this only affects workers who get federal funding for their pensions. To the extent that an employee's government pension is dependent upon the stock market, those employees will see their pensions destroyed by the same economic forces that destroy normal pension funds. Needless to say, the government will not be able to make good on any guarantees of public or private pensions. But, fortunately, as many pensioners get poorer, they will qualify for Social Security, welfare, and Medicaid.

Again, all these cuts will be highly unpopular, but with no ability to borrow money anymore and a rapidly shrinking tax base, the government will simply have no choice but to cut spending—a situation many states are already facing now in the Bubblequake.

Big Spending Cuts Will Need to Be Coupled with Big Increases in Taxes

Probably the only thing more unpopular than big spending cuts will be big tax increases. Many people will be out of work and those who are working will see their incomes lowered by their employers and their standard of living squeezed down dramatically by the collapse of real estate and stock market values. So they will *not* be happy about tax increases.

But, the same problems that make increasing taxes so unpopular also make it very necessary. With a massively declining tax base, the government cannot fund even its drastically reduced spending program. And inflation alone will not be enough. The amount of inflation needed to erase the need to raise taxes would destroy our modern economy and would be counterproductive.

Total tax rates on working individuals will range from 30 to 70 percent of total income. Better enforcement of tax collections will also be key to the government increasing its revenues to live within its means. Withholding will become increasingly common on all types of income, including interest, dividends, capital gains and 1099 income. There will also be more requirements for electronic reporting of items such as withholding and relevant bank account information, making quick, cheap and effective electronic auditing much easier.

A Big Change in the Post-Dollar-Bubble World: Not Enough Jobs

The most important difference in the post-dollar bubble world from the pre-dollar bubble world won't be drastically lower stock or real estate prices, but interestingly, jobs. On a day-to-day level, the lack of jobs will be what affects people the most. Many people lucky enough to have jobs will move down the ladder, not up. For example, a former senior accountant at an accounting firm might have to take a job as a bookkeeper or very junior accountant at a business, and at much lower pay, rather than at an accounting firm. Employees will work longer hours for less pay and in less appealing conditions. Benefits will be gone or reduced and competition for jobs will be fierce. Just about everyone will know they could be easily replaced.

However, it won't be anything like the Great Depression of 1929 because of two important differences:

1. The nation will be much wealthier, so few will suffer like they did in the Great Depression.
2. Paradoxically, because we are much wealthier, unemployment will be much higher, likely in the 40 to 60 percent range, when counting the discouraged unemployed.

Unemployment can be much higher when the nation is wealthier because people don't have to have jobs. Unemployed people can live with parents, children, relatives, or friends. Plus, there will be a solid safety net of welfare from the government, although people who are used to today's prosperity will consider the net abysmally low.

In the Depression, if there were a job paying pennies for picking oranges (as in *The Grapes of Wrath*) you'd take it because you had to. In our much wealthier society, the people who do have jobs will be much better paid and will help support friends and relatives who are unemployed.

As is normal, high unemployment will hit disproportionately hard on new entrants into the work force and older workers. So unemployment will be very high for those under 30. However, in the post-dollar-bubble world, unemployment will also be exceptionally high for older workers, since they will have an especially difficult time finding a new job if they lose their current one. This will mean extremely high unemployment for those over 55. We are already seeing some of these trends in Phase I of the Bubblequake.

With unemployment in the 40 to 60 percent range, GDP will also drop by a similar amount, but again, even with a 50 percent drop, that would still be a $7 trillion economy in today's dollars. That's still pretty big bucks. However, it won't feel like big bucks. And that is another big difference between the post-dollar-bubble world and the Great Depression: The psychological pain will be much greater for us today.

The Post-Dollar-Bubble World versus The Great Depression of 1929

In many ways, our coming troubles will be far easier on us than what folks had to endure 80 years ago. But it will actually feel a whole lot worse to us because, compared to the heights of the high-flying bubble economy, life in the post-dollar-bubble world will be quite a fall. Following are the key differences between the coming global mega-depression and the Great Depression.

(Continued)

Great Depression of 1929	Mega-Depression Ahead
Lasted 10 years	Will last more than 20 years
GNP down 25 percent	GNP down 50 percent (but still *way* above 1929 level)
25-percent unemployment	40 to 60 percent unemployment
Real estate, stocks, bonds down 50 percent from peak values	Real estate, stocks, bonds down 90 percent from peak values
For most, living standards already low and became even lower	In developed world, living standards very high and will drop to moderate
Survival-level living	A bigger drop than in 1929, but not survival-level living
Inadequate, limited welfare	Universal and adequate welfare
Limited basic government services	Decline from peak, but adequate government services
Moderate public distress	High public distress due to big drop compared to life in bubble economy

The Loss of Businesses Will Be a Dramatic Change for the Business Community

With a 50-percent drop in GDP, at least half of the businesses in the United States will close their doors. Many of those that stay open will have gone through bankruptcy. Part of the reason for the high bankruptcy rate is that bankruptcy will become an important competitive tool for lowering business costs. Once many competitors do it, a firm may have no choice but to file for bankruptcy to remain competitive, too. We expect to see this kind of competitive bankruptcy to begin happening long before the dollar and government debt bubbles burst in Phase II, the Aftershock.

Small businesses will be hit disproportionately hard and new small business opportunities will be quite limited. Entrepreneurship will be extremely difficult due to a lack of demand for goods and services, especially new goods and services. The lack of small businesses will greatly change the face of the local business community.

Of course, the financial industry, which will have been badly battered prior to the dollar bubble pop, will be hit hard by high interest rates, high inflation rates, and the lack of any government support or guarantees. Needless to say, if the government can't pay its own debts, it can hardly guarantee the debts of anyone else. Nearly all banks and insurance companies will be insolvent in such a situation.

This is another striking difference between the post-dollar-bubble world and the Great Depression. Although many banks failed during the Depression, many banks survived as did major insurance companies and stock brokerage firms. Even in Phase I, we have already seen many financial institutions that survived the Depression unable to survive the first popping of the bubbles. When the biggest bubble pops—the dollar bubble—the survival rate will be exceptionally low.

Banks will still be able to process transactions, but their ability to make anything more than basic inventory loans (and similar asset-based loans) will be severely limited. Even inventory loans will be difficult to come by. Whole life insurance companies will be insolvent but term life insurance will be available as will property and casualty insurance for basic needs. Of course, the value of most real property will greatly decrease so not as much casualty insurance will be needed.

Longer Term Impacts of the Dollar Bubble Collapse—Economy Gets a Bit Chaotic for a While

The high unemployment and high bankruptcy rates of the post-dollar-bubble economy, combined with a greatly pared down government will, for a while, create an unusual set of economic conditions. For example, in such a chaotic economic situation, there will be little incentive for people to pay their mortgages or other debts. Many of their creditors will be insolvent and there will be no significant market for selling the properties. Much of the management of these debts will be handed over to an overwhelmed government with little interest in foreclosure. Even if it did foreclose, who would it possibly sell the properties to? And there will be no serious financing available for buyers at that point, anyway. Certainly, the government won't be able to provide financing.

A good decision for many people will be to simply stop paying their debts. Even rent may not be worth paying as evictions could become increasingly politically difficult for elected sheriffs to carry out. Plus, it will be difficult for landlords to find good tenants to replace the bad ones. Debt repayment will become a bit lawless during this period.

Businesses will follow a similar path as individuals. They will stop paying mortgages and other debts and even limit the rent they pay to what is needed to fund basic utilities and maintenance. They won't be making much money and if they have to pay rent above basic costs, in many cases, they will go under—something the landlord doesn't want to see either since there are no good tenants to replace them.

As a result of all this, squatters will be increasingly common for businesses, and even more common for individuals since it will be politically difficult, and of little economic advantage, to throw tenants out. Local governments will have very tight budgets and won't have the resources to spend on throwing people (and voters) out of their homes so that the landlord can have a vacant property with no prospects of rental. This situation will not last forever, but in the meantime, people will take advantage of it.

Eventually, big reforms will be made to resolve these and other problems (see Appendix B), but that is still a ways off.

No New "New Deal"

While some people now say they are worried about drifting toward socialism or "sharing the wealth," in fact there won't be much wealth to share. Instead of the rich funding the poor, the middle class will shoulder most of that burden by paying very high taxes to fund nearly all of the enormous number of people on welfare. Instead of shared wealth we will have "shared poverty."

With the government essentially in default on its loans, it will have no way to raise money for its welfare programs, other than through taxes. And since there will be so few wealthy people left to tax, that leaves only the middle class and the much smaller upper-middle class to carry the load. Still, working and paying very high taxes, averaging 50 percent of total income, will be better than not working at all.

Like the Great Fire of London

In 1666, 90 percent of London burned. There are similarities between that massive fire, and today's economy—how it got to where it is today, and where it is going. The buildings in London at that time had serious problems with how they were constructed. Fire prevention had not been a priority, and building codes were non-existent or not enforced. Like the rising bubble economy, there was little in place to impede a disaster.

When the fire first started, only minimal and ineffectual efforts were made at early fire-fighting. People didn't think it would become that much of a problem (think home price declines in 2006 and 2007). Later, the growing blaze began to consume more and more of London (think financial crisis in the 2008). Finally, substantially more effort was made to try to contain the growing blaze (think Obama in 2009). But, at this later stage, the London fire proved impossible to put out, and the city all but burnt to the ground (think the dollar bubble collapse). Finally, after many years, London was rebuilt, better and safer than ever before, with all the changes necessary to keep it safe from having such a devastating fire again.

We, too, will rebuild an economy better and safer than ever before.

Foreign Investors Will Slowly Come Back to the United States

With the dollar so low, investments in U.S. companies and real estate will eventually become attractively priced. In this environment, foreigners will once again become an attractive source of capital for the United States—only at much lower levels. The bad economy will scare away most foreign investors. Still, some will be drawn in by the extremely low prices.

However, unlike today, purchases of U.S. companies will not necessarily be made via the stock market, but more as direct purchases of companies out of liquidation and further direct investments to repair and improve those companies. The United States will need to work hard to lure foreign investors. The key will be attractive tax incentives for business investments and major reforms in the enforcement of foreclosure and eviction for real estate investments, and bankruptcy. These will be highly unpopular moves by the government and, hence, it could take some time to garner the necessary political support. Of course, without these investments, the United States will continue to suffer so there is a strong incentive to encourage such investments.

The Difficult Economy Will Create Social Unrest, but Not Social Chaos

There won't be a massive level of violence in the streets but there will be dramatically increased stresses on individuals due to the immense economic pressures. Divorces will increase and domestic violence will increase. Expect more killings of family and friends by distraught people who have lost so much economically, but still have plenty of guns handy to express their anger and depression. We are already seeing the early signs of this in late 2008. The number of killings could ultimately increase enough that there is a backlash against guns, similar to the after effects of the Long Island Railroad killings, but much stronger. So, there won't be a lot of violence in the streets against the government, but plenty of violence at home and in the workplace.

But that doesn't mean that people will be happy with government. Quite the opposite. Enormous anger at government will break down some partisan barriers. For a while, there won't be a partisan direction so much as just enormous anger at government and government officials. Government officials will likely react by becoming more reclusive and less interactive with their constituents. No matter what they do, people won't like it. And people won't like their elected officials either, who will be voted in and out of office fairly quickly. It will be a very uncomfortable time for elected officials.

Eventually, a new political direction will evolve that will be quite partisan, just like past changes in the United States, such as the Revolutionary War or the Civil War, only that this one certainly will not require a war. The focus of this change will be rather mild, relative to the violent wars of our past. This time, the focus will be on improving economic productivity and reforming the economy.

We're Gonna Need Bigger Barrels

A common caricature of the Great Depression was a drawing of someone so poor they couldn't afford clothes, so they hung a wooden barrel around themselves instead. It became a symbol of poverty in the Depression. Well, in the post-dollar-bubble collapse we're gonna need some barrels, too, but they will have to be bigger barrels because, unlike the Great Depression, this time everyone will be very well fed. In fact, *too* well fed. After the dollar bubble pops, obesity will be a major problem. It already is now, and it's going to get a lot worse. There will be no lack of money for cheap, high calorie, food. And there will be no lack of stresses that will cause many people to overeat.

Hanging around the house with no job, eating chips, and playing stolen video games, and watching stolen movies is not a recipe for physical fitness. And the stresses from both finances and strained interpersonal relations caused by problematic finances will drive many people to the refrigerator. It doesn't take much stress to push someone to overeat with all the low-cost, high-calorie foods we now have available to us. In the post-dollar-bubble world, there will be high stress and high-calorie food in abundance, and a whopping obesity epidemic to match.

Life Will Be Much Better Than in the Great Depression, but It Will Feel Much Worse

As mentioned earlier, the psychological pain will be much greater than the Great Depression, even though the physical conditions will be much better. This is because expectations were so very high prior to the Bubblequake; much higher than before the Great Depression. Real estate had gone up phenomenally, stock values had gone up phenomenally, and money was easy, not only in the United States but overseas, as well. It seemed like a new billionaire was born every minute.

Long-term blue chip stocks, like Apple, could still rise 3,000 percent in a few years, even after the tech bubble burst. Life was good, very good and, except for a few bumps, it had been very good for decades, since the dollar bubble began in 1982. As many people liked to crow, it was the longest boom in post World War II history.

And people expected it to continue, even if not at quite the same levels as before. They wouldn't need to save for retirement, the booming stock market and the booming real estate market would take care of that. Most people felt they didn't really need to save at all. The economy would never go down much and certainly the job market would always remain relatively strong.

When all that comes to a screeching halt, Americans will be reeling with a tremendous feeling of shock and awe. In addition to the rise in divorces, family fights, killings, and so on, that we mentioned earlier, it will also lead to more clinical depression.

Yes, one of the biggest differences between the Great Depression and the post-dollar-bubble world will be depression! There will be much more of it after the Aftershock. Fortunately for those suffering from depression, the medicines to treat it are much better now and we will see a large increase in the use of anti-depressants. We will also see an increase in the use of that age-old remedy for depression: alcohol. However, many of the alcohol providers, especially the vintners, will also be depressed because the increase will be entirely in low-cost alcohol. High-cost alcohol in every form will see a dramatic decline, forcing many vintners and other high-end alcohol producers into bankruptcy, along with many other high-end goods makers (remember, the discretionary spending bubble will be fully popped at this point).

Former Wall Street titans will be depressed, too. A lot of these guys have no idea what it takes to build wealth without a rising bubble economy. To get a feel for what it was like to make big money prior to the bubble economy, we suggest readers take a look at *From Wall Street to Main Street* (Cambridge University Press, 1999) about how Charlie Merrill and other very impressive individuals created Merrill Lynch. It was quite difficult and risky and required a lot of very good judgment. It was not a *Master of the Universe* story or *Barbarians at the Gate*, as during the rising bubble economy. It took tremendously hard work and it paid off very well. But it certainly was not easy money.

The Friends and Family Plan

There's no question there will be a lot of anger and social unrest in the post-dollar-bubble economy. Many people have asked if there will be a great deal of political unrest and political violence, even possibly a dictator. We do not think there will be much political violence. Political anger will mostly drive voters to the polls and drive politicians out of office more frequently (no more 97-percent re-election rates for Congress), with a great deal of criticism being leveled at all politicians, even those who are doing a good job under the circumstances.

However, we do think there will be a sharp rise in violence against one particular group: friends and family (including co-workers). We are already seeing an up-tick in that today. In March 2009, four separate families were massacred, not by a stranger but by the man of the house. We also expect to see more workplace violence. Friends and family are obvious targets for people who are angry and distressed over finances and work, because they are convenient and don't take precautions against being shot, unlike the politicians who will take precautions. So, although an armed uprising is highly unlikely, a great deal of violence against friends and family is almost certain.

The only silver lining to this dreadful situation may be that, after a while, people will become unhappy enough with the high levels of violence that they consider ways of reducing it that were previously unthinkable in the United States, such as gun control. Given the lack of guns in Europe and Japan, we would not expect to see such a large amount of lethal violence against friends and family there, although it may increase somewhat over today's levels. The anger will be there, like the United States, but the tools to convert that anger into quick and easy killings are not.

The Good News: Increased Productivity in our Service Sector (Health Care, Education, Government Services) Will Make the United States Far Wealthier than Before

The good news is that we can, and ultimately will, transform the economy by increasing real productivity. This massive potential increase in productivity can bring us out of the Bubblequake as fast as we will make the changes to increase productivity. The faster and more fundamental the changes are, the faster the economy and our wealth will grow. But it will require some very basic changes that will take some time to become politically feasible.

The productivity changes we are talking about will have to focus on the service sector of our economy—because it is the largest part of our economy—and not the manufacturing sector, which has so often been the primary focus of productivity improvements. Not that there aren't some productivity improvements to be made in manufacturing, but since it is only 10 to 15 percent of the economy, improvements there won't have the same transformative impact. The primary focus of productivity improvements will have to be on our three largest service areas:

1. Health care
2. Education
3. Government Services, including the military, police, prisons, and so forth

Also important will be other major service sectors, such as transportation services, retailing, financial services, food services, travel services, and utilities. The key to our future growth will be dramatic improvements in these key service areas of the economy. The faster we can make these improvements, the faster we can get out of the post-dollar-bubble mess. It's that simple.

Our future books will provide details on how to improve productivity in each of the key sectors of the economy. We are fully prepared to write such a book right now, but few people would be interested in reading it. Once the dollar and government debt bubbles pop, our audience will likely widen. We'd like these books to stimulate conversation on how to move productivity forward. We would expect these to be "fierce conversations" as Susan Scott put it in her excellent book of the same name. There will be lots of disagreement and resistance to any change but the net result of these national conversations, which could last many years due to their controversial nature, will be greatly improved economic productivity, leading to tremendous non-bubble economic growth.

So that's the silver lining to the post-dollar-bubble world. The collapse of the bubble economy will force us to confront our fundamental problems and make changes to our government and society to improve productivity. We would have to do this in any event to improve the economy even if we didn't have a bubble economy. The only difference is that we wouldn't have gone through all the suffering created by the bubble economy if we had focused instead on improving productivity and not focused on blowing economic bubbles.

On the other hand, those rising bubbles were sure fun while they lasted. However, people in the post-dollar-bubble world will quickly forget all the fun when faced with the grim realities of a post-bubble-economy America. It's important to remember that during this time, the entire world will suffer, more than we will here. They, too, will have to confront the realities of improving their productivity in a post-bubble-economy world. In fact, for many countries, like those in Africa, this will be far more urgent than in the United States. Once productivity improvements are made, life will be much better for everyone, indeed.

For more information on the post-dollar-bubble world of the mega depression, go to www.aftershock.economy.com/chapter10.

Epilogue

SAY GOOD-BYE TO THE AGE OF EXCESS

It's sad to see it all go. It was the Party of the Century and not just in the United States, but around the world as well. The Age of Excess was like no other time in U.S. history and there will never be a time like it again because we do learn from our mistakes, even if painfully so. And how quickly we will forget the good times and how good they were when faced with the "shock and awe" of the Aftershock that will end the Age of Excess. So, this epilogue is dedicated to reminding us how good the Age of Excess really was.

But where do we begin? There was so much excess. First, there were all the corporate executives and investment bankers who made hundreds of millions of dollars making terrible business mistakes that destroyed the value of their companies. And better yet, the government bailed out their companies while the executives kept all the money they made from making the decisions that destroyed their companies, and they got some nice bonuses to boot. And why not? The government could always borrow so much money, it really didn't matter. Why hold anyone accountable when we're all in this party together, right?

And let's not forget all the great Internet companies whose values kept going up, up, up even though their revenues and profits did not. We knew they were worth a lot of money because sooner or later some other company was bound to buy them at massively overvalued prices. And why should the acquiring company worry about overvaluation? Their stock never suffered from their bad decisions; it just kept going up, up, up along with the rest of the stock market, despite terrible management.

That same party thinking worked wonders for private equity firms, the true Masters of the Universe. Their strategy was simple:

always pay a higher price to buy a company than anyone else and then just let the ever-rising stock market make you billions when you sold it later. Some private equity firms made billions just by taking themselves public, because everyone on Wall Street knew that their strategy of buying companies at very high prices was foolproof.

Even folks on Main Street got to play at the party, too. Lots of credit cards and home equity lines of credit made everyday life very festive, indeed. We got to enjoy lots of big screen TVs, the latest computers, and all sorts of new gadgets and gizmos at the party. And with retirement stock market accounts rising so rapidly, why not put everything in stocks, including our future social security? Remember that one?

Even if stocks didn't go up every year, you could always count on your home as a great investment. No matter how much the price went up, we just knew it would never, ever go back down very much. Market cycles only worked in the up direction, right? Even if your income didn't rise very much, the value of your house could easily double in a few years. We didn't entirely know why, but something really good must have been happening somewhere. Whatever it was, we didn't care. It was all part of the joy of the Age of Excess. In the Age of Excess, you didn't have to think too much about why things were so good, they just were.

Even better, in the Age of Excess, good jobs never, ever disappeared. If you lost one, you could always just hop onto another— like catching the next train leaving the station. And plenty of jobs meant you didn't have to waste perfectly good money by putting it in a savings account. Let those poor Chinese peasants who made all the stuff we bought do all the saving. Besides, saving money was downright un-American. If you saved, you were hurting the economy. And look what happened when we finally stopped buying so much and started saving a little in late 2008—the economy really started to tank. If we had just kept spending like we did before, we'd still be doing just fine.

Speaking of which, don't forget that in the Age of Excess, patriotism means doing your part to help in a war. That certainly doesn't mean tax increases—in World War II, tax rates were as high as 75 percent. No, it actually means you need your taxes decreased for all of your suffering from high taxes. It also doesn't mean a draft or volunteering for the war. In World War II, over half of Congress volunteered for the war.

In World War I, Charlie Merrill, the founder of Merrill Lynch, was so interested in volunteering for the war that he drove down from New York to Fort Myers in Washington to speed up his enlistment process. In the Iraq War, there were so many Titans of Wall Street volunteering that they had to set up a separate sign-up window at the Pentagon! (Not really.)

Of course, patriotism also doesn't mean cutting your consumption to help out the boys fighting the war. No, what it means to be a patriot in the Age of Excess is to put those "We Support Our Troops" stickers on your car. In fact, to be more patriotic, you should buy more cars to put more stickers on, especially if those cars are one of those hot new BMWs or Mercedes. Wow, now that's real support. To show how much we supported our troops, by 2008 we had purchased 35 million more cars than we had registered drivers. That's a lot of cars to put stickers on! If only we had done that in World War II, imagine the difference it would have made. But, that wasn't war in the Age of Excess where war has no cost.

And, finally, who could forget that in the Age of Excess, the government has no limit on how much it can borrow. If we hit a rough patch in the economy, we just convert to the bailout economy. Made a business mistake or a personal financial mistake? No problem; the government will just borrow money to bail you out. Bailouts are easy and the government wouldn't think of raising taxes to do bailouts when it can so easily borrow so much money at such low interest rates. That's just part of being the U.S. government in the Age of Excess. No money, no worry; the government can just borrow what it takes to tide us over. Is there any limit to what the government can borrow? Well, why worry about it? Something good must be happening to let the government borrow so much money. And that's after it has already borrowed $10 trillion and hasn't been able to pay back a penny of that debt. It's almost magical. But whatever it was, in the Age of Excess, you didn't have to think too much about why things were so good—they just were.

Too bad it had to end.

To participate in discussions on the issues brought up in this book, go to our blog site, www.aftershockeconomy.com/blogs or subscribe to our newsletter at www.aftershockeconomy.com/newsletter.

Appendix A

FORCES DRIVING THE COLLAPSE
OF THE BUBBLES

As discussed throughout the book, there are multiple forces that have led to the collapse of the various bubbles. In this appendix, we will outline those forces as they pertain to the following bubbles:

1. Real Estate
2. Stock Market
3. Private Debt
4. Discretionary Spending

Forces Driving the Collapse of the Real Estate Bubble

The discussion below is primarily about the first phase of the housing bubble pop (during the Bubblequake), which is where we are currently. The second phase of the housing bubble pop will occur when the dollar bubble pops (during the Aftershock). At that point, the main driving forces on the real estate market will be the very high interest rates and the truly terrible economy, which will devastate housing prices. Those two forces combined will have a much larger impact on the housing market than all of the forces in Phase I combined. But, before we get to Phase II, we have to go through Phase I. So, the forces affecting the housing market in Phase I follow:

Driving Force 1: Rising or Declining Home Prices Drive Home Prices.   The first and most important driver is the most obvious, but often the least talked about. Home prices themselves are one of the biggest drivers of home prices. People like to buy homes if home prices are going up. They don't like to buy them if they are going down. It's obvious but it is probably the biggest single factor pushing home prices down now. Of course, many people are buying homes now because they don't feel prices will keep falling much longer. However, if many of these people who are buying homes now keep losing money, there will be fewer people to follow. And that is already starting to happen. According to the *Washington Post*, in the Washington DC area, 62 percent of home sellers in Q1 2009 accepted less than they paid for their homes. That number will only increase in the future, thus scaring off buyers who thought the home price decline was ending soon.

Homes are an unusual good. If prices rise, people want to buy more—even forming lines to get the next hot new condo or house on the market or creating bidding wars. But, when the price is falling people lose interest in buying—no more lines at the new condo developments, no more bidding wars. That's because a home is both a good and an investment. Although people buy it as a good that they use, they are also sensitive to the investment issues because they have to be—it is also an investment.

As a side note on how fast people change, Washington, DC used to have lines at many of its new condo developments in 2004 and 2005. Our office in Reston is surrounded by new condo developments. Now, the supply of new condos in the DC area would last more than 13 years at the current sales rate. That's a breathtaking change, particularly after many condos have been taken off the market and turned into rental units.

Driving Force 2: Learning the Down Side of the Power of Leverage.   This fear of buying a home when prices are falling is greatly increased due to the down side of leverage. Investors, especially real estate investors, know the power of leverage to boost their profitability. During the boom a buyer could put down 5 percent in cash and see their cash investment increase 200 percent in value in a year if their home value went up just 10 percent.

The down side is equally true. If someone puts down 5 percent, they could see their entire cash investment wiped out in far less than a year with home prices falling an average of 14 percent. In places like Miami, where home prices have fallen almost 30 percent in a year, their entire cash investment would be gone in *two months*. For most people, that's a big problem. And, as more banks require higher down payments of 10 percent or more, people have even more cash at risk. That makes them even more reluctant to buy.

So, the prospect of quickly losing 100 percent of your cash investment in a house in less than a year in most major cities will continue to be a big drag on the home market and greatly compounds the problem of falling home prices.

Driving Force 3: Collapse and Death of the "Innovative" Mortgage Business.   Innovative mortgages were the key to driving up prices in the housing bubble. Obviously the lack of those mortgages will be a key force driving prices down. As the most "innovative" mortgage companies go bankrupt and the Fed cracks down on risky lending practices, the key force that drove prices up will be gone.

People seem to think that by getting rid of these risky mortgages we are helping the situation. We're not. We're hurting prices badly by doing so. I'm not saying we should keep them. It was never a sustainable business model. It flew in the face of any real financial analysis or economic analysis. But, to say that the removal of these risky and "innovative" practices will not dramatically hurt home prices equally flies in the face of any real financial or economic analysis. It is critical.

The only reason we have put this as third in our priority of driving forces is that much of the closure of this industry has already happened. Alt-A loans are very hard to find. Lenders are definitely looking to verify income. Option ARMs aren't offered any more. Introductory-rate adjustable mortgages are very hard to find. No-money-down mortgages have vanished. Low-money-down mortgages (5 percent or less) are hard to get, except through the FHA.

But even though much of the industry has closed, the lack of these mortgages puts continuing pressure on housing prices for several years to come. One could argue that to fully adjust for this issue alone, housing prices should return to the levels they were at in 2001, before they helped create skyrocketing housing prices. Although we wouldn't make the argument that the entire bubble in home prices since 2001 would go away due to this factor, clearly it will cause enormous downward pressure on home prices that will eventually push them much closer to the prices they were at in 2001.

At a presentation co-author Robert Wiedemer made on America's Bubble Economy, he was asked how the government could help the housing market since he said in the summer of 2008 that the government's foreclosure bailout program wasn't going to do very much. Borrowing a page from the recent "mortgage innovators" he suggested the Triple Zero plan. In this plan, the government would offer mortgages at Zero percent interest, Zero money down with Zero credit check. Now that would bring housing prices back up!

Bob wasn't kidding. It really would work—in the short term. But it's a little too easy for people to see the long-term fundamental problems in the plan for it to gain popular support. Too bad more people didn't see the same problems in the innovative mortgages that were so important to creating the housing bubble.

Driving Force 4: Job Loss and Growing Perceived Job Insecurity. Perhaps the biggest new force putting downward pressure on home prices in 2009 is job loss and job insecurity. Traditionally, this is the major reason that home prices are put under pressure—many people have lost their jobs, run out of savings and can't pay their mortgage payment due to a bad economy. The fact that we were facing a foreclosure crisis and massive housing price declines in a good economy in the first half of 2008, even when we had little job loss tells you how vulnerable home prices were (and are) to a major decline.

The slowing economy has already caused job growth to stop and significant job loss to begin. But there has still been a lot of positive economic momentum from the past. For example, commercial construction hit an all-time high in July 2008, offsetting much of the decline in housing construction. Local and state governments went on a hiring spree in 2007 and the first half of 2008. That growth is coming to a screeching halt with local and state budgets being hammered by lower tax receipts.

In addition, commercial construction is likely to decline with the credit squeeze and lack of demand for new construction. The American Institute of Architects Architectural Billings Index (ABI) turned highly negative in late 2008, foreshadowing much less commercial construction in the future because billings for architects were declining.

Other areas of the economy will feel continued pressure—areas such as real estate, financial services, retailing, restaurants, hotels, entertainment, and airlines. Even the medical business is starting to slow as people buy fewer drugs and hospitals postpone large capital purchases. More importantly, with less home construction there will be fewer new hospitals and professional buildings built in the suburbs to serve those clients. The same goes for restaurants, retail, entertainment, new schools, and day care. New home construction drives a lot of secondary construction in those areas.

Some industries will continue to take body blows, such as the auto industry and home building industry. Both will be pounded severely in 2009 and 2010 as interest in homebuying continues to decline and interest in buying cars, especially the big trucks and SUVs that American car companies make, will decline even from its current low levels.

All of this will contribute to noticeable job loss in 2009 and 2010, unlike 2008 where it was more restricted to some industries like home construction and autos. More importantly, perception of job insecurity will increase dramatically. This is a much wider phenomenon than job loss and, hence, much more important. Even in a major recession, such as 1981, when unemployment rose to almost 11 percent, relatively few people lost their jobs. However, a very large percentage, 30 to 40 percent, felt some level of perceived (rightly or wrongly) job insecurity. They were worried they might lose their jobs and it affected their spending habits, especially on large purchases such as cars and homes. When people have perceived job insecurity, they will postpone those big purchases. They don't give up on them; they just postpone them. But that's all it takes for much more downward pressure to be put on home prices. In addition, that postponement of major purchases in itself slows the economy down, thus creating a negative feedback loop and putting further downward pressure on home prices.

Driving Force 5: Foreclosures. Why haven't we listed foreclosures higher in priority? It sure is talked about a lot. Foreclosures are talked about because they are the most brutal and politically sensitive part of the housing crisis. Nothing is worse than watching someone being forcibly thrown out of their home. It is clearly something that attracts government attention and a lot of media attention. And it happened at a stunning rate in 2008 that continues into 2009, despite efforts by the federal government to limit or halt foreclosures. Moody's Economy.com and the FDIC estimate that the number of foreclosures in 2009 will hit 1.6 million, up from less than 400,000 in 2006. And that number could go much higher as the number of mortgages that are delinquent or in the process of foreclosure has soared from just over 5 percent in 2007 to 13 percent in Q1 2009 according to the Mortgage Bankers Association.

However, foreclosures themselves are not as important as the previous forces in pushing down home prices. Instead, it is part of a lengthy legal process that keeps homes off the market. Only once that home is put on the market does it put downward pressure on home prices by adding to the inventory of unoccupied homes for sale.

However, it is important to remember than only about one-third of homes put into foreclosure actually end up in the lenders' hands. It will be brought home to you if you attend a foreclosure. They are often held on the steps of the county courthouse. Often, very few of the homes will be bought by the many bidders attending the auction. The lenders will buy them. Eventually the lenders will put them on the market, but it might take time and they might price them too high to move for a while. That's one reason we have such a backlog of unoccupied homes for sale—banks are still pricing the homes too high. Eventually, the banks will have to lower the price, but that doesn't help their profits because it forces a greater markdown on the loans than they may have already taken.

The other two-thirds of the homes that don't get taken back by the lenders represent a real time bomb for home prices. The reason they aren't taken back is that some arrangement has been made to postpone foreclosure—either the bank agrees to some change in the mortgage that allows the homeowner to keep the home or the homeowner comes up with some extra money to keep it from being taken by the bank. However, even in good times, about half of those homes that avoid foreclosure the first time, fall back into foreclosure. With falling home equity levels and a worsening economy, the percentage of homes falling back into foreclosure and into the lenders' hands is likely to stay high and get higher. As those homes go back into foreclosure and go back on the market, that will put further downward pressure on home prices.

How Much Will Government Intervention to Prevent Foreclosures Stop the Housing Price Collapse?   Well, not that much. Not only was the bill passed by Congress and the Bush administration in the summer of 2008 inadequate, but further attempts by the Obama administration in early 2009 will also be inadequate, partly because so many of the homes being foreclosed on have no equity value. When the homes have no equity value, the lender can't refinance the loan because there is no collateral for the loan. The government will likely make some efforts to help in this area, but they will probably be inadequate. Job losses will further compound the foreclosure problem because people can't pay any reasonable mortgage payment if they don't have a job. The government will have a hard time dealing with that problem.

The most important problem is that these anti-foreclosure measures don't attack the heart of the problem—falling home equity. The biggest single cause of foreclosure is falling home equity levels. As home equity levels fall to zero or become negative, people have much less interest in maintaining their home payments. When the home equity level gets highly negative, such as 20 percent or more, many homeowners figure they will never pay it off and quit. As mentioned in Chapter 2, over 20 percent of home mortgages now have no equity. In some parts of the country, it is not that hard to just stop paying your mortgage and send the keys to the lender.

It would be hard for Congress to pass a law that would raise home equity levels. It is a massive and very expensive problem. Anything short of the Triple Zero plan mentioned earlier would not be adequate.

When equity levels become negative it is very hard for lenders to work out a deal to avoid foreclosure. There is no equity basis for a new loan of the size needed to pay off the old loan. The problem is not that the person has temporarily lost his job and he just needs a break. The problem is a permanent loss of value in the asset.

If banks made it easy to just write off 20 to 30 percent of your mortgage, many people would take them up on that offer. Why not do it if the bank is encouraging it? But the banks just can't afford to do that, especially in a rapidly declining market. The government can try to subsidize the banks, and it is doing that to some extent, but it is adding to the bigger problem of the dollar bubble.

In addition, for homebuyers whose loans have been sold into a mortgage-backed security, the trustee managing that security is often limited by the legal restrictions on the mortgage-backed security in the number of loans the trustee can modify. That number is usually pretty low—less than 5 percent. It makes sense though, because the investors bought the loans thinking they were AAA safe and were going to get 100 percent of their principal back. But this makes it difficult to modify loans to avoid foreclosure in such circumstances. And during the boom, a lot of mortgages were sold into mortgage-backed securities.

The bottom line is that there are a lot of reasons that home prices are declining, and foreclosures are one of them. But government aid to help prevent foreclosures will do little to keep prices from declining because the aid is small relative to the need, and there are so many other factors pushing home prices down.

Driving Force 6: Higher Down Payments are an Inevitability in a Declining Home Market. Even with the bailout, Freddie Mac and Fannie Mae will require increasingly higher down payments on the loans they buy, given declining home prices. To be prudent, they must. In fact, they are already doing it. So if private mortgage insurance goes under, Fannie and Freddie will likely have to raise minimum down payments even higher to make up for that. Private mortgage insurance is one of the main reasons Fannie and Freddie can keep buying loans with only a 10 percent down payment. The private mortgage insurance company is taking the entire risk up to 20 percent.

So, just by Fannie's and Freddie's actions alone, down payments will rise. This is a huge problem for the housing industry. As any mortgage broker knows, big down payments are a real downer for homebuyers. Especially when home prices are falling, buyers will feel they are taking even more risk by having to put up a big down payment.

The FHA is trying to alleviate some of this problem by offering loans with only a 3 percent down payment required. Of course, there is massive risk in doing this. There are a number of restrictions on its loans, including the need for income verification and a limit on how large of a loan it can cover. These restrictions vary depending on the location of the home.

Even with the limitations, the FHA now handles almost 20 percent of the mortgage market, up from less than 5 percent a few years ago. Of course, with such low down payments the FHA will eventually be experiencing large losses on their loans. With only

3 percent down, loans in many markets will be underwater in months. Already, several dozen FHA loans are now defaulting every week before they have even made ONE mortgage payment. How can the FHA feel comfortable in taking a 3 percent down payment when house prices are falling nationwide by 14 percent a year and in some areas by more than 25 percent a year? Ultimately, a 3 percent loan program will not be viable and may be scaled back. Of course that is part of the larger question of how much in losses the government is going to be willing and able to take.

However, when the dollar bubble pops, the government will no longer be able to refinance its debt or back FHA loans, and they will go into default. The repercussions of such a default on home prices will be devastating.

But, even if the government keeps subsidizing losses for the FHA, down payments will likely be increasing dramatically over the next couple of years for all other loans. This will put huge downward pressure on home prices.

Buyer and Seller Panic—The Final Chapter in Phase I's Housing Crisis

The final chapter on how the whole housing price collapse plays out will be buyer and seller panic. At some point, all of these forces that are pushing down home prices will eventually change people's beliefs. That means, at some point, a lot of sellers won't hold their homes off the market in hopes of higher prices. They've seen the enormous amount of money they have already lost and are becoming quite concerned they will lose even more if they don't sell and sell quickly at whatever price they can get.

Unfortunately, rather than solving the problem, this exacerbates the problem because the falling prices that result will eventually start to panic buyers even though it may help move more homes in the short term. These buyers, who were already a little nervous about buying homes due to past housing declines, now become really nervous. You'll hear, "Honey, why don't we just wait out the storm and see what happens? I know Mary and Frank took a real hit on the home they bought."

They will begin taking our advice, which is to not buy a home until prices rebound. Why try to buy a home when it is falling in price? How much are you really going to save by catching it as it is falling rather than waiting until it has started to recover? Eventually people realize they will lose nothing by waiting and will only save money. That is when buyer panic sets in. Buyers become very reluctant to buy and prices start to plummet. It is a self-fulfilling prophecy.

Aren't There Any Forces Pushing Home Prices Up?   Well yes, and we have just listed many of them—low job loss, the availability of private mortgage insurance, and so on. But these forces keeping prices up will soon change and become downward forces.

We have said before, the most important force keeping home prices up now is people's belief that prices will go up. Once that belief changes, home prices will decline quite rapidly. Currently, it is an enormous force keeping home prices up, both for buyers and sellers.

Whenever someone tells you that they're sure home prices will go up again, ask them why? Can they give you several solid reasons that won't wither under the fire of good economic and financial cross examination?

The Housing Price Collapse Has Bottomed Out!   This was a refrain you heard almost monthly during the early stages of the collapse in 2006 and even into 2007. Every month an analyst or economist would point to an uptick in some statistic and announce that the housing crisis was over—it had reached bottom. Of course, this was most common among analysts or economists closely related to real estate or home construction, but it was pretty common outside of those fields as well.

In 2008, after these analysts had missed the mark so many times and it was quite obvious that the housing market was nowhere near turning around, the mantra changed.

The new mantra, especially after any uptick in housing statistics (although there weren't many by then), was that the housing market *will* bottom out in—fill in the blank—6 months, 12 months, the end of the year, the end of next year.

You would think that after being proved wrong so many times before, that these analysts and economists would have no credibility left at all. But, amazingly enough, they did. It makes sense because they are telling people what they want to hear. So, the last thing anybody wants to do is take away credibility from people telling you what you want to hear. Instead, the focus by many is still to try to take away credibility from people who are not telling you what you want to hear, even if they are right!

It's a good lesson to remember as you watch others analyze the housing market in 2009 and 2010.

When the Prices of Used Homes Fall, New Home Prices Fall, and so Will Construction.   The same factors affecting used home prices will affect new home prices. However, it has a much bigger impact on the economy because people don't buy as many new homes. That forces down home construction, which is a huge driver of the U.S. economy not only because of the purchase of the home, but also because of all the related purchases of furniture, appliances and other home-related goods and services. The more home prices keep going down, the fewer new homes will be sold, thus putting further pressure on the economy and people's interest in and ability to buy new homes.

The Myth That People Have to Buy Homes.   One of the key aspects to remember when looking at home purchases is that anyone who has the credit and income history to qualify for a mortgage, especially today, is probably already pretty well housed. They aren't giving mortgages to homeless people—at least not anymore (ha-ha!). People who qualify for a mortgage don't have to buy a home; they would like to buy a home to upgrade their standard of living and to build up some home equity. Hence, the decision to purchase a new home is much more discretionary than is sometimes indicated in many economic reports.

Forces Driving the Collapse of the Stock Market Bubble

Following are the driving forces behind the collapse of the stock market bubble.

Driving Force 1: Mergers and Acquisitions Got Hit

Although the massive wave of mergers and acquisitions (M&A) that was driven by the private equity bubble was a key element of the big upturn in the stock market from 2006 to 2007, M&A by corporations had also been growing rapidly. In fact, according to Mergerstat, the value of U.S. M&A activity grew from $823 billion in 2004 to a peak of nearly $1.5 trillion in 2006, and $1.3 trillion in 2007 before falling back to $823 billion in 2008.

But, once the debt-fueled private equity bubble began to get hit, the resulting declining stock market and tighter credit put the brakes on corporate M&A. Although it was more resilient than private equity-driven M&A, corporations lost their appetite for acquisitions, especially after the big drop in the market in late 2008. In fact, due to that big drop in the market, most of the acquisitions made during the M&A frenzy of 2006 and 2007 have lost a significant part of their value, often forcing large write downs of goodwill in 2008 and 2009. The tremendous drop in M&A greatly dampened the stock market frenzy that had driven it up so substantially in the 2006 to 2007 period. Showing no signs of returning any time soon in 2009 or 2010, the lack of a large number of high-priced M&A deals will keep a lid on growth in the stock market.

Driving Force 2: Stock Buybacks Got Hit

Stock buybacks were all the rage in 2006 and 2007. Almost every day another corporation was announcing a major stock buyback program as a way to boost their stock price. Some of it was fueled by the large amount of cash many corporations had and some of it was fueled by debt. Either way, it meant a lot of upward pressure on the stock market. In fact, according to Standard & Poor's, share buybacks by the S&P 500 soared from just under $50 billion in Q3 2004 to over $160 billion at its peak in Q3 2007. Now that upward pressure has almost vanished as buybacks have gone the way of the M&A frenzy.

In fact, some of the same corporations that were buying stock are actually trying to sell stock to boost their capital position and offset rapidly growing debt. Of course, these offerings are almost always at a much lower price than what they paid to buy their stock a couple of years ago, showing how foolish it was to do the stock buybacks in the first place.

Driving Force 3: Home Construction (and Related Services) Gets Hit Even Harder

Home construction and related services (mostly financial) and related purchases (appliances, furniture, etc.) comprise one of the biggest industries in the United States, producing over $600 billion in construction revenues alone at its peak in 2006, according to the U.S. Census Bureau. With related services and spending, the total would rise to nearly $1 trillion.

However, as everyone knows, home construction has been hit hard with new housing starts (single-family and multi-family units) falling from 2.15 million at its peak in 2005 to an annual rate of 494,000 in April 2009, according to the U.S. Census Bureau. Even more important, it will be hit even harder since the annualized sales rate of single family homes by the end of 2009 is likely to go below 250,000 units and below 150,000 units by the end of 2010 (after adjusting for cancellations of sales). The number of housing starts will have to follow sales down.

Even though sales are down, homebuilders have been building more homes than they are selling partly because of past momentum and partly because they need to sell the expensive land they bought. If they can't sell that land, they risk bankruptcy. Of course, if they build homes on the land and can't sell the homes, they will certainly go bankrupt. It's a situation of damned if you do and damned if you don't. Hence, expect all the major publicly traded home construction companies to go bankrupt in the next few years.

The pressure on the economy and ultimately the stock market from such a massive decline (over 70 percent) in the revenues of such an important part of the economy is enormous. It's also not just the construction jobs that are lost, but the materials supplier jobs as well. Everything from air conditioners, to kitchen equipment, to concrete, to paint, to drywall is affected. All of those supplies have to be manufactured and much of it is manufactured in the United States. And, don't forget, two-thirds of the cost of a home is in the financing, so a lot of real estate related financial services jobs will also get hit hard. The collapse of the housing construction industry has already put pressure on the stock market, but it will continue to put downward pressure on the market in 2009 and 2010.

Driving Force 4: Consumer Spending

Consumer Spending, makes up 70 percent of the economy. It gets hit due to:

A. Loss of home equity
B. Loss of stock value

Driving Force 4A: Loss of Home Equity.   George Will wrote a column for *Newsweek* back when oil prices were first heading up in 2005. A number of people in the media commented on how quiet everyone was about increases in the price of gasoline. And they were quiet. But George Will said simply that when America had just seen an increase in its home equity value of $2.6 trillion, it was hard to worry about an increase in oil prices that amounted only to $100 billion. I think it was an excellent observation.

But now I would make a similar observation, just in reverse. Total extraction of home equity through sales, refinancing, and home equity loans has fallen by more than 50 percent from its peak in 2005 of $1 trillion. That has had a tremendously chilling effect on America's consumption psyche, but that doesn't mean it translates directly into less consumer spending immediately. The effects could be delayed. For one thing, not all home equity extraction goes into consumption; much of it was put back into homes. People might be selling their homes in California for retirement homes elsewhere. People might be selling their first homes to buy a much bigger second home, and so on.

Part of what made the housing boom possible was the boom itself. By creating so much home equity, it gave people the necessary down payment to buy bigger homes. Or it helped to boom retirement housing. Or it gave people more confidence in putting down large down payments or buying more expensive homes than they would have otherwise.

But there is no question that at least a part, if not a good part, of home equity extraction went into consumption.

In the case of home equity loans (a large part of home equity extraction), we can be very sure it went for consumption. In fact, one intelligent comment Alan Greenspan made was about home equity loans. It is worth repeating. In the late 1990s when stock prices were going up, there was a lot of talk about how the wealth effect from a booming stock market was helping to boost consumer spending. Greenspan's comment on this was, yes, the wealth effect probably had some impact on increased consumer spending, but that the much greater impact was from home equity loans. His point was that when a person's stock portfolio goes up in value, they don't usually cash it in immediately and go out and buy something. The person might feel a little more flush and spend a bit more, but the stock gain is primarily kept in stock. However, when a person gets a home equity loan, that person is almost certain to spend 100 percent of that money on consumption, and usually pretty quickly.

Home equity loans have a big impact on consumer spending. They had a big impact during the 1990s when house prices were rising modestly and they were having a much bigger impact when house prices have risen very rapidly. A wonderful statistic worth repeating that demonstrates this point is that 30 percent of the cars and trucks bought in California during 2007 were bought with home equity loans. Wow.

As some have said, home equity loans turned people's homes into a giant ATM. So true. However, home equity lines of credit are no longer increasing and many are being reduced as home prices fall. Unused remaining equity lines are being eliminated in areas where home prices are falling dramatically, such as California and Florida, which felt so much of the home equity spending boom.

Banks are also reducing the amount of the home's appraised value that people borrow on. Where at one time the banks would happily loan up to 100 percent of the home's value, that number has dropped precipitously during the housing crash to 95 percent to 90 percent to 85 percent and now at many banks, the most they will lend is 80 percent of the appraised value. All of this decrease in home equity lines of credit spells big problems down the road for consumer discretionary spending. Some effects are already starting to show up.

Driving Force 4B: Loss of Stock Value.   Just as declining wealth from home equity has a negative effect on consumer spending, declining wealth from a declining stock market also has a negative effect on consumer spending. As we mentioned earlier, we subscribe to Alan Greenspan's belief that the wealth effect from the stock market is far less important to consumer spending than home equity, but it still has its effect, especially so now.

By itself, if there were something to offset it, a stock market decline would have limited effect. But, when combined with a massive loss of home equity and a rapidly slowing economy, it creates a small version of a perfect storm in the consumer's mind. Also, the longer the market stays down, the larger the storm that will brew. Plus, the size of the decline contributes to the storm—the bigger the decline, the bigger the storm.

There is one other aspect to this market that people overlook. At 7000 or below, the Dow is back down to its 1996 levels. That means the stock market has gone nowhere in 13 years. That's a long time. That wears on people's consumption psyche as well. If you add in inflation over that time, an investor has actually lost more than 15 percent of the value of their stock. No long-term growth there. And that's assuming they bought the stock in 1996. If they bought it later than 1996, they have lost money PLUS the losses due to inflation. And if they bought when the market was at 14,000 in 2007, they have lost a lot of money.

Also, at the higher end of the consumption scale, many people's wealth is more heavily concentrated in just a few stocks, such as Lehman Brothers or Bear Stearns employees. Some of those stocks have seen dramatic declines of 80 percent or more, hammering many higher income and higher consumption households. It's the unspoken carnage of the recent stock market because it primarily affects higher income people, but these are often high-consumption people who also buy a lot of stock. You can be sure that both consumption and stock purchases will be down for this group.

Combined with all the other problems, the stock market performance of the last year becomes a little disheartening and takes the wind out of some consumers who are happy to spend cash or borrow on their credit cards because they know tomorrow will be a better day. This is another downward force on consumer spending, the economy and the stock market.

Driving Force 5: Business Investment and Spending Will Follow Consumer Spending

It would be surprising that with consumer spending down, we would see business investment increase. It's hard to see businesses gearing up for more sales in this environment. In fact, according to the Bureau of Economic Analysis, private fixed investment, including equipment, software and construction, fell by 38 percent in Q1 2009 versus Q4 2008.

This huge decline in spending is showing up in declining purchases of all kinds of business goods from machine tools to information technology to construction equipment. Even the energy industry, which had seen big increases before, will see huge declines. The number of oil and gas drilling rigs operating in the United States will decline more than 70 percent in 2009 from its peak in late 2008. At its peak, the U.S. had more than twice as many drilling rigs operating on its soil as the rest of the world combined. New ethanol plants are going nowhere and even utilities are delaying plans for new facilities. Exports of business-related capital goods are falling fast given the collapsing economies of Japan, the Middle East, and Western Europe. This is a huge change from 2008 when export growth was strong and was even used by cheerleaders as another reason the economy and the stock market were unlikely to fall very much.

Of course, a key part of business spending and investment that will almost flatline in the next couple of years is commercial construction. That will have a huge effect on the economy. The commercial construction boom in 2008 took up quite a bit of the slack in the economy left by the declining housing market, but, as mentioned earlier, this is about to turn around in a big way.

You can see it easily in Washington, DC. Construction cranes filled the sky in 2008, working on projects everywhere from bridges to a baseball stadium, to hotels, to office buildings, entertainment venues, shopping areas, and of course, lots of condos in the city. In the suburbs there was an enormous amount of the same—retail, restaurants, condos, hotels, offices, schools, churches, roads, and so on.

By the end of 2009 most of those cranes will be gone and they won't be replaced. Both in the city and in the suburbs commercial construction is about to come to a screeching halt. Lack of financing and lack of demand is killing new commercial projects. Some government construction will continue—roads, schools, office buildings, and so on, but local and state governments are now under significant budget pressure due to the housing price collapse. Unlike the federal government, the local governments can't borrow infinite amounts of money at low interest rates.

The same is true across America—we are overbuilt in offices, condos, retail, hotels, and restaurants. You name it and we're overbuilt. Demand is declining and supply has been increasing dramatically. For that reason, many developers won't build and those who do want to build are having trouble getting financing, and for very good reason. Their projects will likely lose money and the lenders are much more wary.

As a side note, the commercial mortgage-backed security market has also collapsed. It is little talked about, but it is similar in many ways to the residential mortgage backed securities market.

It is not as big, but it is still big—over $200 billion in 2007 according to Dealogic. It was also powering a lot of the buying and selling activity in commercial real estate recently. But it has changed bigtime. The market fell apart in 2008, and in 2009 we may barely sell $10 billion in commercial mortgage-backed securities. This has affected commercial real estate dramatically. In Washington, DC, commercial real estate transactions have fallen by more than half. The financing just isn't there for these transactions.

This huge downturn in commercial construction will eliminate all the new jobs created when these new hotels, retail stores, and restaurants open.

Will Sovereign Wealth Funds Drive Up the Stock Market?

Not too long ago this would have been a serious question. Now it's laughable, and more importantly almost completely forgotten. Remember de-coupling? The idea was that the Chinese economy was not driven by the U.S. economy and therefore could help buffer the U.S. recession. Now that is laughable and also completely forgotten.

The reason we mention these issues is to show how desperate and creative stock analysts and economists are to cheerlead the stock market and the economy. They didn't really believe these ideas. That's why they are completely forgotten so quickly. They were just more attempts to cheerlead the market.

The key point is that these types of cheerleading arguments won't stop. More are sure to come and you should be on guard against them. This is a typical cheerleading tactic—to take a short trend (a few sovereign wealth funds investing in U.S. banks at discount prices) and expand to a general trend that is a very positive long-term trend for the stock market. People love to believe these ideas so they are very common, but they are never based on good analysis. It's just opportunistic cheerleading by analysts and economists desperate to try to boost the market.

Forces Driving the Collapse of the Private Debt Bubble

Following is a discussion of the forces that led to the collapse of the private debt bubble.

It's hard to imagine how America's bankers and financial institutions could make so many bad loans, but they did. We have listed below some of the key areas that are going to cause huge problems for private debt and ultimately cause the private debt bubble to collapse.

Like the housing bubble and stock bubbles, the private debt bubble will pop in two phases. In Phase I (the Bubblequake) bad loans in each of the categories listed below go bad. In Phase II (the Aftershock) good loans go bad.

Driving Force 1: Innovative Home Mortgages.   There are still plenty of innovative home mortgages, including Alt-A loans and Option ARM loans that were made earlier, that will likely run into severe difficulties in the next couple of years.

When interest rates rise due to increasing perceived risk and higher inflation, many of the regular adjustable-rate loans, which have had little problem so far due to incredibly low interest rates, will rise as well. That will force many of those loans underwater and they will go bad. Finally, prime loans will also start to go bad at a higher rate, with rising unemployment and sinking home equity values.

In looking at the mortgage market, it's important to realize that toxic assets can become more toxic. As home values fall, the value of the assets backing up toxic and non-toxic loans falls as well. That means rising defaults and increasing write-offs. This is not a matter of simply writing off sub-prime loans, it is a dynamic situation where bank losses will be increasing as long as home values continue to fall and more people find themselves with serious negative equity in their homes.

Driving Force 2: Commercial Real Estate Loans.   This will be one of the big new debt problems in 2010. The values of commercial real estate are falling rapidly. It is obvious that with a sharp drop in retailing that the value of shopping centers will fall, but we also have an oversupply of office buildings. More importantly, the price of those office and retail buildings was in a bubble during the last few years due to a huge influx of cash from commercial mortgage-backed securities and big investments from leveraged real estate investment trusts, or REITs (like the largest shopping center operator in the United States, General Growth Properties, which recently went bankrupt)—life insurance companies and other financial entities, such as Lehman Brothers.

Also, some of those loans had short terms to take advantage of lower interest rates, and will be coming due in 2010 and 2011 when many of these loans will be underwater due to their rapidly falling value. In many areas, such as Washington DC, New York, and Los Angeles, commercial property values have fallen by 30 percent or more. In addition to retail space and office buildings, hotels have been hit by a big drop in demand due to the recession. Revenue per available room has declined 15 percent and will certainly keep declining. There has also been a huge increase in supply—over 100,000 new hotel rooms will be built in 2009 and another 100,000 new rooms in 2010.

All of this means there will be a wave of commercial loans that are underwater. In addition, many will need to be re-financed because they were short-term, creating a bit of a perfect storm for commercial real estate loans in the next year. These bad loans mean more write-offs for the banks and more pressure on the private debt bubble.

The wave of bad commercial real estate loans is another reason that banks won't or can't lend for new construction now. That will help bring commercial construction to a grinding halt. Not that the banks should be lending for more construction—we are overbuilt and overpriced in almost every commercial real estate category. And, for reasons described in this book, we won't have an economic rebound that works off the inventory.

Driving Force 3: Credit Card Loans.   One of the wonderful aspects of the Age of Excess was the incredible abundance of credit cards. Billions and billions of pieces of direct mail were sent out to everyone possible, including prisoners and dogs, to encourage them to sign up for yet another credit card. Deceased relatives were also a favorite target of credit card companies, as all of the authors have seen personally. As a side note, that is changing—in Q1 2009 only 500 million direct mail pieces were sent out, down from 1 billion in Q4 2008.

With such an abundance of credit, it's no surprise the credit card companies made a lot of bad credit card loans. But they expected that, which is why they charge such high interest rates and fees. What they didn't expect was for the economy to go bad. Again, like everyone else was thinking, the economy has never really gone bad in almost 30 years, why should it go bad now? But it is starting to go bad and so are credit card loans.

A typical rule used by the credit card companies is that default rates track the unemployment rate. With low unemployment rates, the credit card companies have enjoyed low default rates. But as unemployment goes over 10 percent default rates are going even higher than 10 percent. That's no surprise given the over abundance of credit cards. Credit cards are so easy not to pay (they don't take your house or car) and if money's tight, many people just stop paying because they didn't have a lot of financial muscle to begin with. As mentioned in Chapter 2, most major credit card companies have around 30 percent of their credit cards with sub-prime borrowers. That's a lot of risk in a bad economy that is getting worse. Much of that risk will turn to bad loans and big losses for the banks behind them, most notably Bank of America, Chase, and Citibank, which have created or bought much of the credit card business in the country.

The much-needed credit card reforms passed in spring 2009 will increase bank losses even further since they cut into the high fees and interest rates that were critical to making money when banks make such terrible loans.

Of course, banks will have to cut back on the amount of credit they offer, which will further hurt consumer spending and the economy. When bubbles pop, the good times don't just stop—they go into reverse!

Driving Force 4: Loans to Companies That Are Now in Trouble or Going Out of Business.   Not only were banks pretty loose on credit to consumers, they were also pretty loose on loans to businesses. It was all part of the private debt bubble. Again, since the economy never goes bad, what's the risk in lending money to businesses?

Well, there isn't that much risk when the bubble economy is very good, but it can change in a heartbeat when the bubble economy, especially the discretionary spending bubble, starts to pop like it is now. Businesses that at one time made plenty of money are finding their sales declining and their profits evaporating. Many businesses are already having difficulties making payments or are closing down. Housing bubble related businesses, such as construction firms, are causing huge problems for smaller banks around the country that made so much money lending to them during the bubble.

Many large businesses also leveraged up very highly during the recent private debt bubble. Some did it because of leveraged buyouts but others did it because the money was so cheap and provided an easy way to get cash. Again, as long as the economy stayed good and interest rates stayed low, everything would be fine. Now we are seeing the highest percentage in our history of debt by the S&P 500 being rated at junk or lower. The risk of that going bad in an increasingly bad economy is huge. It's easy to see why everyone wants to cheerlead the economy because if it gets worse, a lot of bubble dominoes are about to fall.

All These Bad Loans in a *Good* Economy! Wait Until It's a Bad Economy and Good Loans Go Bad!   Many of the loans described above would have gone bad even in a relatively good economy simply because they were made with very optimistic assumptions that the growth of the last few years would keep going and going. Even now, the economy is still relatively good. Real job losses have only begun since the fall 2008 credit crisis, and mortgage rates and inflation are still very low. In fact, in the first half of 2009, interest rates were at record low levels spurring a refinancing boom.

As recently as June 2009, unemployment was at 9.5 percent. That's still well below the 10.8-percent peak of the early 1980s recession. Part of the reason we underestimate how bad things are going economically is that we have had a major drop in asset values—both stocks and real estate. The other reason is that things have been so good lately. In April 2008, unemployment was at 5 percent.

But as we have explained in the book, our analysis of the fundamental economic conditions shows this changing in a big way. When it does change and we hit the triple double-digit scenario described in Chapter 3, where we have a double-digit interest rate, inflation rate and unemployment rate, many of the good loans in bankers' portfolios that wouldn't have gone bad even in a slightly recessionary economy, will go bad. The toxicity of bank loans will increase causing much greater losses in their portfolios.

Won't Government Bailouts Solve the Problem? Yes, the government can try to bail out all of the bad loans we just mentioned, but that doesn't keep the private debt bubble from bursting; it just shifts the losses to the government. The losses are being created by fundamental economic conditions. The government can't and isn't changing that. All it is doing is absorbing the losses. And yes, the government can handle far more losses than the mortgage market or the credit card market or the commercial real estate market or the commercial loan market can, but these losses can get pretty big. As they get bigger, even the government's ability to handle losses gets stretched because it came to the loss bailout game with over $10 trillion in debt itself.

As we pointed out in Chapter 3, ultimately, the government's many lenders will get worried and some will begin to pull back on the government's credit line, just as many bankers would if they became more worried about the creditworthiness of a borrower. So the banker's bad loans have encouraged the government—which has already gotten itself into $10 trillion of debt it can't pay off—to take on even more debt. It solves a short-term problem, but it creates a much more massive problem when the dollar bubble bursts, forcing the government debt bubble to burst.

In Phase II, Good Loans Go Bad—30-Year Fixed Rate Mortgages Are a Great Example. People wonder how we could have made so many bad loans in the past. Well, just look at bankers today. They are making enormous numbers of terribly bad loans. The 30-year fixed rate mortgage is a great example. How could anyone make a 30-year loan commitment at 5 percent? That means you think that interest rates or inflation will not rise above 5 percent for 30 years. Given the Federal Reserve's current actions to save banks and the enormous and rapidly growing debt levels, it is absolutely beyond conception that someone could really believe that. But believe it they do. It's incredible. Even historically speaking, we have had interest rates as high as 18 percent in the early 1980s. Why would anyone bet such big money for so little return, that it would never happen again?

Plus, the same mistake is being made all the time when banks lend to businesses. The feeling is that the economy is close to bottoming out and these businesses won't have any problem paying off more debt or refinancing old debt. The feeling seems to be that if they have paid their debt in the past, they can certainly pay it off in the future.

Wow, what a shock it will be when Phase II hits. Not only will all the loans made under those unreasonably good assumptions go bad, but even the best of loans, such as inventory loans to Wal-Mart, will have trouble with the extremely high inflation rates and the instability of the U.S. and world economy in the Aftershock.

The bottom line is that people are expecting everything to get better and are absolutely unprepared if it does not. That's a mistake bankers should not make. And when things truly go in a historically unprecedented downward direction in the Aftershock, bankers will see even the best of their loans go bad.

The Credit Crisis Is Over! You don't hear this mantra much any more even though it was very popular in spring 2008. (How quickly we forget!) The reality is that the credit crisis won't be over until the housing price collapse stops. It was the housing price collapse that kicked off the massive losses in mortgage backed securities and those losses won't stop until prices stop declining. There's no way to put a number on it since it is a moving target. If someone is putting a number on it, they're likely wrong—on the low side. House prices are going to keep declining for quite some time. All we know is that the final number on the losses, when it does arrive, will be massive.

Forces Driving the Collapse of the Discretionary Spending Bubble

The forces driving the collapse of the discretionary spending bubble are much less complex than the forces driving the housing, stock and private debt bubbles. We are also much more aware of them because everyone is a consumer and feels the pressures directly. Hence, most of these forces were discussed in adequate detail in Chapter 2. But to keep the symmetry of this appendix, we will present a brief review of those driving forces:

Driving Force 1: Home Equity Extraction Declines

As we discussed in Chapter 2, the housing bubble was the first bubble to pop, and that put pressure on consumers by eliminating the massive home equity they were tapping to finance their discretionary spending. This cash came from home equity loans, home sales, and the feeling that there was no reason to save, since your house was doing all the saving you could ever do, and then some. This very important driving force of the discretionary spending bubble is collapsing at a good pace and will continue to put pressure on the discretionary spending bubble.

Driving Force 2: Credit Cards Melt

Like the Wicked Witch of the West, credit cards are melting, melting, melting, albeit much more slowly. Consumers can no longer refinance them with home equity loans. Banks are pulling back on credit lines as more and more consumers default. Fewer new credit cards are being offered. Unemployment is rising further pushing up credit card defaults. Consumers may also be feeling tapped out: Household debt as a percentage of disposable debt has risen from around 60 percent in the early 1980s to almost 130 percent today, according to the federal Reserve. At the end of 2008, credit card companies had $13.8 trillion in debt—almost as much as our total GDP. It is a downward spiral that is hard to control. The end result is that much less discretionary spending is possible.

Driving Force 3: Assets Decline

Although the economy has been relatively modestly hit, assets have been devastated. Households have seen their net worth drop by $12.9 trillion from Q2 2007 to Q1 2009, according to the Federal Reserve. It's an unprecedented drop in asset value creating a real feeling of "shock and awe." Consumers who are in a state of shock and awe don't feel much like partying it up with their spending. Even high-end consumer psyches have been hit—Tiffany's New York store sales have fallen over 40 percent, and the over-$50,000 jewelry has just stopped selling. This feeling of shock and awe will only get worse if asset values continue to decline, as our analysis shows they will, putting more downward pressure on the discretionary spending bubble.

Driving Force 4: Jobs Decline/Hiring Collapses

In a non-bubble economy, the traditional damper on consumer spending is job loss. This very important factor has only recently come into play in Q4 2008, and increasing job loss will put more pressure on the discretionary spending bubble. More importantly, according to a survey of employers by Manpower, Inc. in Q2 2009, over 65 percent of employers were not planning to increase their work force. So hiring has slowed to a crawl. This is also showing up in the ranks of the long-term unemployed. People not only fear unemployment, but longer-term unemployment due to the difficulty in finding a new job. And it's the fear that drives down discretionary spending.

Driving Force 5: Spending Mentality Dies

The reverse of all of the above: rapidly rising home equity that was easy to tap, huge increases in credit cards, huge increases in asset values, and an economy that always provided good jobs except for slight interruptions, created a huge consumer spending mentality. Hundreds of new retail chains and consumer products companies were born during this boom. Consumers thought the good times would never end—no need to save when you can spend instead! Ha-ha-ha. What fun it was! If a little debt is no problem then a lot of debt doesn't really matter either.

That mentality is starting to change. Not as dramatically as you might expect, but it is changing. That spending mentality will begin to change very noticeably in 2010 when people realize that this isn't just another economic downturn and they start to think that asset values have fallen for a long time, if not permanently.

The Aftershock Hits.   When the Aftershock hits, the discretionary spending world changes completely. At that point, we're not just getting rid of the bubble—we're starting to change very fundamentally the ways and amounts we consume. The money simply isn't there anymore for anything like the kind of spending we are used to with inflation, huge declines in asset values, and extremely high unemployment pounding consumers. The fear and anger is very high, and discretionary spending becomes enemy #1 on people's budgets. At that point, many things that people now consider essential become discretionary, including many medical and education expenses as well as governmental expenses. It's a whole different world that is difficult to comprehend today.

To find out about additional driving forces in the Bubble Economy, go to www.aftershockeconomy.com/appendixa.

Appendix B

HOW WE CAN (AND WILL) SOLVE
OUR ECONOMIC PROBLEMS

The reforms needed to solve our economic problems will require significant changes to certain aspects of the status quo. These changes are politically explosive and will not be made until the massive pain of the coming Aftershock and global mega-depression forces us to make fundamental changes that now would be politically impossible.

A good analogy is the Great Fire of London. It was fairly obvious, even in the seventeenth century, how major urban fires could be prevented and how a city should be built to be more fireproof and less vulnerable to extremely large fires. However, the political reforms that would have been required to make London safer from large fires were so great that the changes needed to prevent a fire were never implemented before the Great Fire.

But, as is often the case, ignoring a potential problem was not enough to prevent it from happening.

Eventually, a serious fire broke out and destroyed almost all of London. Once London was destroyed, people became far less resistant to making the big political reforms needed to keep it from recurring. Previously resisted reforms were rapidly implemented and London never had a fire of that magnitude again.

The same will be true for the global mega-depression. It is a one-time event and it will never be repeated because, after it happens, reforms will be put in place to prevent it from happening again. Right now, people will say that this is impossible, but just like the Great Fire of London, once we get thoroughly burned, radical reforms will eventually be made.

Seven major sets of reforms will be required to solve our economic problems in the long-term:

1. Political reforms
2. Productivity enhancements
3. Bubble prevention
4. Financial reforms
5. Economic reforms
6. Capital creation (after the capital markets have failed)
7. Targeted stimulation

Political Reforms and Productivity Enhancements Have to Come First

Two sets of reforms will create the fundamental bedrock upon which all the other reforms will be built: (1) political reforms and (2) productivity enhancements. Without a start based on these two basic reforms, nothing else can easily proceed in a workable manner.

After we begin the necessary political reforms and productivity enhancements, we will be able to start efforts to bring about economic stabilization, including bubble prevention, financial reforms, capital creation, and then finally move on to targeted stimulation, which will be the final basis for the recovery.

Political Reforms

It will eventually become obvious to people that the mega-depression was largely a governmental failure. The political reforms to help prevent these failures would include:

- Campaign finance reform
- Media reform
- Lobbying reform
- Improving governmental efficiency

As we mentioned earlier, these reforms would be impossible in today's environment or would be so watered down as to be ineffective. However, after the mega-depression hits, once unthinkable reforms will become quite thinkable and will ultimately become law.

This appendix was written to give the reader a broad overview of what will be needed to solve our economic problems. It was not meant to be a detailed description or it would become too long—almost a book within a book. However, the detailed description is available on our web site at: www.aftershockeconomy.com/politicalreforms.

Productivity Improvements

This seems to be a no-brainer and easy to do, but in fact it is not. Once we understand what is involved in productivity improvements we will understand that every action that would actually improve productivity is a political minefield. However, if there are no productivity improvements, the stimulus we will be using will not work due to the radically altered consumption patterns that were caused by the bubble collapse. To bring back reasonable consumption patterns we must have productivity growth.

We divide the economy into 10 productivity improvement sectors. A brief example of the kind of productivity improvements we are discussing can be found at our website, www.aftershockeconomy.com/auto, on the auto industry. Of course, this is just one of many improvements needed for the Transportation Sector, which is sector 6 of the 10 productivity improvement sectors. Improving productivity is a lot of work, but the benefits are enormous and there is no way around it. You can't blow bubbles forever, as we are about to find out.

More information on productivity improvements in the other sectors, as well as a complete listing of the sector divisions, is given on our web site at www.aftershockeconomy.com/productivity.

Economic Stabilization Reforms Come Next

Once the underlying issues of government reforms and productivity improvements are well on their way to being resolved, we can move on to economic stabilization reforms. Economic reforms will generate investments and consumer confidence, and ensure that the popping bubbles that created the mega-depression never happen again.

Bubble Prevention

Bubble prevention reforms are made to ensure that the economy will never collapse again in a set of punctured bubbles. Bubble prevention is accomplished as one broad overall reform. However, each type of asset requires a different technique to prevent bubbles from occurring again. The five major asset types are:

1. Real estate
2. Stocks and derivatives
3. Foreign exchange
4. Bonds
5. Gold

Like the political reforms, more detailed information on each of the five bubble prevention reforms is given on our web site at: www.aftershockeconomy.com/bubbleprevention.

Financial Reforms

These reforms are designed for a dual purpose:

1. To ensure that the financial system is an aggressive, open, free market system that is highly entrepreneurial.
2. It is as free as possible of any systemic risk so that the financial system can never again collapse with devastating consequences.

Without these two sets of reforms everyone, including investors, consumers, and workers, will be so concerned about another financial collapse that they will not take the risks or actions necessary to re-start the economy.

There are three basic reforms that need to be implemented. These are:

1. Private loan reforms and default prevention
2. Government debt (and government financial guarantee) reforms and default prevention
3. Banking and brokerage reform

Again, so as not to overly lengthen the book and still provide plenty of detail for the reader, the detailed description of these three reforms is given on our web site at www.aftershockeconomy .com/financialreforms.

Note: If at this point you are interested enough in these issues to just read the entire detailed version without having to go back and forth between the book and the web site, please go to www.aftershockeconomy.com/appendixb.

Economic Reforms: Drastically Reducing Inflation and Unemployment While Balancing Trade

These are the three major problems of the Mega-Depression, with inflation being at extraordinarily high levels all over the world, international trade having virtually collapsed, and unemployment being very high everywhere. We explain how to virtually eliminate inflation, have robust, balanced international trade, and how to deal with what will seem like an intractable unemployment problem on our web site at www.aftershockeconomy.com/economicreforms.

Inflation will be addressed by the implementation of EPRITS (Electronic Property Rights Transfer System). Unemployment will be addressed by welfare and employment/unemployment benefit reforms. Balanced trade will be addressed through the implementation of the IMU (International Monetary Unit), which was discussed in Chapter 9, and International EPRITS.

Create Capital (After the Capital Markets Have Failed)

No one in the world wants to save or invest capital after the extreme losses that have been suffered in the Aftershock. Even in the face of this skepticism, there are some techniques for generating a modest amount of equity capital, but to really get the economy growing rapidly in the future requires vast amounts of very cheap capital. We cannot even generate such vast amounts of low-cost capital today. In the midst of the Mega-Depression it will be a very daunting task, but we explain how the people will accomplish this goal.

It will require the development of two radically new methods of capital accumulation, which are:

1. Capital accumulation requirements
2. Insured balanced and revised retirement plans

These two methods are described in detail on our web site, www.aftershockeconomy.com/capitalcreation.

Targeted Stimulation

After all the above reforms are under way, we will have finally reached the Holy Grail of economic recovery and growth. This is what most people would like to do immediately, but for it to be effective it must be done on a huge scale, which means that it is extremely expensive—and this is even truer with the economy in a Mega-Depression. Thus, there is no choice but to do it right the first time. That's why proper preparation is needed so that when the targeted stimulation is undertaken, the economy will reasonably rapidly go back to full employment and then continue at a full employment level without continuous stimulation.

This is, in fact, not only possible, but it is what we are going to do. In fact, at a later stage, the world economy, including the U.S. economy, as a result of targeted stimulation and many other reforms occurring past the megadepression recovery period, will actually create an economy that is locked into a condition of very low unemployment (less than one tenth of a percent) and very limited inflation (far less than one tenth of a percent).

Targeted stimulation will be focused on two main areas:

1. Capital goods (including industrial goods)
2. Discretionary spending

The targeted stimulation for these two areas is described in more detail at: www.aftershockeconomy.com/stimulation.

In closing, all of the reforms mentioned earlier will create a very productive, interesting and enjoyable world and economy, but getting there will be very difficult due to the political obstacles that will be placed in the path of these necessary reforms. Eventually, we will get there.

This appendix on megadepression recovery was necessarily very brief, so please use the website for additional information, since most of the content had to be placed on the website. Please go to www.aftershockeconomy.com/appendixb for these details.

Bibliography

Allaire, Marc, and Marty Kearney. *Understanding LEAPS.* Boston, MA: McGraw-Hill, 2003.

Altman, Daniel. "Uncle Sam, Deadbeat Debtor?" *New York Times,* July 23, 2006.

Athanasoulis, Stefano, and Robert J. Shiller. "The Significance of the Market Portfolio." *Review of Financial Studies,* 13(2) (2000): 301–29.

Athanasoulis, Stefano, and Robert J. Shiller. "World Income Components: Discovering and Implementing Risk Sharing Opportunities." *American Economic Review,* 91(4) (2001): 1031–54.

Ballinger, Kenneth. *Miami Millions: The Dance of the Dollars in the Great Florida Land Boom of 1925.* Miami, FL: Franklin Press, 1936.

Batra, Ravi. *The Great Depression of 1990: Why It's Got to Happen, How to Protect Yourself,* Rev. ed. New York: Simon & Schuster, 1987.

Berman, Dennis K. "Fistfuls of Dollars Fuel the M&A Engine." *Wall Street Journal,* January 3, 2006.

Blinder, Alan S. and Janet L. Yellen, *The Fabulous Decade: Macroeconomic Lessons from the 1990s.* New York: Century Foundation Press, 2001.

Bonner, Bill, and Addison Wiggin. *Empire of Debt: The Rise of an Epic Financial Crisis.* Hoboken, NJ: John Wiley & Sons, 2006.

Borio, Claudio, and Patrick McGuire. "Twin Peaks in Equity and Housing Prices?" *Quarterly Review,* March 2004, pp. 79–93.

Browning, E.S., and Justin Lahart. "Is Easy Money Going Down the Drain? Anxious Markets Closely Watch Push by World's Central Banks to Cut Off a Speculative Binge." *Wall Street Journal,* June 5, 2006.

Bruno, Michael, and William Easterly. "Inflation Crises and Long-Run Growth." *Journal of Monetary Economics,* 41(1) (1998): 2–26.

Buffett, Warren E. "Chairman's Letter to Shareholders." Berkshire Hathaway, Inc. 2005 Annual Report.

Bulgatz, Joseph. *Ponzi Schemes, Invaders from Mars, and Other Extraordinary Pop Delusions, and the Madness of Crowds.* New York: Harmony, 1992.

Case, Karl E., Jr., and Robert J. Shiller. "The Efficiency of the Market for Single Family Homes." *American Economic Review,* 79(1) (March 1989): 125–37.

Cassidy, John. *Dot.con: How America Lost Its Mind and Money in the Internet Era.* New York: Perennial Currents, 2003.

Clements, Jonathan. "The Debt Bubble Threatens to Derail Many Baby Boomers' Retirement Plans." *Wall Street Journal,* March 8, 2006.

Cooper, Jim. "A Truer Measure of America's Ballooning Deficit." *Financial Times* (London), May 1, 2006.

Coronado, Julia Lynn, and Steven A. Sharpe. "Did Pension Plan Accounting Contribute to a Stock Market Bubble?" Washington, D.C. Board of Governors of the Federal Reserve System, Finance and Economics Discussion Series No. 2003-38, 2003.

Cutler, David, James Poterba, and Lawrence Summers. "What Moves Stock Prices?" *Journal of Portfolio Management,* 15(3) (1989): 4–12.

"Danger—Explosive Loans." *Business Week,* October 23, 2006.

Delasantellis, Julian. "U.S. Living on Borrowed Time—and Money." *Asia Times Online,* March 24, 2006. *www.atimes.com/atimes/Global_Economy/Hc24Dj01.html*

Dent, Harry S. *The Roaring 2000s: Building the Wealth & Lifestyle You Desire in the Greatest Boom in History.* New York: Simon & Schuster, 1998.

Duncan, Richard. *The Dollar Crisis: Causes, Consequences, Cures.* Hoboken, NJ: John Wiley & Sons, 2005.

Easterlin, Richard. "Does Economic Growth Improve the Human Lot?" in *Nationals and Households in Economic Growth: Essays in Honor of Moses Abramovitz,* ed. Paul David and Melvin Reder. New York: Academic Press, 1974.

Eichengreen, Barry. *Golden Fetters: The Gold Standard and the Great Depression: 1919–1939.* New York: Oxford University Press, 1992.

Fisher, Irving. *The Stock Market Crash – and After.* New York: Macmillan, 1930.

Friedman, Milton. *Money Mischief: Episodes in Monetary History.* New York: Harcourt Brace Jovanovich, 1992.

Froot, Kenneth, and Maurice Obstfeld. "Intrinsic Bubbles: The Case of Stock Prices. *American Economic Review,* 81 (1991): 1189–1214.

Galbraith, John Kenneth. "The 1929 Parallel." *Atlantic Online,* January 1987, www.theatlantic.com/doc/198701/galbraith.

Galbraith, John Kenneth. *The Affluent Society.* New York: New American Library, 1995.

Galbraith, John Kenneth. *The Great Crash: 1929,* 2nd ed. Boston: Houston Mifflin.

"Goldman Sachs: On Top of the World. In Its Taste for Risk, the World's Leading Investment Bank Epitomizes the Modern Financial System." *The Economist,* April 27, 2006.

Gordon, Robert J. "U.S. Productivity Growth Since 1879: One Big Wave?" *American Economic Review,* 89(2) (1999): 123–28.

Jung, Jeeman, and Robert J. Shiller. "Samuelson's Dictum and the Stock Market." *Economic Inquiry,* 2005.

Katona, George. *Psychological Economics.* New York: Elsevier, 1975.

Keynes, John Maynard. *The General Theory of Employment, Interest and Money,* New York: Harcourt Brace and World, 1961.

Kindleberger, Charles P. *Manias, Panics and Crashes: A History of Financial Crises,* 2nd ed. London: Macmillan, 1989.

Ip, Greg. "Richest Americans' Income Share Jumps Sharply." *Wall Street Journal,* September 23, 2006.

James, Harold. *The End of Globalization: Lessons from the Great Depression.* Cambridge, MA: Harvard University Press, 2001, chapter 3, 125, 142.

Kaufman, Henry. "How the Fed Lost Its Groove." *Wall Street Journal,* August 14, 2006.

Keynes, John Maynard. *A Tract on Monetary Reform.* London: Macmillan, 1923.

Krugman, Paul. "How Fast Can the U.S. Economy Grow?" *Harvard Business Review,* 75 (1977): 123–29.

Lindert, Peter. *Growing Public: Social Spending and Economic Growth Since the Eighteenth Century.* New York: Cambridge University Press, 2004.

Lowenstein, Roger. *Origins of the Crash: The Great Bubble and Its Undoing.* New York: Penguin Press, 2004, 2.

Lucas, Robert E. "Asset Prices in an Exchange Economy." *Econometrica,* 46 (1978): 1429–45.

Mandel, Michael. "Bubble, Bubble, Who's in Trouble?" *Business Week,* June 15, 2006.

McGrattan, Ellen R., and Edward C. Prescott. "Is the Stock Market Overvalued?" *Federal Reserve Bank of Minneapolis Quarterly Review,* 24 (2000): 20–40.

Melzer, Allan H. "Monetary and Other Explanations of the Start of the Great Depression." *Journal of Monetary Economics,* 2 (1976): 455–71.

Perkins, Edwin J. *Wall Street to Main Street.* Cambridge, UK: Cambridge University Press, 1999.

Posen, Adam S. "It Takes More than a Bubble to Become Japan." *Institute for International Economics Working Paper No. 03-9,* October 2003.

Prechter, Robert R. *At the Crest of the Tidal Wave: A Forecast for the Great Bear Market.* New York: John Wiley & Sons, 1995.

Prechter, Robert R. *Conquer the Crash: You Can Survive and Prosper in a Deflationary Depression.* Hoboken, NJ: John Wiley & Sons, 2003.

Pressman, Steven. "On Financial Frauds and Their Causes: Investor Overconfidence." *American Journal of Economics and Sociology,* 57 (1998): 405–21.

Robinson, Jerry. *Bankruptcy of Our Nation.* New Leaf Publishing Group/New Leaf Press, 2009

Romer, Christina. "The Great Crash and the Onset of the Great Depression." *Quarterly Journal of Economics,* 105, (1990): 597–624.

Rosenberg, Yuval. "The Boomer Bust." *Fortune,* June 19, 2006.

Samuelson, Robert J. "A Financial 'Time Bomb'?" *Washington Post,* March 12, 2003.

Samuelson, Robert J. *The Good Life and Its Discontents: The American Dream in the Age of Entitlement, 1945–1995.* New York: Crown, 1995.

Shiller, Robert J. "Measuring Bubble Expectations and Investor Confidence." *Journal of Psychology and Markets,* 1(1) (2000): 49–60.

Stovall, Sam. *The Seven Rules of Wall Street.* New York. McGraw-Hill: 2009.

Summers, Lawrence H., and Victoria P. Summers. "When Financial Markets Wore Well: A Cautious Case for a Securities Transactions Tax." *Journal of Financial Securities Research,* 3(2–3) (1988): 163–88.

Turk, James. *The Coming Collapse of the Dollar and How to Profit from It: Make a Fortune by Investing in Gold and Other Hard Assets.* New York: Currency, 2004.

Wanniski, Jude. *The Way the World Works,* 2nd ed. New York: Simon & Schuster, 1982.

Wiedemer, James. *The Homeowners Guide to Foreclosure: How to Protect Your Home and Your Rights,* 2nd ed. Kaplan Publishing, June 3, 2008.

Wiggin, Addison. *The Demise of the Dollar … and Why It's Great for Your Investments.* Hoboken, NJ: John Wiley & Sons, 2005.

Will, George F. "Guaranteed Collisions." *Washington Post,* May 15, 2005.

"World Finance: The Coming Storm for Banks." *The Economist,* February 20, 2004.

Index